Books by Kevin Crossley-Holland

POEMS

The Rain-Giver
The Dream-House
Time's Oriel
Waterslain
The Painting-Room
New and Selected Poems 1965-1990
The Language of Yes

Moored Man
The Mountains of Norfolk: New and Selected Poems
The Breaking Hour
Seahenge
Gravity for Beginners

TRANSLATIONS

The Battle of Maldon and Other Old English Poems
Beowulf

The Exeter Book Riddles
The Anglo-Saxon World

MEMOIR

The Hidden Roads

MYTHOLOGY

The Norse Myths

HISTORY AND TRAVEL

The Stones Remain   Pieces of Land

DRAMA

The Wuffings

AS EDITOR

Running to Paradise: An Introductory Selection of the Poems of W.B. Yeats

Winter's Tales for Children 3

Winter's Tales 14

New Poetry 2

The Faber Book of Northern Legends

The Riddle Book

Northern Lights. Legends, Sagas and Folk-Tales

The Mirror of Britain (series)

The Oxford Book of Travel Verse

Folk-Tales of the British Isles

FOR CHILDREN

Havelok the Dane

King Horn

The Green Children

The Callow Pit Coffer

Wordhoard

The Pedlar of Swaffham

The Sea-Stranger

Green Glades Rising: The Anglo-Saxons

The Fire-Brother

The Earth-Father

The Wildman

The Dead Moon

Beowulf

The Mabinogion (with Gwyn Thomas)

Axe-Age, Wolf-Age: A Selection of Norse Myths

Storm

The Fox and The Cat: Animal Tales from Grimm (with Susanne Lugert)

British Folk Tales

The Quest for Olwen (with Gwyn Thomas)

Wulf

Under the Sun and Over the Moon

Sleeping Nanna

Sea Tongue

Tales from Europe

Long Tom and the Dead Hand

The Tale of Taliesin (with Gwyn Thomas)

The Labours of Herakles

The Green Children (*new version*)

The Old Stories: Tales from East Anglia and the Fen Country

Short! A Book of Very Short Stories

The King Who Was and Will Be

Arthur: The Seeing Stone

Enchantment

The Ugly Duckling

Arthur: At the Crossing-Places

Viking! Myths of Gods and Monsters

Arthur: King of the Middle March

Gatty's Tale

Outsiders

Waterslain Angels

Bracelet of Bones

Scramasax

Heartsong

The Norse Myths

Norse Tales

Between Worlds: Folktales of Britain and Ireland

Arthur: The Always King

The Ice Coffin

New Leaves on an Old Tree

First published in 2023
by Propolis Books

The Book Hive,
53 London Street,
Norwich, NR2 1HL

All rights reserved
© Kevin Crossley-Holland 2023

The right of Kevin Crossley-Holland to be identified
as the author of this work has been asserted
in accordance with the Copyright,
Designs and Patents Act, 1988

A CIP record for this book
is available from the British Library

ISBN 9781916905146

Endpaper image ©Andrew Rafferty. 'Tides' from *Seahenge: A Journey*
Cover design by Niki Medlik
www.studio-medlikova.com
Text design and typesetting · benstudios.co.uk

Printed and bound by TJ Books Limited,
Padstow, Cornwall

www.thebookhive.co.uk

New Leaves on an Old Tree

Kevin Crossley-Holland

A Writer's Portfolio

propolis

For Sue Bradbury with gratitude and love

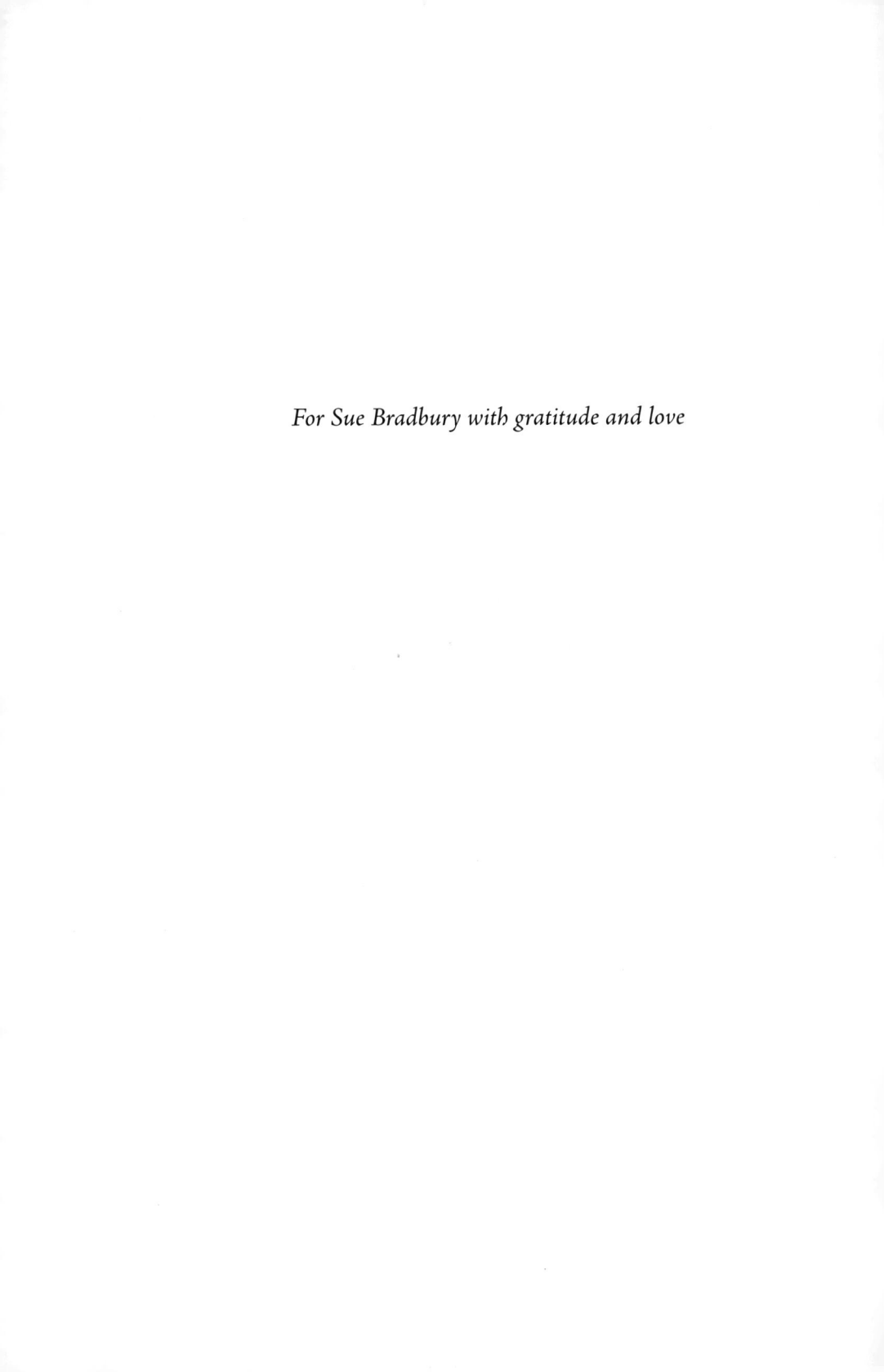

CONTENTS

Storytelling 1
We, the Story: Traditional Tales that Relate Us 2
On Katharine Briggs' *Folk Tales of Britain* 23
Different, – but oh how like! 31
Which Eye Can You See Me With?: Interpreting Folk Tales 51

Butterfly Soul 72

Anglo-Saxon Poetry 75
An Old House Packed with Memories 76
Word ond Andgiet: On Translating Anglo-Saxon Poetry 79
The Anglo-Saxon Elegies 91
The Exeter Book Riddles 101
The Cross Crucified: An Introduction to 'The Dream of the Rood' 110

From 'The Dream of the Rood' 122

Authors and Books 127
Rosemary Sutcliff: *The Eagle of the Ninth* 128
T. H. White: *The Once and Future King* 136
George Crabbe: 'Peter Grimes' 145
Footprints on the Grass: Of Gardens and Children's Books 155
Michael Longley: Breathing on the Embers 180
Annie's Wonderland: On receiving the Carnegie Medal for *Storm* 183
The King Within Each of Us 187
A Sort of Song of Everything: *Gatty's Tale* and Music 200

From *Storm* 207

In Tandem 209
   Collaborations with Artists 210
   'Tump' and 'Altar' from *Seahenge* 234
   Collaborations with Composers 237
   The Girl from Aleppo (Everyday Wonders) 249
   On Writing a Libretto 252
   From *The Wildman* 258

Norse 261
   Look North 263
   Axe-age, Wolf-age 272
   On Ian Crockatt's *Crimsoning the Eagle's Claw* 275
   From *The Death of Balder* 277

Places 281
   On *The Oxford Book of Travel Verse* 282
   The Kings of the Irish 297
   Let There be Light 313
   Scolt Head 320
   Until the Dragon Comes 332
   Festival of the Phoenix 342
   In a Norfolk Garden: An Idyll for Peter and Margaret Scupham 346

Bibliography 351
Sources 358
Acknowledgements 360

STORYTELLING

Story is the most potent word in the English language.

At once individual and social, it's the chief and most crucial channel by which we humans communicate with each other.

The great writer Barry Lopez, whose profound reverence for nature was underpinned by humanitarian and spiritual sensitivities akin to those of Thoreau and John Muir, was asked why he decided to be a writer.

"I can tell you in two words," he said. "To help. I am a traditional storyteller. This activity is not about yourself. It's about culture, and your job is to help."

Lopez led by example and exhortation. He wrote to my wife twenty-six years ago: "I'm barely ahead of you but must say the insight at 50, looking back, came down to this: the work you've done lies ahead of you again. You've another 30 years to give us all, and we eagerly await it. I hope… that from this day you flourish as grandly as you have."

I wholeheartedly share Lopez's views about story and the value of story. I always have. That's why this section comes first in my portfolio.

We, The Story

Traditional Tales that Relate Us

When I think of my early childhood, I hear sounds. The sound of the music of many cultures, spinning at seventy-eight revolutions per minute on our old gramophone; the sound of my father singing-and-saying traditional tales from north and south, east and west, sometimes accompanying himself on his Welsh harp.

When I advance to my teenage years, I see faces: not only "your Roman-Saxon-Danish-Norman English", as Daniel Defoe has it in *The True-Born Englishman*, but faces from every continent and ethnic group on this middle-earth. A rainbow of visitors to our creaky old London house in the unfashionable part of Hampstead.

Some of these visitors stayed. Some stayed for years! And some have never gone away.

I recall Mihran, a doe-eyed Armenian student, a brilliant young violinist – later the leader of a celebrated American orchestra. It was as natural for him to share stories as to share food, and the stories with which he nourished us were from his own life. Mihran said that in his village, the hairdresser was a very busy man; there was always a queue in his shop. One day the village wise man came to have his hair cut. "You'll have to wait." "I've no time." "You'll have to wait your turn." "I'll tell you what," said the wise man. And he took off his head! He took off his head and put it down on a chair – in its place in the queue. Then the head said, "All right! I'll leave my head here. I'll be back in half an hour."

I recall Hari, a young East Indian architect, who lived with us for two years, and called my mother 'Mummy'. I furiously resigned from our pukka – yes, pukka! – local lawn tennis club because his application for membership was turned down. "No blacks, old boy!" I was told. "No Jews! Nothing personal." When I was nineteen, I wrote an unpublished novel, called *Debendranath*, and Debendranath was really Hari. Yes, I thought of Hari as my brother.

Such stories! Such friendships! Such diversity! The dance of life.

Then how am I to account for the fact that the man writing this has sometimes had ugly thoughts or unsavoury feelings? At time, I have connived with nationalist or racist talk by remaining silent when I should have objected. But worse, I, a writer, custodian of language, have heard myself using the very language that perpetuates offensive cultural stereotypes. And again: despite my belief that all humans are of equal value, I have found myself thinking that the death of Bosnian and Croatian and Serbian children is somehow more grievous than the death of starving children in Somalia. Was Jimmy Carter speaking for most of us when he said, "I try not to be racist and wouldn't call myself a racist, but I have feelings that border on it"?

Some years ago, Bill Clinton declared, "There is no them; there is only us", but it is, I fear, part of human nature to think in terms of 'us' and 'them'. Very young children learn to group and name so as to communicate. My ten-year-old daughter tells me she likes girls and hates boys (though some boys, she adds, can be admitted as friends). And, looking at people around me, I categorise them by gender and colour and religion and education and language and sexual proclivity and age and class and income and sense of style.

The great Anglo-American poet W.H. Auden made the point in his poem 'Law Like Love' that we all fashion the world in our own image – we all see it according to our own lights:

> Law, say the gardeners, is the sun,
> Law is the one
> All gardeners obey
> To-morrow, yesterday, to-day.

Law is the wisdom of the old,
The impotent grandfathers feebly scold;
The grandchildren put out a treble tongue,
Law is the senses of the young.

Law, says the priest with a priestly look,
Expounding to an unpriestly people,
Law is the words in my priestly book,
Law is my pulpit and my steeple.

Law, says the judge as he looks down his nose,
Speaking clearly and most severely,
Law is as I've told you before,

Law is as you know I suppose,
Law is but let me explain it once more,
Law is The Law.

This kind of parochialism may be human and droll, but it is also dangerous. Each of us is morally obliged to use our imagination and intelligence to try to understand one another's point of view. *Audi partem alteram*, said St. Augustine in his *Confessions*. Hear the other side. Failure to do this has two direct consequences. The first is that we will be parties to continuing social injustice. The second is that we will have, and will pass on to our children, a warped view of history.

Let me take one topical instance. How did publishers of children's books respond to the quincentennial celebration of Columbus's voyage to the New World? By publishing a succession of books that blindly perpetuate a Eurocentric standpoint, extolling Columbus and his motives (adventure, overcoming obstacles, opening up new land, riches) and ignoring the terrible havoc and appalling genocide wrought upon a vast array of American Indian cultures numbering some seventy-five million people, between two and eighteen million of whom lived in the area now known as the United States.

Writing in the admirable *Hungry Mind Review*, the educationalist Herb Kohl says of these books: "I am deeply disturbed by their cultural myopia… there is too much offense and insult in them… Children must look at the violence that led to the remaking of this continent." For the record, the one book Kohl praises – and he praises it highly – is Jane Yolen's *Encounter*, which is written from the perspective of a Taino Indian boy who witnesses the landing of Columbus and his party in Dominica.

I have often returned to a magnificent book: *America in 1492* edited by Alvin M. Josephy, Jr. It offers a stunning series of perspectives on the origins, environment, customs, values, religion, artistic, and technological achievement of the Indian peoples before the arrival of Columbus. In the afterword, Vine Deloria, Jr. – a Standing Rock Sioux known for many distinguished books on the history of Indian-White relations – writes:

> Increasingly, American Indians are understanding the European invasion as a failure. That is to say, in spite of severe oppression, almost complete displacement, and substantial loss of religion and culture, Indians have not been completely defeated. Indeed, the hallmark of today's Indian psyche is the realization that the worst has now passed and that it is the white man with his careless attitude towards life and the environment who is actually in danger of extinction.

The European invasion was a triumph. The European invasion was a failure. Just one example! Wherever one turns, and to whichever period of America's past, it is plain that we are all caught up in a massive and complex struggle to rewrite the past and understand identity.

The reason humans falsify history is to show their forebears did right, or at least acted from the very best of motives, and to justify present and future action. True, we may not be responsible for the sins of our fathers, but we do certainly have responsibilities arising from them: we are morally obliged to see them plain and ensure they do not recur. We need our wits, we need action, and we need great stamina to confront and redeem the damage done to others and to ourselves by blind self-justification; the perpetuation of ridiculous stereotypes, and generations of social injustice.

> 1800's in this town
> fourteen longhouses were destroyed
> by not these people here.
> not these people
> burned the crops and chopped down
> all the peach trees.
> not these people, those people
> preserve peaches, even now.

So says the poet Lucille Clifton in her sequence of poems, 'in white america'. She talks of giving a poetry reading, "my eyes bright, my mouth smiling, my singed hands burning". "It is late in white America," she says.

"It is late in white America." It is late in white Europe. It is late in Australia. In New Zealand. It is late, very late, in white South Africa.

I'm aware the truth of this is widely recognised in Minnesota. "The great moral tasks" as they have been called by the poet Wendell Berry in *The Hidden Wound*, "of honesty and peace and neighbourliness and brotherhood and the care of the earth" are part of the daily agenda here in a way that would astonish many of my fellow Englishmen. Please forgive me, therefore, for my presumption in what I call talking turtle – that is to say, sticking my neck out.

We can proceed through the word. This is what Confucius has to say in *The Great Digest* (translated by Ezra Pound):

> …wanting good government in their own states, they first established order in their own families; wanting order in the home, they first disciplined themselves; desiring self-discipline, they rectified their own hearts; and wanting to rectify their hearts, they sought precise verbal definitions of their inarticulate thoughts (the tones given off by the heart)…

Let us, then, try to find the precise words, the words which identify our deepest longings. And let us find stories which – by embodying these longings – enable children to understand themselves and to have courage. Traditional tales that relate us – that tell us who we are and connect us to one another.

The sort of tale I have in mind is not easy to categorise. It may belong to any one of the three tiers of traditional tale: myth, legend and folk tale. It may belong to any one of many thematic groups: creation myth, for instance, or hero-tale, or wonder tale. And you won't find it in a motif-index of folk literature. There is nothing for it: we must do some digging for ourselves.

At the heart of the tale I am describing is a paradox. It makes two apparently opposing points. Firstly, it says, 'each one of us in *one*, is singular, completely and utterly different from any other one'. And then, in the same breath, the story says 'we are the same, all of us, and together we are one, and only together are we one'.

I have two such tales to lay before you – one myth, one folk tale. These are both tales I have worked on, and they both come from my own north-west European culture. I hope I do not have to apologise for that.

The first story is one of the racy, ice-bright Norse myths, and it is, I think, one of the world's great tragic stories. The gods and goddesses know that the life of Balder, god of innocence and beauty, is threatened; and they know that if innocence and beauty are eclipsed, the whole of creation will hasten to its end:

> They thought of all the ways in which one can die; they named each earth-thing, sea-thing and sky-thing that can cause sudden death. Then Balder's mother, Frigg, began to travel through the nine worlds and get each and every substance to swear an oath that it would not harm Balder.
>
> Fire swore an oath. Water swore an oath. Iron and each kind of metal swore an oath. The stones swore oaths. Nothing could stay Frigg from her mission, or resist her sweet troubled persuasion. Earth swore an oath. The trees swore oaths. Each kind of illness swore an oath. Balder's mother was untiring and painstaking. All the animals swore an oath and so did every sidling snake.

But there is one little bush growing west of Valhalla from which Frigg does not win a promise: a sprig of mistletoe. "That's so young and tender I didn't bother with it," says Frigg. Learning of this, the Trickster Loki pounces. Like many another Trickster figure, Loki starts off as a cunning, selfish, unreliable, sometimes comic cheat. He is always landing the gods in deep water and then bailing them out again. But as time goes on, this quite playful figure turns into a cruel and vindictive destroyer, committed to the overthrow of the gods.

> Loki fashions a dart from the mistletoe twig, puts it into the hand of Loki's blind brother Hod, and guides Hod's hand...
>
> The mistletoe flew through the hall and it struck Balder. It pierced him and passed right through him. The god fell on his face. He was dead.
>
> There was no sound in Gladsheim, no sound, only the roaring of silence. The gods could not speak. They looked at the fairest and most wise of them all, shining and lifeless...

In a scene of heart-breaking intensity and anguish, gods, giants, dwarfs, humans, animals – representatives of the whole of creation – gather on the seashore to give Balder a ship-burial. But already one of the gods, Hermod, is galloping down to the underworld to discover what ransom the gods will have to pay to bring Balder back from the dead.

Hel, the monster-woman who rules Niflheim, realm of the dead, states her price:

"If each and every thing in the nine worlds, dead and alive, weeps for Balder, let him return to Asgard. But if anything demurs, if even one thing will not weep, Balder must remain in Niflheim."

Then the gods sent out messengers to every corner of the nine worlds. And all that they asked was that dead Balder should be wept away from Hel. As each substance had sworn an oath before that it would not harm Balder, each substance now wept. Fire wept, iron and every other metal wept, the stones wept, earth wept, the trees wept, every kind of illness wept, all the animals wept. All the birds wept, every kind of poisonous plant wept, and so did every sidling snake – just as these things weep when they are covered with rime and begin to thaw again.

The god's messengers were making their way back to Asgard and they all felt they had overlooked nothing. Then they came across a giantess sitting in a cave.

"What is your name?" asked one.

"Thokk," said the giantess.

Then the messengers explained their mission and asked Thokk to weep as all things had wept, weep and weep Balder away from Hel.

The giantess glowered at the messengers, and then she answered sourly, "Thokk will weep dry tears over Balder's funeral. I never cared for the Old Man's son – alive or dead, I have no use for him. Let Hel hold what she has."

Despite the messengers' prayers and entreaties, Thokk refused to say another word. She would not recant, and she would not weep.

Then the messengers left her; they mournfully crossed Bifrost, the rainbow bridge. And what they had to say was clear from the manner of their coming.

The gods and goddesses ached; they felt old and confused and unable and weary. And not one of them doubted that Thokk, the giantess in the cave, was also Loki.

This great myth is concerned with several pairs of opposites: life and death, love and hate, innocence and guile, action and passivity. But above all, to my mind, it is concerned with individuality and universality.

Each object in the nine worlds has to swear not to harm Balder; each object has to weep him back from the world of the dead. In both instances, one thing, one life – first the sprig of mistletoe and then the giantess Thokk – fails to do so.

Here are the words of a wise English educationalist, Christian Schiller:

> There is more than one way of observing. You can observe like a camera. There is the object, 'it'; here am I, 'I'… I note carefully the shape, colour, pattern, texture, accurately and exactly… and if I make a record of my observations accurately and skilfully it will be an exact reproduction of the object, a record of what would be seen by any observer at that place at that time. Such a record is objective. There is the object, 'it'; here am I, 'I'. There is in the record nothing relating me as an individual person to what I have observed.
>
> There is, however, another sort of observation. I look at this flower. It is just a flower with a shape, a colour, a pattern, and texture. But as my attention focuses more sharply my feeling is aroused and I perceive that this flower is not just a flower, any more than you are just a man or a woman: you are unique. There is nothing else in the

world just like you; there is nothing else in the world just like this flower. And I begin to observe this flower as I observe you, with a relationship between 'I', here, and another unique being, 'you', there. There is a bond between us, the flower and I; we are each unique beings in the same world.

Like the Norse myth about Balder, Schiller's words affirm specificity and deny generalisation. They recognise the limited and impersonal value of categorisation, and I believe that, in our daily lives, it is precisely this observation and celebration of individuality – of what Gerard Manley Hopkins calls 'thisness' – that leads on to a respect for difference, a delight in difference, be it difference of gender, colour, or religious belief.

In the myth of Balder, the price of the failure of the individual to swear or to weep is that the forces of evil are unleashed. The inhabitants of the nine worlds – the entire universe – are destined to fight and destroy one another. That is to say, the action or inaction of an individual directly brings about a universal condition.

When I say that the myth of Balder is concerned with universality, I do not have in mind some Eurocentric value system. I mean, rather, that every single thing shares life, every human and grasshopper and leaf and stone; I mean we are all children of time, more alike than unalike; and I mean that the actions of one influence the whole.

"My friend," says Black Elk, the Sioux holy man, "I am going to tell you the story of my life… and if it were only the story of my life I think I would not tell it… It is the story of all life that is holy and is good to tell, and of us two-leggeds sharing it with the four-leggeds and the wings of the air and all green things; for these are children of one mother and their father is one Spirit."

This is the world in which each and every object relates to the others, has a function, and has its own story.

Traditional tales entertain and instruct. they are metaphors which tell us indirectly, as all story tells indirectly, about human experience and understanding.

In a sense, too, such tales are memories. They are dramatised distillations of wisdom, each one created and recreated by many people in many places at many times.

The early Spanish chronicler Gonzalo Fernández de Oviedo y Valdés heard the Taíno Indians of the Greater Antilles sing songs at their feasts or *areytos* (a term suggesting remembrance or recall), and to my mind his words perfectly sum up the essential functions of traditional tale:

> Their songs are their books and memorials, transmitted from generation to generation, from fathers to sons, and from those who are alive today to those who will arrive... Thanks to their *areytos* they could recall things of their past... They had *areytos* in their principal feasts or to celebrate a victory over their enemies, or when a cacique [tribal chieftain] was married, or at any occasion in which one looked for pleasure.

If a writer is to recreate traditional material for children he or she – why don't I say we? – we plainly have responsibilities. Before I advance to my second story, let me rehearse some of them.

Our first responsibility is to our material. We should try to get some sense of the field – the whole body of tales – we are working in, so as to make the most judicious selection. Children need old favourites, of course, but there are many equally fine tales virtually unknown, still waiting in the margins.

The matter of which tales we select calls not only for literary judgement but may also raise questions of social responsibility.

Let me quote a letter I recently received from Marianne Carus, editor of the children's literary magazine *Cricket*. After accepting one of my retellings, she went on to say:

> You know that I love your style – we all do at *Cricket* – but the content of the tales is rather problematic for us: comments about the devil, religion, violent deaths, cutting out hearts, etc., all this is too strong, too sophisticated for the average American family. A sad statement, but I am sure you are aware of all the demagoguery in this country right now. We get hundreds of letters (and unfortunately also cancellations) if we happen to upset any of these pressure groups.

When I replied to Marianne's letter, I told her a little tale from Maria Tatar's *The Hard Facts of the Grimms' Fairy Tales*:

> There was once a young boy whose pedagogically solemn parents resolved to do everything in their power to prevent their child from developing superstitious fears. They banned fairy tales from the household and saw to it that witches, giants, and other cannibalistic fiends were never once mentioned in the child's presence. All went according to plan until one night the parents awoke to the shrill cries of their son. Startled, they rushed to his bed only to learn that he was afraid of sleeping in the dark. They were even more startled after they asked the boy why he was afraid of sleeping in the dark, for the child's answer, punctuated by sobs, was: "There's a complex hiding under my bed."

I accept, naturally, that each country and culture has its own values, customs, and expectations, and I'm aware that there are a very few traditional tales so shocking that it would be unwise to set them before children. But these apart, we are more likely to damage children than nurture them if we pretend there are no terrors when children know perfectly well that there are. A tale names, it expresses what children already instinctively know, it therefore helps them to understand their own thoughts and feelings. In my opinion, the question of what is acceptable for children has rather little to do with material and a very great deal to do with interpretation and tone.

The way in which children relate to fact and story at the point where it touches their own experience is amusingly made by the great Czech poet Miroslav Holub in his poem 'Napoleon':

> Children, when was
> Napoleon Bonaparte born,
> asks teacher.
>
> A thousand years ago, the children say.
> A hundred years ago, the children say.
> Last year, the children say.
> No one knows.
>
> Children, what did
> Napoleon Bonaparte do,
> asks teacher.
>
> Won a war, the children say.
> Lost a war, the children say.
> No one knows.
>
> Our butcher had a dog
> called Napoleon,
> says Frantisek.
>
> The butcher used to beat him and the dog died
> of hunger
> a year ago.
>
> And all the children are now sorry
> for Napoleon.

Then there is another minefield. Can a writer feel free to speak for another culture, or must that be left to a member of that culture? Must I confine myself to writing about white north-west Europeans?

Let's see where this tack leads me. I am to write only about north-west Europeans. Or, more strictly, only about the British. No! About the English! Must also I turn my back on women and write only about men – boys and men?

Do I have to close the book on Shakespeare's Othello and Defoe's Man Friday and Longfellow's Hiawatha? What about Madame Butterfly, and Porgy and Bess?

The absurdity of this narrow-minded position is obvious. For where could it possibly lead us but to bigotry, and dangerous notions of nationalism and racial purity? No one has a monopoly of the truth. As writers, we should be fully aware of the dangers of perpetuating stereotypes (American Indians have suffered a great deal in this respect), and conscious of how immensely difficult it is to speak for the minds and hearts of people with beliefs and values different to our own. But we must also allow our intelligence and imagination to take us where they will.

I am entirely in sympathy with the views expressed by Linda Crawford (and friends) in their absorbing and practical book of conversations for multicultural understanding, *To Hold Us Together*:

> I know of a course in cultural pluralism given at a large university in which no one is permitted to talk about any culture, and students discuss only subjects about which they can speak with validity, like sibling conflict (only if they have siblings, of course). Another alternative is to keep doing the best we can by our homework, by talking to many people of diverse origins, by exercising a rigorous integrity, by admitting to ourselves and others that that we are not experts about any culture, not even our own, of which we are merely one example.

Writers for children have another responsibility: to our craft. To begin with, I suggest we make an attempt to read the first written versions of tales that interest us. It is scarcely good enough to work, as so many writers do, from derivatives: to work from sources that are in themselves interpretations and recreations.

And then there is the question of what forms we will use for our retellings. Michael Marland, distinguished educationalist and headmaster of a multicultural school in London, made the point to me the other day that writers should be aware of, and sensitive to, the art forms indigenous to the people with whose material they are working. Narrative? Non-narrative? Prose? Poetry? Market-led Western publishers, he pointed out, maintain the dominance of the narrative short story; and in this, we may all be complicit in cultural colonisation.

But even if we decide on prose narration, there are plenty of ways in which we can proceed. We may act as editors, remaining in the shadows. We may follow the form if not the letter of the original before us. We may tell a story as a tale within a tale – a traditional device which happens to be in line with the self-referring interest in form which is one of the characteristics of the late twentieth-century fiction. Again, writers may choose to step into a tale and tell it, as it were, from inside out. I've found this method particularly useful when it revolves around some outsider. For example, from my *The Wildman*:

> Don't ask me my name. I've hear you have names. I have no name.
>
> They say this is how I was born. A great wave bored down a river, and at the mouth of the river it ran up against a great wave of the sea. The coupled waves kicked like legs and whirled like arms and swayed like hips; sticks in the water snapped like bones and the seaweed bulged like gristle and muscle. In this way the waves rose. When they fell, I was there.

This is the voice of the Wildman, hauled out of the sea by some surprised fishermen on the east coast of England. This poor Wildman is insulted, imprisoned, and tortured:

Then they let me go, they let me dive into the water. It coursed through my long hair. I laughed and passed under the first net and the second net and the third net. I was free. but why am I only free away from those who are like me, with those who are not like me? Why is the sea my home?

They were all shouting and waving their arms, and jumping up and down at the edge of the water. They were all calling out across the grey wavelets. Why? Did they want me to be their friend?

I wanted to go back. I wanted them as friends...

It is the very nature of traditional tale to progress rapidly from A to Z, and to write a tale as monologue enables one to do just that while at the same time suggesting states of mind and heart.

I pushed this form one step further in my *Sea Tongue*, recreating a traditional tale as a kind of sound-story for different voices (or for one voice playing different parts). The voices belong to the different elements in the tale. Imagine, if you will, the North Sea, a cliff, a church perched on the cliff, and old bellwoman:

I am the bellwoman. There! those lights, stuttering and bouncing. There's a boat out there, and maybe ten.

Up, up these saucer steps as fast as I can. up! Here in this mouldy room, I'll ring and ring and ring, and set heaven itself singing, until my palms are raw. I'll drown the sea-god.

I am the sea-god. And I keep clapping my luminous hands. Come this way, fisherman, over the seal's bath and here along the cockle-path. Here are the slick quicksands, and they will have you. Fisherman, come this way over the gulls' road and the herring-haunt! Here, against this crumbling cliff. Give me your boat.

I am the boat...

In the course of this short tale, the bellwoman speaks, and the bell; the sea-god speaks; the dead speak; the living, the church, the boat, the night-storm, the morning, the fisherman: each speaks. I took my lead, of course, from 'The Death of Balder', and simply acted on the recognition that everything in our universe, every stick and stone, has its own life and voice.

And then there is the matter of language! Writers must choose language – and remember, there are many Englishes! – appropriate to the tale; language in itself quick, clean, taut, true. Words like windows that do not draw attention to themselves but enable you to see through them! Do not doubt that such words have infinite power.

Perhaps humans have always known the divine energy of the word. The classical Mayan *Popol Vuh* describes the creation as an act of speech:

> The Mother said this,
> And the father:
> "Should it only be still,
> Or should it not be silent
> Under the trees
> And shrubs?"...
> And when they thought
> And spoke,
> At a stroke there came to be
> And were created
> Deer
> And birds.

"In the beginning was the Word, and Word was with God, and the Word was God": the astonishing first verse of St. John's Gospel. And Maori storytellers:

> The breath of life,
> The spirit of life,

The word of life,
It flies to you and you and you,
Always the word.

My second story comes from late twelfth-century England. it is set in a village called Woolpit in the county of Suffolk, where I have lived for the past ten years, and it is called 'The Green Children'.

I first heard this story as a boy from my father. Then I retold it as a picture-story book in 1966. And just three years ago, working with the composer Nicola LeFanu, I turned it into an opera for children. The American premiere was presented by the Twin Cities Opera Guild. The performances took place at the World Theater in May 1991, under the baton of Philip Brunelle, and the soloists included Maria Jette, Janis Hardy and James McKeel, while the student librettists, composers and performers came from the Arts High School, Central Junior High School, Convent of the Visitation School, J. J. Hill School, Oak Grove Intermediate School and Prairie Creek Community School.

First, a rapid outline of the tale as we have it from Ralph of Coggeshall, Abbot of a Cistercian monastery. During his own lifetime, tells Ralph, two children with green skin, brother and sister, had been found near the village of Woolpit. The villagers took them to the manor house of the local landowner, Sir Richard de Calne. The children were unable to speak English, and wouldn't eat good Suffolk food, but finally they ate green beans. The Woolpit priest baptised the children, and began to teach them English, but before long the green boy fell sick and died.

When she had learned English, the green girl told the people of Woolpit an amazing tale about her own country. It was under the earth, she said, and everything there was green; it was divided from another, much brighter land by a broad river. She and her brother had been minding their sheep, but one strayed into a cave. They went into the cave after it, heard the sound of bells, followed them, and came out on the face of the earth. And when, later, the green girl and her bother searched for the way back home, it was no longer there.

The green girl stayed on in Woolpit. And in time, she married a farmer from Lynn, forty miles away...

I believe this haunting tale raised profound questions about prejudice, tolerance and the nature of home. And it is these that Nicola and I addressed when we turned 'The Green Children' into an opera.

For how were the green children treated when they first appeared in Woolpit? You can be sure that many of the Suffolk villagers, confronted by difference, not just difference of colour but cultural difference, seized up with suspicion and fear:

> They'll wreck our crops!
> They come from Old Nick!
> She'll steal my man!
> We'll all fall sick!

But the villagers' suspicion that the children might be ghosts or evil spirits or worse, and their desire to have them chucked out or branded or even put to death, doubtless began to change when the little green boy became ill. They witnessed the green girl's grief; seeing her to be a child of time, like themselves, they may have begun to identify with her and accept her.

The green girl's description of her own country, to which it seems she cannot return, invites us all to consider what we understand by 'home'. Where is your home? Where is mine? And in the opera, replying to the green girl's assertion "I must go home", the villagers sing:

> Stay here! Stay with us!
> Stay here with us!

> I'm black, he's yellow,
> We're pink, they're green.
>
> But our hopes and our fears-
> They are the same.

I wonder whether, when the green girl met and married the farmer from Lynn, her ideas about home began to crystallise. "What is home?" I have her sing. "First it's your mother and your father. It's the first cot that you sleep in, and the room with your belongings." That is how it is for us all, to begin with. But time passes, we grow up, and our sense of home develops. It may not lose those first elements but embraces new ones: friendship, love, a shared language. Home, that is to say, is the common ground where one tries to understand and is understood; where one accepts and is accepted. "Not just this place, not just that place," sings the green girl, "it's true, your home can be the world."

The opera ends with a round – a recognition of the dance of time, the endless cycle of life and death and life:

> This world is greening,
> Greening is growing,
> Growing is living,
> Living is blessing,
> Sowing and reaping
> Through the year's turning,
> Dying to living,
> Song without ending.

Like 'The Death of Balder', then, 'The Green Children' – preoccupied with difference, prejudice, acceptance, shared values – has at its heart the theme of individuality and universality: each one of us in one, is singular, completely and utterly different from any other one; we are the same, all of us, and together we are one, and only together are we one.

I am not quite sure I know what the precise words, the magic words that identify our deepest longings, are. But perhaps they are simple: perhaps just a revised version of the list of personal pronouns. I, thou, you, we. *Niin, giin, giin, niinawind. Mai, aap, tum, hum. Wo, ni, ni men, wo men.*

Maybe Bill Clinton was right after all! Shall we try to do away with 'he' and 'she' and 'they' altogether? For, as Linda Crawford says in *To Hold Us Together*, "it seems that the deeper we look, the more we are willing to grant humanity to those who are unlike us, and it begins to seem as though they are who we are, that there is so little difference between us it is not worth mentioning."

"As though they are who we are." The great James Baldwin in his essay 'Here Be Dragons' went one passionate and moving step further:

> ...we are all androgynous, not only because we are all born of a woman impregnated by the seed of a man but because each of us, helplessly and forever, contains the other – male in female, female in male, white in black and black in white. We are part of each other.

I and thou and you: we, the story! Let us find the tales and share the tales which celebrate this truth.

On Katharine Briggs' *Folk Tales of Britain*

Let me declare my hand at once. This glorious compendium has sat at my elbow and lain beside my pillow for the last forty years, and is without question the book I'd want to take with me to a desert island.

The first part contains folk narratives, which inhabit the fictional Never Never Land and are set in 'Once upon a time'. The second part consists of legends – stories that were believed by their early narrators to be true. These are rooted in time and place and often refer to individuals: some still remembered, some lost in the dark drumroll of years. That's the crucial distinction.

So what categories of legend are there? And what kinds of delight do these books offer? And is Philip Pullman justified in calling the dictionary as a whole "one of the great books of Britain"?

During the Middle Ages, some historians thought it fitting to incorporate legends into their work. I'm thinking not so much of a writer like Geoffrey of Monmouth, who was a master of invention – virtually a Romantic novelist – as of men like the Cistercian Abbot of Coggeshall, Ralph, who in his *Chronicon Anglicanum* (written sometime between 1187 and 1218) carefully records the discovery of two green children at Woolpit and "a certain wild man captured in the sea" at Orford, both in Suffolk, as well as describing what happened to them.

But accounts such as these are by nature occasional and scattershot, and the truth is that although the Middle Ages seethed with superstition, it was largely oral in transmission. Almost ninety per cent of today's English villages are named in the Domesday Book, and each village had its own ghost – just as most still do – while many people were aware of nearby black dogs or changelings or fairies or witches. These 'wonders', rumours, customs, memories, and folk beliefs were told at the hearth, and passed from generation to generation, but very few of them were actually written down because most of the 'folk' were illiterate.

So it is probably right to think of the chief cause for the first decline of folk legend and folk narrative as being the advent of printing and literacy. This is certainly what John Aubrey argued in his *Remaines of Gentilisme and Judaisme* (1686–7):

> Before Printing, Old-wives Tales were ingeniose, and since Printing came in fashion, till a little before the Civill-warres, the ordinary sort of People were not taught to reade. Now-a-dayes Bookes are common, and most of the poor people understand letters; and the many good Bookes, and variety of Turnes of Affaires, have putt all the old Fables out of doors: and the divine art of Printing and Gunpowder have frightened away Robin-goodfellow and the Fayries.

The other reason why folk belief and folk tale suffered was that many rural communities began to break up during the Industrial Revolution, while others were depleted by emigration to the United States of America, especially from Ireland. This was memorably described (and regretted) by the Dublin bookseller and antiquarian Patrick Kennedy in his *Legendary Fictions of the Irish Celts* (1866):

> Taking into consideration the diminishing of our population by want and emigration, and the general diffusion of booklearning, such as it is, and the growing taste for the rubbishy tales of the penny and halfpenny journals, we have in these latter times been haunted with the horrid thought that the memory of tales heard in boyhood would be irrecoverably lost.

True, during the eighteenth and nineteenth centuries a number of antiquaries recorded folk tales along with descriptions of physical remains, folklore and brief biographies of local notables, but it was during the nineteenth century that they began to work in the field as opposed to relying on earlier literary sources, and in the process became genuine folklorists. The story of how, all over Europe, the collection of folk tales started as a serious hobby and ended as a science is an inspiring and even a thrilling one, best documented by Richard Dorson in *The British Folklorists: A History* (1968). And it is, above all, the work of these men and women, and the tales they collected, that Katharine Briggs draws on in her magisterial *omnium gatherum*.

There are many more kinds of legend than one might imagine, and in so far as Dr Briggs has had to impose some order on her material – there are well over one thousand legends here – she prints them alphabetically within the following fourteen categories: Black Dogs, Bogies, Devils, Dragons, Fairies, Ghosts, Giants, The Supernatural, Witches, Historical Traditions, Local Legends, Origin Myths, Saints, and Miscellaneous Legends.

This may sound rather intimidating, but each time I engage with this book, even for the purposes of research, it is akin to going on the most fascinating walk with a tactful, knowledgeable, maybe ghostly companion! One sets off, as one must, at the beginning but before you've gone more than a few steps you're distracted by some wonder; you dawdle, you pick up speed, your companion points out something you would otherwise have missed.

Thus the first category is Black Dogs, dangerous and benevolent, actual and ghostly, including Padfoot, the Warwickshire Hooter, the Lancashire Skriker and the dreadful, howling saucer-eyed Barguest (which can also be a pig or a goat), as well as the calf-sized Shuck who once accompanied a Viking to England and still trots past my doorstep on the north Norfolk coast.

From here, it's only a hop-and-skip to the stories in the Bogies category, including the one about the most appalling bogie of all, Nuckelavee :

> The lower part... was like a great horse, with flappers like fins about his legs, with a mouth as wide as a whale's, from whence came breath like steam from a brewing-kettle... On him sat, or rather seemed to grow from his back, a huge man... But what to Tammie appeared most horrible of all, was that the monster was skinless...

Maybe it's a natural progression from Nuckelavee to a British dragon or two – more than one hundred villages boast their own dragon tales – or maybe it's time to escape from slithy toves and the sound of slughorns into the world of fairy folk, by far the most appealing but also the most chancy of supernatural beings, sometimes rewarding humans, sometimes exacting a price for disrespect. Fairies are apt to take on features of the landscapes they inhabit, as well as the temperaments of their inhabitants, so while East Anglian bogies and boggarts tend to be hairy and earthy and plain-speaking, Celtic fairies are wild, often hauntingly beautiful, and the legends about them leavened with imaginative detail.

Dr Briggs has no truck with "self-styled witches" who claim to be perpetuating a Bronze Age fertility religion, but gives full rein to the old belief in witchcraft "with its ill-will, forespelling and sympathetic magic", as well as pointing to present-day survivals of actual belief. Indeed, if my walking companion were still alive, I could lead her straight to an example of that.

But no, Dr Briggs died in 1980, and so it seems entirely appropriate that *Folk Tales of Britain* should contain such immensely strong sections on ghosts of all kinds (surely the most widely held of all folk beliefs) and on supernatural legends of second sight, wraiths, visions of events faraway in place or time, and wholly inexplicable happenings.

In these volumes, Katharine Briggs represents not only monkish chroniclers, antiquaries and semi-scientific collectors, but also twentieth-century folklorists armed with tape recorders, intent on preserving legends without the literary adornment that often characterises nineteenth-century versions. And the cornerstone of Briggs's achievement plainly lies in her selection of the legends themselves, most reprinted in full but some shortened and many summarised, so as to provide the very greatest possible range of tale-type (complete story, that is to say) and of motif, voice, time, and place.

No less impressive is the scholarly but accessible paraphernalia with which Dr Briggs underpins this great story-hoard: her terse introductions, her incomparable bibliography and Index of Tale-Types, above all her lively and informative notes on individual tales. In his preface to *Folk Tales of Britain: Narratives*, Philip Pullman introduces her and hails her impeccable scholarship and authority, and to my mind she is well-nigh pitch perfect in the way she satisfies the needs of folklorists without overtaxing the general reader.

Earlier, I asked what kinds of delight this seminal dictionary offers. And I suppose the first is the one alluded to by Patrick Kennedy: the memory of tales we heard in childhood. As children, many if not most of us heard traditional tales before going on to read them for ourselves. We listened, we memorised, we engaged, we identified, and they left such an indelible impression on us that to revisit them may bring us close to tears.

The second delight has to do with locality. Those readers living in Britain, or familiar with these islands, will quickly encounter a story rooted in their own county, even in their own village. This may be one of the Historical Traditions embodying memories of wars and renowned individuals, some predictable, such as King Alfred ('*Engle hyrde, Engle deorling*' he was called in the Middle Ages; the shepherd of the English, the darling of the English), or Coeur de

Lion, or the much vilified Oliver Cromwell; or may be one of the Local Legends, some scarcely known beyond our own communities, some achieving a much wider purchase, such as the tradition that King Arthur and his knights lie sleeping under a hill, and will one day emerge and drive all the nasty Angles and Saxons and Frisians and Jutes back across the German Ocean.

When we encounter and assimilate any local, doorstep story – something momentous or a mere trifle – it becomes part of our own story. It's like a milepost leading from now to then, reminding us how fruitful it always is to think of our shared story in terms of layers: layers of time, layers of scape natural and manmade; layers of language, layers of traditional tale.

Before long, one finds oneself tuning in to the voices of individual storytellers, and senses their delight in telling a tale. One learns to identify the areas of interest of specific collectors and recognises the different ways in which they choose to record their legends. But what these tales have in common is even more significant than what separates them: they're almost all driven by event, unconcerned with the emotions of the individuals caught up in them. This, for instance, is how a Scottish mother and her maid get rid of a changeling and recover the 'real child' in 'The Caerlaverock Changeling':

> At midnight the chimney-top was covered up, and every chink and granny stopped. The fire was blown till it was glowing hot, and the maid speedily undressed the child and tossed him on to the burning coals. He shrieked and yelled in the most dreadful manner; and in an instant the fairies were heard moaning on every side, and rattling at the windows, door, and chimney. "In the name of God, bring back the bairn," cried the lass. The window flew up, the real child was laid on the mother's lap, and the wee deil flew up the chimney laughing.

So it comes as something of a jolt when, just now and then, Katharine Briggs slips into the mix one of Child's *Ballads*, with their powerful (if traditional) imagery, dramatic situations and naked emotions, such as 'The Unquiet Grave':

> The twelvemonth and a day being up,
> The dead began to speak:
> "Oh who sits weeping on my grave,
> And will not let me sleep?"
>
> "'Tis I, my love, sits on your grave,
> And will not let you sleep;
> For I crave one kiss of your clay-cold lips,
> And that is all I seek."
>
> "You crave one kiss of my clay-cold lips;
> But my breath smells earthy strong;
> If you have one kiss of my clay-cold lips
> Your time will not be long."

All these delights, then, and yet perhaps the greatest one of all is the way in which we come face to face time and again with the shrewdness, the earthiness, the sheer knowingness, the salty wit, the shoulder-to-shoulderness in the face of danger or death, the sturdy philosophical acceptance of our human comedy in the huge cast of characters caught up in these tales. Here is the full gamut of human experience and response, love and hate, hope and fear, courage and cowardice, patience and impetuosity, humour and humility, and even while admiring them for their strengths, one cannot but love human beings all the more for their failings and stupidity.

But there is something else. Many of these legends embody an awareness that however much we know, there is even more we do not know. So while they may be no-nonsense and down to earth, they're also humble and open-minded. High-flown and highfalutin only in the language of the most literary of their collectors, and seldom making use of simile or metaphor, their characters keep their ears to the ground and hear all manner of wonders.

And what could be more tantalising, more haunting, than to hear a snatch of fairy music, as some human beings claim to have done? That song of the seal: "I am a man upon the land, I am a selkie in the sea..." Or the voices of the fairies at Knockgrafton, "each mingling and blending with the others so strangely, that they seemed to be one, though all singing different strains..."

There is one unforgettable Cornish legend, collected and retold by a number of nineteenth-century folklorists, which tells 'How Joan Lost the Sight of One Eye' (and which we will come to presently). To my mind, it's a metaphor. We can view this world around us in two different ways, it seems to say: with the eye that observes the physical, material, verifiable world, and with the eye of the imagination. Not only this: the story demonstrates how each of us needs both eyes, both ways of seeing, if we're to engage to the full with life here on Middle-earth.

I know of no book that invites us all to do so more wholeheartedly. *Folk Tales of Britain* is at once a national monument and an inexhaustible springboard for storytellers, writers, and artists working in many disciplines. It is indeed one of the great books of Britain. Read it, listen to it, and you will hear the hum and underhum of our island story.

Different, – but oh how like!

In his poem, 'Yes, it was the Mountain Echo', William Wordsworth declares, "Like, – but oh how different!" The voice and echo, he says, the oral source and its repetition, are less similar than dissimilar.

Well, maybe! But as one reflects on what responsibilities oral storytellers and writers may have, and what strategies they may devise, one may well conclude that it is not a matter of "Like, – but oh how different!" but, rather, "Different, – but oh how like!" So that, with apologies to Mr Wordsworth, I claim as my title.

What I have to say falls into five unequal parts: first an attempt at a redefinition of traditional tale; then some brief comments on accounts of storytelling; so into the meat of the matter with a discussion of the storyteller's responsibilities and of ways of retelling tales I have found fruitful; finally, a few remarks on the educational uses of tale.

*

To my mind, a traditional tale may be a myth or a folk tale and is in either case a metaphor which entertains and instructs: a narrative in the first instance oral, which is the product of no single person, place or time, and which has been retuned and sometimes reclothed by those who have transmitted it.

A myth is a story within a loosely-knit cycle of narratives which together amount to a sacred history. This history is panoptic. It assigns human beings their place within the entire order of creation, but its first matter is not women or men but their giant shadows, the goddesses and gods. Myth looks back, myth looks forward, myth explains and warns. Always, it is concerned with the welfare of women and men not only as social animals but as spiritual beings.

A folk tale is the generic term for many different kinds of narrative, always brief enough to be digested at one sitting. The cast of thousands consists of humans, animals, and supernatural beings of all kinds (as well as talking plants, trees, and natural phenomena), but never the celestial beings who created them. The character of folk tale is direct narrative, in which the emphasis is on action as opposed to idea or feeling, and its purpose is to illustrate the whole gamut of non-religious human experience – all the longings and rewards and sorrows and frustrations and hazards and absurdities of our lives.

The folk tale tree is laden with fruit of many shapes, sizes, and colours: etiological (or ætiological) tales that inhabit the borders of myth as they explain origins and causes – how, for example, the body of the Muckle Mester Stoor Worm turned into the islands of Orkney and Shetland and Faroe and Iceland; tales of fabulous beasts – Jacqueline Simpson identifies more than one hundred villages in Britain with their own distinct dragon stories; tales of shape-changers; giant stories; stories of heroes and strong men, and saints and devils. Then there are fairy tales, involving supernatural beings and magic – it is incorrect to speak of 'folk and fairy tales' as two genres, for the latter is simply one species of the former; there are wonder tales; jocular tales; fables; nursery tales.

In addition to these categories, there is that kind of tale in which a moment of definable or indefinable historical actuality is embedded within any amount of fantastic invention. Most ghost stories belong in this category. And so do those stories we call legends, or folk legends.

How is it that Richard Whittington, philanthropic Lord Mayor of London, became hero of a tale in which his cat made his fortune on the Barbary Coast? And how come the thirteenth-century abbot of a Cistercian monastery at Coggeshall describes a wild man – a relative of the wodewose and the merman, a man completely covered with hair – and the way in which he was hoicked out of the sea by fishermen at Orford in Suffolk?

What actually happened? In such tales, what is fact, what fiction, and how did they come to combine? These are the fascinating and largely unanswerable questions always begged by legend.

I sometimes think it is useful to think of a legend in this way. An oyster gets a piece of grit inside its shell. "Ugh!" it says, or slobbers, or whatever oysters do. "Ugh! My shoulder's itching!" So what does this oyster do about it? It exudes its own balm; it surrounds the source of its itch with that nacreous substance we call pearl. Likewise, a legend has at its heart a piece of grit: a moment of historical substance. Around it there gathers and grows an accretion, the filaments of imagination. Grit and invention: together they form the pearl of legend.

Will you step for a moment into your early childhood? The village or street where you lived. Is there anyone living nearby whom you – and maybe your friends – suppose about, talk about, maybe even worry about? Is he really a werewolf? Is she a witch?

Most of us can think of such a person: someone who set our imagination racing, someone we've continued to think of from time to time, adding and subtracting to and from the persona – part fact and part fantasy – whom we created years ago.

In the seaside village in north Norfolk where I spent my holidays as a boy, just a mile away from where I now live, there was a woman called Sheila Disney. She had slightly webbed fingers and webbed feet. I think she did! Anyhow, she told me once she was descended from a seal, and I saw no reason to disbelieve her. After all, I knew that Shetlandic tale about a sealwoman who marries a fisherman, and gives birth to human children. But Miss Disney – everyone called her Diz – also told me she was an eastern, English cousin of the great Walt! I think she did. And she had a moustache! This sealwoman barked, and she scared me stupid; she taught me to swim, after a fashion; and wading along the muddy creek, she used to catch her breakfast – some luckless passing flatfish – with her feet. Not so long ago, I wrote a verse about her:

> Easterlies have sandpapered her larynx.
> Webbed fingers, webbed feet:
> last child of a seal family.
>
> There is a blue flame at her hearth, blue mussels
> at her board.
> Her bath is the gannet's bath.
>
> Rents one windy room at the top of a ladder.
> Reeks of kelp.
>
> "Suffer the little children," she barks,
> and the children – all the little ones
> are enchanted.
>
> She has stroked through the indigo of
> Dead Man's Pool
> and returned with secrets.
>
> They slip their moorings. They
> tack towards her glittering eyes…

You see? A hopeless mixture! Memory of actuality and deliberate invention which, at this late date, can scarcely be separated. This is what legend is; and you and I, we have all created our own legends.

*

There is nothing so fascinating as coming to grips with process, whether it be watchmaking or furniture-making, bell-ringing or learning to fly. And when that process is one we have attempted ourselves, we compare, we learn, and we enjoy a sense of almost conspiratorial intimacy. That is why I often go back to accounts by folklorists of the oral storyteller in action:

> Her memory kept a firm grip on all the stories. She herself knew that this gift was not granted to everyone, and that there were many who could remember nothing connectedly. She told her stories thoughtfully, accurately, with wonderful vividness, and evidently had delight in doing so.

That is how Jacob and Wilhelm Grimm described a village woman from near Kassel who provided them with a number of tales during the first decade of the nineteenth century.

My second storyteller is the redoubtable Peig Sayers, who lived on the Blasket Islands until they were evacuated in the 1930s. She recorded many tales on Ediphone cylinders and, in the words of folklore collector Seosamh Ó Dálaigh:

> Great artist and wise woman that she was, Peig would at once switch from gravity to gaiety, for she was a light-hearted woman, and her changes of mood and face were like the changes of running water. As she talked her hands would be working too: a little slap of the palms to cap a phrase, a flash of the thumb over her shoulder to mark a mystery, a hand hushed to mouth for mischief or whispered secrecy.

The third of my accounts was written by John Francis Campbell of Islay. He and his team of Gælic speakers collected no fewer than 791 tales (there are 86 in his four-volume *Popular Tales of the West Highlands*, 1860–2), and in this vivid passage he sets the storyteller in context:

> One woman was industriously weaving in a corner, another was carding wool, and a girl was spinning dexterously with a distaff

made of a rough-forked birch-branch, and a spindle which was little better than a splinter of fir. In the warm nook behind the fire sat a girl with one of those strange foreign faces which are occasionally to be seen in the Western Isles, and which are often supposed by their neighbours to mark the descendants of the Spanish crews of the wrecked Armada... Old men and young lads, newly returned from the eastern fishing, sat about on benches fixed to the wall, and smoked and listened; and Macdonald sat on a low stool in the midst, and chanted forth his lays amid suitable remarks and ejaculations of praise and sympathy. One of the poems was the 'Lay of Diarmaid'... "Och! och! – aw! is not that sad?" said the women when Diarmaid was expiring.

Now let me isolate and slightly expand the qualities ascribed to these storytellers:

i) Memory – that is to say the establishing of the storyteller as part of the tradition through reliable recall; anything less sows seeds of doubt; and each story has its own sequence, shape and proportions as surely as an egg-timer has a waist.

ii) Thoughtfulness – the storyteller cares for and gives proper weight to each character and action; (s)he is involved in a tale but may also stand outside it and comment on it.

iii) Accuracy – mastery of language; no action or thought or feeling or description is greater than the language which expresses it.

iv) Vividness – the use of words to make memorable images and memorable sounds.

v) Constant changes of mood – a folk tale is always fast on its feet and embodies a wide range of emotion.

vi) Use of face and hands – while words tell a story, expression and gesture enact it.

vii) Delight – delight in story and delight in the art of storytelling; delight in the act of sharing which, as Jack Zipes says in *Revisiting the Storyteller*, awakens the storyteller in others and is an act of liberation.

In these short passages, then, there are valuable lessons for oral storytellers and writers alike, as well as indications of some of the elements that separate them.

In a preliterate society, it is customary for the poet and storyteller to undergo formal training. How else can (s)he become guardian of the memory-hoard? In Heroic Age Ireland, for instance, the *filid* (for whom the simple label 'storyteller' is too scant; they also served as poet, magician, lawgiver, judge, and counsellor to the chief) served an apprenticeship of seven years; doubtless he learned from existing practitioners about the very qualities we have just isolated; and he was expected to commit to memory more than 250 tales.

The contemporary storyteller is no longer the living memory of the tribe, unless (s)he is one of the tiny minority who belong to a preliterate society; but for all that, (s)he has responsibilities, and not only those implied in the passages by Grimm, Ó Dálaigh, and Campbell.

To begin with, storytellers – no matter how substantial or modest their aims – will do well to spend some time inhabiting the world of traditional tale: only when they win a decent working knowledge of the canon and can proceed on the basis of comparison – comparison of different motifs, comparison of the same motif from different sources – can they feel fully confident in their choice of matter. And only when they are fully aware of the remarkable amount of leaves on the storytree will they be likely to choose little-known material instead of playing 'follow my leader'. It is encouraging that so many anthologies of folk tales have been published during the last generation, but discouraging that relatively few break substantial new ground in their choice of tale.

I do not mean that we should not engage with and renew 'standards' such as 'Cinderella' (in one of its more than 300 versions!) and 'Sleeping Beauty' and 'Jack and the Beanstalk'. Of course we should. They are tales with unsurpassable characterisation and colour, movement and meaning. What I am saying is that there are very many other great tales that are scarcely known at all, and that they present storytellers both with opportunity and responsibility.

Of their nature, folk tales reconcile people of different gender, colour, race, and nation. Their ground is what humans hold in common, not what divides them. But although many tales may share one motif, the flesh and clothing of each varies greatly from the others, and depends on local circumstance. It follows that the storyteller's second responsibility is, like the first, contextual.

It is scarcely adequate to select and retell or rewrite a tale without having some knowledge of the culture from which that tale comes. With such knowledge, the reteller is likely to avoid a number of obvious traps: the misunderstanding of idea, behaviour or terminology; the exorcising of the humdrum; and the reinforcing of divisive cultural and national stereotypes.

Let the storyteller be assured, on the other hand, that traditional tale is indeed a *jeu sans frontiéres*, and that desirable sensitivity to cultural difference is not to be confused with political correctness, which is reductive and stupid. I give little credence to the notion that, because I am a man and white and Anglo-Saxon – a deadly trio! – I may not give words in a tale to, say, an Aboriginal or Inuit woman, on the grounds that I can have no imaginative empathy with her condition. That way lies madness. It is absurd to argue that an artist can speak for no one but her/ himself.

I think the storyteller's third responsibility is to the chosen tale. Before (s)he reshapes it, (s)he must enter it and allow it to enter her/him. What does the tale say? What does it mean? Does it have more than one meaning? More than two? And if the tale originated in a known place and moment – as is likely with legend – what did it mean to its original audience? What parts of the action are structural and what incidental? Which words of which characters are crucial and which casual?

Only when the teller has really pondered questions of this kind can (s)he feel free to remake it. And of course, in exercising this freedom, the teller may well choose to change the emphasis of a tale so that it speaks to her/his own time and society.

Take, for example, the popular fifteenth-century Norfolk tale of 'The Pedlar of Swaffham': the account of a man who has a dream, and walks halfway across England because of it, only to learn of gold buried in his backyard – a fortune he dedicates to the rebuilding of the local church. Is this story about divine purpose – the way in which absolutely everything that happens is part of God's plan? Is it about the advisability of buying a ticket to heaven? Is it concerned with the importance of dream and intuition? Is it about the value of dogged persistence? Is it about how the greatest treasure is not to be found far afield but on our own doorsteps? Storytellers divided by more than 500 years might very well come to different conclusions about the meaning of such a tale. But provided the contemporary storyteller has carefully questioned the source, and does not arbitrarily impose but elicits and develops meanings, there is nothing whatsoever wrong with that.

The storyteller's fourth responsibility is to craft and language. (S)he must try to find a shape appropriate to meaning, cultural origin, audience, and (s)he must try to find the right words to tell or write the tale. No easy task! I'll confine myself here to a few comments on language, and say something later about craft in relation to my own storytelling strategies.

The language of folk tale, like the action of folk tale, is not complicated or fatty: it is simple and lean. This is because it derives from the oral tradition; because it deals in actions always, and seldom in feelings or ideas; and because it aims to speak to a wide, often unlearned and often youthful audience. The words in our language that describe things, not ideas and feelings, very largely derive from Anglo-Saxon. Womb (*wamb*), man (*mon*), child (*cild*), water (*wæter*), earth (*eorthe*), plough (*ploh*), root (*rot*) – the very fabric of life. The language of folk tale retold in English must surely come from this root too: words that are quick and clean and taut and true. Short words pack the greatest punch.

In the same spirit, the language of folk tale will be rich in nouns and adjectives but have little time for modifiers – sometimes I think we could do without adverbs altogether. And it will not be slowed and sargassoed in a sea of passive verbs; rather, good retellings live and kick in the present and active tense.

The canon of traditional tale; the culture to which a tale belongs; the chosen tale itself; the craft and language: above and beyond these four considerations, oral and literary storytellers share one further responsibility, and that is to their audience.

As their name implies, traditional tales usually have their own histories, and have survived for generations, though I'm aware, of course, of the body of urban legends – such as 'The Hook' and 'The Vanishing Hitchhiker' and 'The Runaway Grandmother' – which are of comparatively recent vintage.

The chief reason why early nineteenth-century European antiquarian and social historians began to write down traditional tales – the trickle of curiosity soon becoming a floodtide of fascination – was because they witnessed the dislocations of the Industrial Revolution. As families moved from green country to black country (what a depth charge those two words have when set side by side!), and from village to city, so as to sustain and develop the manufacturing industries, they leeched and fractured rural communities in a way not seen since the dreadful plagues of the fourteenth century. The arrival of mechanised travel, the growth of literacy, penny newspapers, gas lighting: they too all played a part in undermining family and village as integrated, self-sustaining and self-entertaining units to which more than ninety per cent of the population belonged.

Jacob and Wilhelm Grimm were the first to appreciate the implications of this earthquake, and to set down tales as they heard them from rural folk in Saxony during the first decade of the nineteenth century, for fear they would otherwise be completely forgotten and lost. Since the brothers Grimm and most of those who followed them into the field were recording what was essentially a rural tradition, it is not surprising that, when the tales they set down had a setting to speak of (and many folk tales do not), it was a rural one. Neither is it surprising that when those tales were set in a specific time (and most are not), that time was often generations or centuries before the nineteenth century. In such static and conservative communities, everyone knew one another and knew every grass-blade of gossip, and people only ventured into the local market town, on foot or in a cart, two or three times a year. Time came 'dropping slow', and memory was extended and savoured. "A year ago," we say. "It seems like another century." But our forebears said: "A century ago! It seems like yesterday."

Here, then, is the storyteller's final responsibility: the reconciliation of tale and audience. Her/his tales are almost always rural and very seldom contemporary and yet the great majority of her/his audience live in city, town and suburb, and live at a time when social change has been so great that some characters, actions and attitudes within folk tales may seem unrecognisable, irrelevant or offensive.

The wise woman and the childe and the charcoal-burner: where are they now? The wicked stepmother and the impossibly virtuous third daughter: how can we cope with them? And the casual exhibitions of violence – all the routine beatings and imprisonments and chopping off of heads: are these useful models, especially when our audiences consist of children?

Each oral storyteller and writer interested not in rehashing but recreating and perpetuating traditional tale is bound to consider such difficult issues. But where an audience consists wholly or partly of children, (s)he has further responsibilities, akin to those of parent and teacher.

Since the difference between adult and child is not one of intelligence, sensitivity or the imaginative faculty but, rather, of experience and the lack of it, this is plainly where a storyteller's responsibility lies.

It is not much use pretending to children that there are no horrors in the world, when they know perfectly well that there are. They know it from television and radio; they know it from the newspapers; and they know it from loose talk amongst adults. They know it every day.

So while it is natural to try to protect children from naked atrocities, it is likely to be counterproductive to suppress altogether the vein cruelty in traditional tale – as we have already seen with the story of the cosseted child developing a 'complex' under their bed in the place of a more traditional monster.

What is needed is for the storyteller, like the parent, to become the mediator or broker between children and the raw material of human experience. (S)he must relay it but also interpret it. That is to say, the storyteller must consider and present her/his stories in an ethical light, in which good and bad behaviour have consequences both for individual and society.

This said, I must admit I have come across perhaps half a dozen tales so irredeemably nasty and hopeless that it would be perverse (and perverted) to lay them before children, while there are others so sexually frank or deviant as to be completely inappropriate for the innocent eye and ear. I think, really, that a sensible working rule for the reteller for children is not to regard any subject as taboo, but not to confront children with behaviour or situation in which the only colour is unmitigated dark despair.

These, then, are the five responsibilities shared by oral storyteller and writer. And I believe that careful consideration of them should lie at the heart of our re-enacting of traditional tale.

*

The staple diet of oral storyteller and writer alike is third person narrative: she said this, he saw that, they did the other. Or else, in the interests of immediacy: he says, she sees, they do.

But in reviewing the storyteller's responsibilities, I suggested that (s)he must enter a tale and allow it to enter her/him. When this happens, the process of creation begins. And the cornerstone of remaking is the selection of the form which best enables the reteller to reveal the strength of her/his material and best supports the message or moral, however well hidden, that (s)he wishes to convey.

This doesn't mean that the storyteller is duty bound to invade and take over and recast each tale (s)he uses. We all know of originals so well judged and word-bright that we may do best to leave them more or less as they are, and play the role not of remaker but editor. I have sometimes found this to be the right course of action with the century-old versions by Joseph Jacobs.

In the same way, the storyteller may sometimes find her/his primary role is as translator. In retelling astounding tales such as 'Long Tom and the Dead Hand' and 'Samuel's Ghost', collected by Mrs Balfour during the 1980s, I have frankly done little more than come to grips with archaic Lincolnshire dialect, and translate into modern English.

But let me describe three rather more radical strategies I have found fruitful when retelling traditional tale, which can be used by writer and storyteller alike.

One characteristic of our times has been the ubiquity of the outsider. I mean people driven from their homes by oppression, hunger, or illness; herded into encampments which begin as temporary and end up as more or less permanent. I mean all those people who – by virtue of colour, culture or creed – find themselves alone or in very small minorities within the societies they live in. I mean the children of travellers in British primary and secondary schools. I mean the people in my own Norfolk village who were not born here but are, as I am, 'furriners'. I suppose I also mean, by extension, that part of each of us that believes (s)he is a square peg in a round hole, and doesn't really quite fit in.

There are many traditional tales in which the separateness of the central character(s) is the very point of the tale. When A encounters X, Y and Z, what happens? Is there friction? Are they unable to rub along or do they come to accept they're all members of the same alphabet? The telling of tales revolving around conflict, resolution, and tolerance – and even delight in difference – is valuable work. And because the central character is – at first anyhow – an isolated figure, there may be a case for reflecting this in the form of the retelling. How? Simply by telling the tale in the first person, from the viewpoint of the central character. At once, the reteller is working with 'I' and 'they'.

This device has two further advantages. It enables the figure to reveal something of her/his thoughts and feelings without interrupting the rapid progression typical of traditional tale. And it enables the reteller directly to describe the familiar with new eyes.

The second of my three strategies takes its lead from the conviction of the medieval theologian, Duns Scotus, that each element of our planet – each stick and stone and granule of earth – has its own quiddity, if only we have time to dream our way into it; and from the recognition by Native Americans that each element has its own voice, if only we listen to it.

In considering how to retell the legend of church bells ringing underwater to warn sailors of danger – a tradition common to Dunwich in Suffolk and Mundesley in Norfolk, and to Cardigan Bay, and Lancashire, and Brittany – I was guided by the fact that this is a tale in which many distinct and powerful forces are caught up in the conflict: cliff, church, village community, and the dead in the graveyard: are all at risk because of the fury of the night-storm and destructive power of the sea.

So why not, I wondered, give a voice to each of these forces? Why not allow them to tell their own tale? As I drafted the tale 'Sea Tongue', I also hit upon a way of linking the end of each short section with the beginning of the next so as to sustain the narrative's momentum and imitate the tolling of a bell underwater:

> (*end*) I'll undermine the church and its graveyard. I'll chew on the bones of the dead.
>
> (*beginning*) We are the dead. We died in bed, we died on the sword. We fell out of the sky, we swallowed the ocean.

And again:

> (*end*) We live time out, long bundles of bone bedded in the cliff.
>
> (*beginning*) I am the cliff. Keep away from me. I'm jumpy and shrinking, unsure of myself. I may let you down badly.

Whether this form works or not, and whether it is imitable, is for others to say. But I offer it as one way in which form – effectively a fractured narrative – can underpin matter.

My third and last strategy is not so much a matter of form as context, and it arises from the responsibility of reteller, discussed earlier, to reconcile tale and audience. What, in fact, are storyteller and writer to do when most of their material is rural (and ancient) when most of their audience is urban (and youthful)?

One answer is both simple and exacting: strip a tale down to its bare storyline, and then build it up again using modern characters and a modern setting. Sometimes this seems out of the question, because the storyline makes it so. In the case of some of Mrs Balfour's tales, for instance, the huge sucking fen, apparently so empty, in fact so full of threatening supernatural beings – boggarts and bogies and will-o'-the-wykes and squirming dead hands – appears to be so fundamental as to be irreplaceable.

But is this really so? I am thinking of sodden, eerie peat cuttings (such as those on the doorstep of Wilmslow in Cheshire) and of the concrete-and-wasteland of housing estates. There is actually no reason why a reteller should not plant stories such as 'The Dead Moon' and 'Yallery Brown' in such settings.

To do this kind of thing means, of course, that one is laying oneself open to the charge of making artificial transplants. But this would only be the case if the reteller were imaginatively deficient, and changed the setting without changing the cast. What I am suggesting is that writer or storyteller should effectively take an old story as a chassis on which to construct a new one. And this is, of course, precisely what has happened as traditional tales have travelled from generation to generation, country to country, and continent to continent. One storyteller removes the colour local to another, and redresses the bones of the tale with detail and colour familiar to her/his own audience.

I am not arguing that storytellers should always provide their youthful audiences with familiar settings, but that their settings should not always be unfamiliar. Otherwise, we accentuate the distance between retellings and children's experience, and that cannot be right.

Some storytellers may find the prospect of reinventing a tale in this manner rather daunting. I did, when I first tried it in my *British Folk Tales* with 'The Small-Tooth Dog', which begins in a sorry backstreet with a mugging. But take heart! The process is less difficult and more fun than it may seem at first, and it is extremely valuable. At present, the stock of tales with urban or suburban and modern settings is small and largely American; we need to add to it.

*

Parents, teachers and librarians regularly introduce children to traditional tales, while British teachers – in accordance with the National Curriculum – also put them to work in the primary to school classroom.

They ask children predict the endings of tales half-told, to develop their ability to think logically; they use tales as quarries for language-work and character study, and as models for plot-building and descriptive writing; they lead discussions of tales so as to rehearse cause and effect, right and wrong, social consequences, religious beliefs, the existence of magic and the supernatural, the power of names and numbers. Teachers use traditional tales for hot seating (in which a child pretends to be one of the characters in a tale, and answers questions from all comers about her/his thoughts and feelings), and they use tales to point up the difference between thought and action. They use tales as springboards for geography and history projects, and they have children re-enact traditional tale in drama, music, dance and artwork.

All this activity is potentially extremely valuable, but it is also all secondary. I want to assert that none of it is or can be a substitute for a young child's primary experience – hearing or reading the tale itself. This is the moment at which a child may enter into deep communion, revelling in a tale's drama and music and patterning, apprehending without fully understanding that this story is also in some part her/his story, and unaware that (s)he is animating the tradition by sharing in it.

It follows that teachers simply must root around for the best-written versions they can find; and often, I know, this means they will be personally buying books for use in the classroom. It means they must do their utmost, as so many do, to become lively storytellers. And, though funds are invariably limited, it means they must try to bring writers and storytellers into direct contact with children in the classroom.

This is a lot to ask. But I do not think it is overstating the case to say that a child's experience of traditional tale is seminal. It can be a time of intensely-experienced joy; it can lead to a lifelong love of story; and the quality of a child's involvement with the secondary activities described above is likely to be determined by it.

Indeed, I have heard teachers make the point that a child's hearing or reading of story has lasting implications for her/his whole learning capacity, and is especially important in an age when we all have a growing disability to visualise and conceptualise. Research into the human brain indicates that brain activity is high when one is absorbing information through one sensory mode (hearing, for instance, or seeing) but low when one is using two sensory modes (hearing and seeing), as is the case when one watches and listens to television.

It follows that a child whose imagination is quickened by regularly listening to and reading tales will also be developing her/his ability to solve a mathematical problem or set up a science experiment.

*

Of course there are some aspects of the oral tradition the writer cannot assimilate. (S)he cannot raise or lower the voice, or speak in different tones, but only describe such differences:

> "Somebody's been eating my porridge!" said the great, huge bear in his great, rough, gruff voice…"Somebody's been eating my porridge!"

said the middle bear in his middle voice... "Somebody's been eating my porridge!" said the little, small, wee bear in his little, small, wee voice, and somebody has eaten it all up!"

Likewise, the writer cannot speed up or slow down a tale to anything like the same extent as an oral storyteller, and can only hint at the sound of silence.

In her valuable Signal Bookguide, *Traditional Tales*, Mary Steele wrote that "In printed form the traditional tale is really a script for the storyteller speaking, performing, acting a story." These words describe the circular nature of storytelling (water drawn up from the ocean must eventually return to the ocean again!) and contain an implicit reminder to writers that since the first sources of traditional tale were always oral, they will be wise to imitate or find equivalents for such crucial elements of the oral tradition as immediacy and an air, however carefully calculated, of spur-of-the-moment improvisation.

But Steele's words also indicate that writers are denied the use of expression or gesture, ranging from the raised forefinger or eyebrow to a kick of the foot or use of the whole body. The storyteller uses mouthfuls of air and a whole bag of oral and body tricks; the writer uses nothing but written words.

All a writer can offer, therefore, are the fruits of deliberation: well considered shapeliness, so as to begin in expectation, achieve the right balance between a tale's basic structure and extraneous detail, and end in inevitability; and well-considered language, full of edge and colour and verve, so as to point up character, action and mood.

Like, – but oh how different! Different, – but oh how like! When we hear a tale well-told or read a story well-written, the work of some teller or writer with energy and wit and love of the human condition, we experience the same two responses. We know that by identifying, or half-identifying with a tale, we're coming close to ourselves and our fellow humans, and engaging in a kind of healing process. And we feel a delight in story that lasts, like a pervasive scent, long after we've forgotten the ins and outs of a particular tale.

So, in the end, this is what matters most: not this story, or that story, and not the primacy of the oral or the written tradition, but – once upon a time and ever after – the story's telling.

Remember, if you will, the wonderful exchange in Ronald Blythe's *Akenfield*:

> "What was the song, Davie?"
> "Never mind the song – it was the singing that counted."

Which Eye Can You See Me With?

Interpreting Folk Tales

If I look carefully, I can see a high hill. On its chest it wears an enormous badge – a great gleaming cross cut out of the chalk that underlies the springy turf. The shoulders and steep flanks of this hill are covered in a long cloak of beech trees, their leaves so feminine in spring, darkening as the year deepens, brassy in autumn.

At the hem of this cloak, at the very foot of the hill, I can see a cottage; I can see a small square bedroom, dimly-lit. In one corner of this room, there's a bunk bed. On the bottom lies a blue-eyed fair-haired little girl; and on the top a wide-eyed boy – her brother, doubtless! How old are they? Three and six perhaps. There's a man sitting by the bunk. He's leaning forward and cradling something in his arms.

If I listen carefully, I can hear the tap-tap-tapping of a branch at the window – I think it's the branch of an elder tree – and the continuous comfortable quiet shush of night-rain, and now the sound of a harp… Ah! That's what the man is holding: a little Welsh harp. He's plucking it and reciting – or, as the Anglo-Saxons had it, *singan ond secgan* – a tale.

If I listen carefully, I think I can hear his voice. Is it the tale about the cow that ate the piper? Or the tale about the Welsh Lady of the Lake, 'The Lady of Llyn y Fan Fach'? Or the one about the Manx farmer who had no sooner sold his old horse to a fairy than fairy and horse, both of them, disappeared into the ground right in front of him?

No, it's the Irish story of the hunchback Lusmore (Lusmore literally means the great herb, which is the foxglove, *Digitalis purpurea*, a plant with many fairy associations). Listen! The man is singing "Da luan da mort… da luan da mort… da luan da mort."

Monday, Tuesday... Monday, Tuesday, Monday, Tuesday. Have you heard how poor Lusmore was trudging home one evening from market at Caher in Tipperary when he came across a troop of fairies in the old moat at Knockgrafton, singing this rather short-winded song?

Lusmore was spellbound by the singing. 'Though to be sure', he thought to himself, 'there's not much variety to it'. After a while, the hunchback began to hum the melody in tune with the voices; and then, when they paused, he sang out "Wednesday."

"Monday, Tuesday..." sang the voices and Lusmore sang with them, "Monday, Tuesday, Monday, Tuesday..." And then, for a second time, "Wednesday."

When the little people heard Lusmore, they were delighted. They skipped and eddied up the bank, and swirled him down to the bottom of the moat in a whirlwind of cries and laughter. The hunchback was twirled round and round, light as a piece of straw, and the fairy fiddlers played faster and faster.

When the world stopped spinning, Lusmore saw he had been swept into a fine fairy pavilion. True, it was rather low ceilinged, but that didn't bother him! The whole place was lit with candles and packed out with little people – little people chattering, eating, playing fiddles and pipes and harps, dancing...

Lusmore was made most welcome: he was given a low stool, and provided with food and drink.

"Grand! I feel grand!" he said as one fairy after another enquired whether he had all he needed, and praised his skill as a singer. "Just grand!" said Lusmore. "I might as well be the king of the whole land!"

Then the music faltered and stopped; the dancers stood still; the feasters put down their knives and forks. Lusmore watched as the little people crowded together in the middle of the pavilion, and began to whisper. Now the hunchback began to feel nervous: "For all your kindness and courtesy," he muttered, "you fairy folk, you're fickle and chancy."

As Lusmore watched, one little man left the huddle and walked up to him. He smiled at Lusmore and solemnly he said:

Lusmore! Lusmore!
That hump you wore,
That hump you bore
On your back is no more;
Look down on the floor!
There's your hump, Lusmore!

As the hunchback looked down, his ugly hump fell from his shoulders and dropped to the ground.

Word of this wonder soon spreads far and wide and, before long, a second and thoroughly peevish hunchback, Jack Madden, tries to capitalise on the fairies' goodwill. He rides in a cart to the old moat at Knockgrafton, and as soon as he hears the fairies singing their new (and improved!) song "Monday, Tuesday, Monday, Tuesday, Monday, Tuesday, Wednesday... he bawls out "THURSDAY" without regard for timing and without thought for pitch. The fairies are enraged. They sweep Jack down to the bottom of the grassy moat and into their fair pavilion. They jostle him and pick at his clothing and bang him with their tiny fists. And the same little man who smiled on Lusmore narrows his eyes at Jack and says

Jack Madden! Jack Madden!
Your words were all wrong
For our sweet lovely song.
You're caught in our throng
And your life we will sadden:
Here's two lumps for Jack Madden.

At this, a troop of twenty of the strongest fairies staggered into the pavilion, carrying Lusmore's hump. They walked over to poor Jack and at once slammed it down on his back, right over his own hump. And as soon as they had done so, it became firmly fixed there, as if it had been nailed down with six-inch nails by the best of carpenters.

This, then, is what one might call a tale about the price of disrespect. But the man with the harp has stopped playing. He's looking up – looking in my direction... How fortunate we were, my younger sister Sally and I! Fairies and changelings and imps and boggarts, ghosts and giants, dragons and black dogs and a whole fabulous bestiary, wise fools and sealwomen and green children: they all passed through our little square nursery.

I wish for my own two daughters, Oenone and Eleanor, the same regular magical grounding, because the majority of folk tales so perfectly satisfy a small child's requirements: they have casts of strongly-delineated characters and strong and rapid storylines; they move unselfconsciously between the actual and the fantastic, as does a child's mind; and they decode the mysterious, often threatening world the child is growing into.

I say that a folk tale can satisfy a small child's requirements. But of course as one grows older one begins to ask questions of it. How old is this tale and how has it survived? When was it first written down? Why are there others like it, or half-like it? And what does it really mean?

What I intend to do is to offer a framework for the knowledge of individual tales which you must already have, survey the many tale-types to be found in the British Isles and introduce just one of them, and suggest some of the strategies available to a reteller of tales for a modern readership.

*

The pioneers of the great nineteenth-century effort to collect folk tales were of course Wilhelm and Jacob Grimm. Their *Kinder- und Hausmärchen*, first published in 1812, was an unmistakable watershed. On one side of the ridge stand the people working as historians or students of Popular Antiquities to whom folk tale was an incidental delight but of no seminal interest – in England one thinks of figures as far removed as the medieval pseudo-historians Gervase of Tilbury and Ralph of Coggeshall, and the seventeenth- and eighteenth-century antiquaries John Aubrey, William Stukeley, and Joseph Strutt. While on the other side of the ridge stand the assiduous semi-scientific fieldworkers of the nineteenth century, the valiant ranks headed by such distinguished folklorists as Asbjørnsen in Norway, Grundtvig in Denmark, and Árnason in Iceland.

The Grimm Brothers brought a quite new methodology to the collection of folk tale. Not only did they leave a magnificent, if sometimes downright cruel, legacy of more than two hundred tales; they also, in the approved modern manner, documented who they had heard a tale from (many of their sources were illiterate) and the circumstances of its collection. I remember, for instance, the village woman from near Kassel who gave the Grimms some of their best tales:

> Her memory kept a firm grip on all the sagas. She herself knew that this gift was not granted to everyone, and there were many who could remember nothing connectedly. She told her stories thoughtfully, accurately, with wonderful vividness, and evidently had delight in doing so. First, she related them from beginning to end, and then, if required, repeated them more slowly, so that after some practice, it was perfectly easy to write from her dictation.

Of course this process of folk tale collection all over Europe soon became a race against time – and against what passes for progress. With the advance of industrialisation and the dislocation of small self-referring communities; with new education laws that meant that almost every child learned how to read; with the proliferation of newspapers and the arrival of electricity; with the excitement of mechanical entertainment; the social importance of folk tales quickly began to diminish. "We have," said the Dublin folklorist and bookseller, Patrick Kennedy, in 1866, "in these latter times been haunted with the horrid thought that the memory of tales heard in boyhood would be irrecoverably lost."

I don't mean to inflict a catalogue of collectors on you – this is about tales and their treatment, not a bibliography! But let me just indicate the shades of interest in, and commitment to, folk tale in the British Isles in the nineteenth century, and identify a few of the names associated with them.

The very first of the British fieldworkers was a man called Thomas Crofton Croker – and we have him to thank, incidentally, for the tale of the two hunchbacks, 'The Legend of Knockgrafton'.

Crofton Croker was an Admiralty Clerk in London and collected the material for his highly successful *Fairy Legends and Traditions of the South of Ireland*, published in 1825, during the course of a number of summer holidays spent in that country. Here at once we see the prototype of the nineteenth-century British folklorist: he is a gifted amateur – and isn't this stance, out of fashion now, just that on which the upper echelons of British society for so long prided themselves? It is easy enough to point to dozens and dozens of men and women who collected tales as a kind of summer sport, in much the same spirit as those Victorian parsons who, after delivering lengthy sermons, used to recreate themselves on Sunday afternoons by cheerfully (and innocently) digging their way into prehistoric tumuli, Iron Age encampments, Roman villas, and the like.

Then there were men like Andrew Lang, Edwin Sidney Hartland and Laurence Gomme who were devoted to the science of folklore, studied its relationship to religion and anthropology, and were founding members of the Folklore Society. There were inspirational figures whose greatest distinction lay in other spheres, but who regularly went out into the field to collect tales, such as the novelist Sir Walter Scott, the philologist Sir John Rhys, and the poet W. B. Yeats. There were men with an occasional interest in folk tale, such as the Poet Laureate Robert Southey, who set down the tale that begins in this way:

> Once upon a time there were Three Bears, who lived together in a house of their own, in a wood. One of them was Little, Small, Wee Bear; and one was Middle-Sized Bear; and the other was Great Huge Bear. They each had a pot for their porridge...

Finally, there were those collectors and writers who were interested in adapting and retelling folk tale, more often than not with children in mind. And the most notable of these is Joseph Jacobs, whose versions of many tales have proved to be more or less standard popular versions, in and out of print now for nearly one hundred years.

*

If you are a specialist, you will categorise folk tales in terms of the motifs they embody; and perhaps you will talk of folk narrative (a tale originally told to entertain and maybe edify, such as nursery tales for young children) and folk legend (a tale that is an account of events actually believed to have happened, as are most ghost stories). But for most of us, it's sensible and practical to group folk tales by theme.

In considering which single category to introduce and illustrate, and rather briefly at that, I have thought about etiological tales – those tales of origins and causes, related to myth, that explain how and why things came to be: how a nation was created, how some feature of the landscape originated. Sometimes it seems that there's no hill or stream in the whole of the British Isles that does not have a story attaching to it. This is the kind of thing Henry James was so aware of when he noted in *English Hours*:

> You feel local custom and tradition – another tone of things – pressing on you from every side. The tone of things is somehow heavier than with us; manners and modes are more absolute and positive; they seem to swarm and thicken the air about you. Morally and physically, it is a denser air than ours.

Then I've reviewed those tales that stand closest to legend – let me designate them Tales of Kings and Heroes. This is where you'll find the magical supermen of early Irish legend, Cuchulain and Fionn mac Cumhaill, and the fated lovers Diarmuid and Grania. And here, too, is the greatest of all British heroes, *Rex quondam, Rexque futurus*, King Arthur – still sleeping (according to one source) under a Welsh mountain, surrounded by his warriors, waiting for the great day when the Black Eagle and Golden Eagle go to war, and he with his warriors will rise and fight all the enemies of Wales and conquer the whole Island of Britain.

The more I looked at the various categories, the more difficult my task became. Do I really, I asked myself, have to pass up Fabulous Beasts, when the British Isles are prey to a pack of wild Black Dogs – the Warwickshire Hooter and the Lancashire Skriker and the Norfolk Shuck – and when more than one hundred villages have their own distinctive dragons?

Do I have to set aside Nursery Tales, and Fables and Jocular Tales, and pass over Tales of Giants and Strong Men, Tales of Saints and Devils, and Wonder Tales? Above all, how can I possibly turn my back on what is arguably the richest category of all: Fairy Tales?

Fairies have many names and manifestations – brownies, pookas, hobgoblins, boggarts, bogles, elves. There are fairies as small as a dollar, and fairies the same size as humans. There are fairies who live on the surface of the earth, and under the earth, in streams, in lakes, and in the sea. Some fairies can fly! Some wish humankind well and help them in various ways; some will not harm humans provided we leave them alone; and some, out of the spirit of mischief or self-interest or real wickedness, can cause serious trouble.

Every area of the British Isles has its own distinctive hoard of fairy tales. In the east of England, for instance, there's a crop of shrewd, earthy, witty tales about boggarts and bogles and other unpleasant customers. But it's the old Celtic kingdoms – Scotland, and Wales, and Man, and Cornwall, and Ireland – that are the true strongholds of the Fairy Tale. And the best Celtic tales are distinguished by a wild, gay, precarious, tear-bright quality that has always distinguished the Celtic from the English (that is to say, Anglo-Saxon) imagination.

In these tales, too, one is frequently aware of rules – rules that constitute the true dividing line between the human and fairy worlds. If a human does not observe them, he or she will suffer – get thrown out of fairyland, or lose a fairy consort, or be landed with a double hunchback…

Have you met Dai, the shepherd, who stepped into a fairy ring high up on a Welsh mountain? The fairies welcome him – indeed they've been expecting him. They tell him he can go wherever he wishes and have whatever he asks for, and that the only thing he must not do is drink from the well:

> Whatever I wanted, they brought it to me. Food, drink, warm water to wash with, a comfortable bed. I wanted harpists, singers, acrobats! Then I wanted to talk to their little children. A whole troop came in, chattering and giggling. They were small as dandelions.
>
> You know what I wanted most? It's always the same, mind. You want what you can't have. That's the old Adam.

After dark, I sneaked out into the garden, see. I ran down to the well. Then I plunged in this hand – and all the coloured fishes, they disappeared. Then I cupped my hands and lowered them into the water...

Oh! What a shriek there was! Glassy and piercing, like the moon in pain. A shriek right round the garden and the palace.

Never mind, I closed my eyes and sipped the water!

The garden and the palace and the little people inside it, they all dissolved. In front of my eyes they just dissolved. Mountain mist.

It was dark, hopeless dark, and I was standing alone on the side of the mountain. Up there, that green patch, see. Standing right in the place where I stepped into the ring.

But, like Dai, I sadly part company with y Twlwyth Teg – the Fair Family, the beautiful people – for the category I have elected to introduce concerns not fairies but ghosts. The reason for my choice is quite simple. I would say that a good fifty per cent of the British nation – adults and children, rural and metropolitan, little-educated and highly-educated, clergy and laity – believe in ghosts. Very many people have had first-hand experience of them. Very many houses and churches have their own resident ghosts and stories associated with them. It's above all through the medium of ghost stories that the ancient folk tale tradition still lives on today.

The human race has always (so far as we can tell) attached great importance to the principle of a decent burial. In piety, the living try to give the deceased final rest and maybe arrange for his transfer from this world to the next, and in fear they try to protect themselves against the possibility of the deceased's return. Many cultures have believed that a corpse left unburied has been wronged and is likely to walk and maybe cause trouble. But those people who have been wronged during their lifetimes are also liable to return as ghosts: in a tale from Cromarty, a woman comes back as a ghost because a promise made to her has been broken; and the ballad of 'The Cruel Mother', in which a mother stabs and hastily buries her newborn twins, illustrates the Christian belief that the unbaptised may return as restless ghosts. But most wronged or slighted ghosts have been physically wronged: in York, a woman and a nurse and a child sometimes appear in a church window, cowering and signalling for help; at Hinckley in Leicestershire people still hear the cries of a boy being flogged to death, and at Littleport in the East Anglian Fens, a lovely long-haired young woman and her baby sometimes clamber aboard the boat of an unsuspecting fisherman – thus escaping the water into which they were once hurled by the girl's murderous father, incensed that his daughter should have conceived an illegitimate child.

There are other reasons why someone may return as a ghost. What's buried or concealed has intrinsic power. Thus there are many tales about people who have hidden something – usually money, of course – during their lifetimes and reappear as ghosts to conduct the living towards it. A less well-known belief is that if someone is buried missing a limb, he or she may return as a ghost. Recently I visited a school in Norfolk which had in its possession an Egyptian mummy. In the 1930s, this mummy was transferred from one coffin to another, and caused a terrific rumpus because a small part of her had been left behind! But nowhere is this belief better expressed than in the comic and gruesome tale of 'Samuel's Ghost'. Young Samuel is incinerated when his cottage is burned down, and he goes to the graveyard to be eaten up by the Great Worm:

"Well!" said the worm. "Where's your body?"

"Please, your worship," said Samuel – he didn't want to anger the worm, naturally – "I'm all here!"

"No," said the worm. "How do you think we can eat you? You must fetch your corpse if you want to rest in the earth."

"But where is it?" said Samuel, scratching his head. "My corpse?"

"Where is it buried?" said the worm.

"It isn't buried," said Samuel. "That's just it. It's ashes. I got burned up."

"Ha!" said the worm. "That's bad. That's very bad. You'll not taste too good."

Samuel didn't know what to say.

"Don't fret," said the worm. "Go and fetch the ashes. Bring them here and we'll do all we can."

So Samuel went back to his burned-out cottage. He looked and looked. He scooped up all the ashes he could find into a sack, and took them off to the great worm.

Samuel opened the sack, and the worm crawled down off the flat stone. It sniffed the ashes and turned them over and over.

"Samuel," said the worm after a while. "Something's missing. You're not all here, Samuel. Where's the rest of you? You'll have to find the rest."

"I've brought all I could find," said Samuel.

"No," the worm said. "There's an arm missing."

"Ah!" said Samuel. "That's right! I lost an arm I had."

"Lost?" said the worm.

"It was cut off," said Samuel.

"You must find it, Samuel."

Samuel frowned. "I don't know where the doctor put it," he said. "I can go and see."

So Samuel hurried off again. He hunted high and low, and after a while he found his arm.

Samuel went straight back to the worm. "Here's the arm," he said. The worm slid off its flat stone and turned the arm over.

"No, Samuel," said the worm. "There's something still missing. Did you lose anything else?"

"Let's see," said Samuel, "Let's see... I lost a nail once, and that never grew again."

"That's it, I reckon!" said the worm. "You've got to find it, Samuel."

"I don't think I'll ever find that, master." said Samuel. "Not one nail. I'll give it a try though."

So Samuel hurried off for the third time. But a nail is just as hard to find as it's easy to lose. Although Samuel searched and searched, he couldn't find anything; so at last he went back to the worm.

"I've searched and searched and I've found nothing," said Samuel. "You must take me without my nail – it's no great loss, is it? Can't you make do without it?"

"No," said the worm. "I can't. And if you can't find it – are you quite certain you can't, Samuel?"

"Certain, worse luck!"

"Then you must walk! You must walk by day and walk by night. I'm very sorry for you, Samuel, but you'll have plenty of company!"

Then all the creeping things and crawling things swarmed round Samuel and turned him out. And unless he has found it, Samuel has been walking and hunting for his nail from that day to this.

Yes, there are many reasons why a person may become a ghost, and likewise many forms that ghost may take. He may be a vampire! (One of the most devastating vampire tales I've ever come across is Augustus Hare's version of 'Croglin Grange' in which the gentility of the English girl who gets bitten in the throat serves as a perfect foil for the horrific vampire. "What has happened," she tells her brother no more than one minute after being bitten, "is most extraordinary and I am very much hurt." Hare tells us that the girl was of "strong disposition". I'll say she was! How Sir John Betjeman would have adored her!)

What other forms can a ghost take? He (or she) may assume human form, or return as a living corpse; he may appear to be what that eclectic nineteenth-century man of letters, the Reverend Sabine

Baring-Gould, called, in a fine phrase, "fog and moonshine"; or he may be a shape-changer.

I have a soft spot for the 'Great Giant of Henllys' who in the course of an exorcism appeared to three Welsh clergymen, first as a horrible monster, then as a roaring lion, then as a raging bull, and then as a wave of the sea. The clergymen keep calm! When the Giant appears once more in his mortal form, they ask him why he assumes such dreadful shapes. "I was bad as a man," says the Giant, "and I am worse now as a devil!" And he vanishes in a flash of fire. But the clergymen haul the Giant back again. They prevail on him to appear in smaller and smaller shapes "until at last he was only a fly, and they conjured him into a tobacco box and threw him into Llynwyn Pool, to lie there for ninety-nine years".

Forlorn, dissatisfied, angry, vindictive: ghosts are imprisoned in a kind of closed circuit. The years pass by but they cannot develop. Rather, they replay to themselves one set of actions over and over again. And left to their own devices, they will continue to do just that for as long as time lasts. But, consciously or unconsciously, it seems humans can break into the path of the current; they can break its continuity. That is where the trouble starts: the closed circuit becomes an open circuit, and potentially dangerous. Despite which I'd say, and often do say to children, that the choice lies with the living. If you don't believe in ghosts, or really do not want to see a ghost, there's very little likelihood that you will. If you do want to see a ghost, well...

*

I am a writer – a poet and a writer for children – not a folklorist. So let me turn at last to the strategies available to the reteller of folk tale. I hope you won't consider it improper if I refer to stories taken from my own *British Folk Tales*; but the truth is that these fifty-five retellings embody my thinking – they were written over a period of four years and deliberately present the old tales and motifs in a wide variety of ways.

The first and most obvious tactic for a reteller is also the most tactful and unassuming. He can just keep out of the way! This is what Joseph Jacobs did in so many instances – he simply tidied up his source and left it at that. So, for instance, when I looked at the beautifully-cadenced language, the formulaic repetitions and simple vocabulary used by Southey in his version of 'The Three Bears', I elected to remain in the shadows, and very closely follow my source. The only alterations of substance were to follow more recent taste in changing Southey's "little old Woman" with an "ugly, dirty head" into Goldilocks – a form she only assumed in 1904 after being called Silver-Hair (1849), Silver-Locks (1858) and Golden Hair (1868) and in dropping Southey's moral asides. Far better, I think, to let the moral reveal itself through the action than to insist upon it!

Some folk tales are written in impenetrable dialect and here, too, the reteller's job may be an exercise in restraint: not so much to recast a tale as to interpret or translate it. The tale of 'Samuel's Ghost', for instance, was collected in Lincolnshire by the redoubtable Mrs Mabel Clothilde Balfour – Robert Louis Stevenson's aunt. Her informant was a little crippled girl aged nine, and Mrs Balfour wrote the tale down just as she heard it from her – in the broadest of dialects. The voice and music of that tale are so much part of its meaning that it seemed unwise to tamper with it. I thought the best thing that I could do was to translate, very lightly edit, and leave it at that.

Another device available to a reteller is to step inside a tale and, as it were, tell it from the inside out. The advantage of a dramatic monologue is that one may enter a mind, offer a singular and sometimes unexpected viewpoint, and utilise all the immediacy and vividness of direct speech. I find it helpful to use this method where a tale portrays an individual or individuals separated from society – an exile, a wanderer, an outsider without anchorage, longing to belong. In the tale where surprised fishermen from Suffolk haul up a wildman in their nets, it's the wildman who speaks: he recounts what has happened to him and describes his thoughts and feelings. And when in Orkney an unmarried girl is found pregnant in mysterious circumstances, it is her daughter who later pieces the events together:

> She was sixteen when I was born. "Bonnie," she murmured, as I fed at her breast. "Bonnie. Brave." She was brave and bonnie.
> The Northern Lights shook their curtains on the night I was born. Clean and cold and burning.
> "And the father," they said. "Who is the father? Where is the father?"
> She said, "I cannot tell."
> "Tell me," whispered her mother. "Tell me," ordered her father. "Tell Mother Church," hissed the minister. "What have you to say?"
> "There is no more to say," she said.
> Wind sang in the shell; sun danced in the scarlet cup; dew softened the ear.
> Days and questions, questions and days. Her mother, her father, her friends, the minister, the elders.
> "I know nothing you do not know," she said. "Why do you ask me if you don't believe me?"
> "Out," they said. "Away. Out of our sight. You and your issue."
> We lived in a bothy by the ocean. One room with no window: it smelt of pine and tar and salt.
> The sea schooled me. I know her changes, her whiplash and switchback and croon. I know the sea-voices, the boom of the bittern, the curlew's cry and the redshank's warning, the shriek of white-tailed sea-eagle and all her sisters. Mine is a sea-voice.
> We scratched the sandy wasteland behind the dune and there we sowed our seeds of corn. We picked sea-peas. Sometimes we went hungry.

It's in the very nature of folk tale, I know, that it should be rapid and ice-bright, closer to saga than novel. Its stuff is direct action, not digression, not cause, not reflection. For all this, it doesn't necessarily seem inappropriate to me if a reteller of tales should choose to be interested not only in the substance of a tale but also in how it is told. This self-referring interest in form is, after all, one of the characteristics of late twentieth-century fiction. So, to take a single example, I have recast the famous tale of the sealwoman – the girl who is obliged to marry a fisherman but, after bearing him three children, returns to her life at sea – as a tale within a tale. One of the sealwoman's daughters puts her ear to a large shell and the shell speaks to her; it tells the girl about her own mother, her own experience. But perhaps this is an old-fashioned technique after all. We have all read those older collections of tales in which the fire flickers, shadows dance, a girl snuggles up to a grandparent, and the grandparent begins to tell a tale.

Folk tales inevitably have their fair share of sexual stereotypes, and the reteller may very well want to challenge them. One has to accept that folk tales generalise the whole range of human character into no more than a few types, but for all that it may not be desirable to perpetuate the long line of ever-so-pretty pea-brained princesses, go-getting heroes, evil stepmothers... One remedy, of course, is for the reteller to select and thereby promote tales that help to offset this imbalance. Another is to alter the gender of a key protagonist. And a third is deliberately to play off a strong woman against a cast of weak men. I have adopted this remedy and used both these devices in my retellings of British folk tales.

What is not so easy to cope with, however, is the casual violence to women that seems to form part of so many folk tales: the way in which woman is so regularly portrayed as passive or helpless or disposable. To return to the sealwoman, for instance: she is simply abducted by the fisherman; she doesn't resist; she calmly accepts her fate. Or think of 'Tom Tit Tot', the witty Suffolk version of 'Rumpelstiltschen'. A girl's mother gives her daughter away to a king and happily agrees that if the girl does not manage to spin five skeins of flax each day, the king may kill her. "Now, there's the flax," says the king, "an' if that ain't spun up this night off goo yar hid." Is this the sort of attitude we want to pass on to our children? Situations such as these are often fundamental to a story's structure and drama, and each reteller must be aware of them, and carefully consider their implications.

While the majority of folk tales are set in a timeless time, some have quite specific historical settings, as often as not medieval. So is there any reason why a tale should not be planted in the present day? Is it not desirable that from time to time it should be? Children will relish it because they immediately recognise and relate to the clothing in which the old motifs are dressed.

I had fun – I think that's the word – retelling an English version of 'Beauty and the Beast' in this way. It's called 'The Small-Tooth Dog' and, set in urban backstreets, it begins with a mugging and attempted robbery. Mr Markham is set upon by three youths, but then a big brindled dog comes round the corner...

> The big brindled dog leaped into the scrum. He ripped the youths' clothes, he bit their calves and arms until they yelped and yelled and ran off. Mr. Markham was left lying on the pavement, a poor fat bundle, his head cradled in his arms.
>
> The big brindled dog gave him a friendly look and Mr. Markham began to unfold and put himself together again. He looked at his cuts and bruises; he looked at the dog and shook his head.
>
> "You've saved me a packet," he said, clasping a hand over the inner pocket of his jacket, "I've got the week's takings in here. More than a thousand pounds."
>
> "I know," said the dog.
>
> "Ah!" said Mr. Markham, and he gave the big brindled dog another, careful look.

The dog bared its teeth in a kind of smile and Mr. Markham saw that they were surprisingly white and neat and small for such a large, shaggy animal.

"Well!" said Mr. Markham. "I'd like to repay you for your kindness. You've saved me a fortune."

"I've saved your life," said the dog, sitting back comfortably on his haunches.

"So I'm going to give you my most precious possession," said Mr. Markham.

"What's that?" asked the dog.

"How would you like the fish?" said Mr. Markham. "It can speak Welsh and Portuguese and Bulgarian and Icelandic and…"

"I would not," said the dog.

"What about the goose, then?" said Mr. Markham. "Would you like the goose? It lays golden eggs."

"I would not," said the dog.

"Well then," said Mr. Markham slowly, "I'll have to offer you the mirror…"

"The mirror?" said the dog.

"If you look into it," said Mr. Markham, "you can see what people are thinking."

"I've no need of that," said the big brindled dog.

"What would you like, then?" said Mr. Markham.

"Nothing like that," replied the dog. "I'll take your daughter. I'll take her back to my house."

"Corinna!" cried Mr. Markham. "Well! A man must keep his word. My most precious possession."

"Me?" cried Corinna. "Not likely!"

"He's not an ordinary dog," said Mr. Markham.

"You're daft as a brush," said Corinna.

"You'll see," said her father. "He's waiting outside the door."

"Crazy!" said Corinna.

But I must leave Corinna here .. I hope you'll want to read the story for yourselves and would only add that I see this resetting – this re-earthing of a folk tale in modern times, with all which that implies, as a fruitful way forward for my own writing.

*

Let me finish here, rather, by describing the tale of 'How Joan Lost the Sight of One Eye', that I see as a kind of metaphor.

Late one night a small dark farmer knocks at the door of a midwife and tells her that his wife is in labour. Farmer – if that's what he is – and midwife gallop up to the farm where, as things turn out, the wife has already delivered herself of her baby – a son. The midwife is disapproving of the farmer's noisy swarm of children, ushers them out of the rather scruffy bedroom where their mother and the new-born baby are lying, and begins to clean up. After a while, the farmer's wife gives the midwife a little pot and asks her to smear some ointment on her baby's eyelids. "But be careful," she says, "not to get any on your own eyes!" We're back in the world of rules again. The midwife waits until the farmer's wife is asleep and, after putting some ointment on the baby's eyelids, smears a little on her own right eyelid…

The moment she does so, quite another sight meets her gaze. With her left eye she sees the simple homely furniture, the squinting baby on her lap, wrapped in an old white shawl, and his mother sleeping on a sagging bedstead. But with her other she sees the baby is wrapped and wound in gauze flecked with silver; his sleeping mother is robed in white silk; and when they return into the room, the midwife sees the children are imps and have squashed noses and pointed ears.

The midwife wisely keeps her mouth shut – an important rule in dealing with the fairies – and gets home safely. The next day, the midwife visits the local market, and while she's there she accosts a petty thief at one of the stalls. The man rounds on her at once.

"Good morning!" he says. "It's you."

"Oh!" says the midwife. "How's your wife… the baby?"

"You can see me then," says the man. "Which eye can you see me with?"

The midwife covers one eye, then the other eye.

"This one," she says.

The little man raises his hand and lightning flashes in the woman's right eye.

Shooting stars! Then complete darkness!

"That's for meddling!" shouts the man. "That's for taking the ointment. You won't be seeing me again!"

And the midwife never sees anyone again, not with her right eye…

There we are! The midwife could see with two eyes: with one eye the world of actual and everyday, with one the world of the imagination. It's true, I know, that by breaking the rules and revealing she has a second way of seeing, she loses that ability; one cannot push the metaphor too far. But to see with two eyes, in two ways… isn't that what storytellers should try to do? We're custodians of the word. And we must try to impart to those children with whom, directly or indirectly, we come into contact, both an awareness of the world in which we live and some sense of the redeeming power of the imagination.

Butterfly Soul

You fell asleep.

I would have fallen asleep too, stretched out under the sun, washed by the lullaby voices in the stream. We were so tired, what with scrambling and searching and shouting all day.

No need to count the missing sheep: I would have fallen asleep too – but I saw your mouth open, and out flew a butterfly as white as first-day snow!

The butterfly flickered over your body and down your left leg, then settled on a swing of grass not near you nor far from you – just the distance of a stone's toss.

I sat up and stood up and followed the butterfly. It fluttered down a sheep-run to the call of the water. It flipped across the stepping stones. It flew through a clump of reeds, in and out, in and out, like the batten in a warp.

On it went, and I still followed it, until it nosed out something lodged in the long grass. The skull of an old horse, gleaming white, home of the winds!

The butterfly went in through one of the eye sockets. It worked its way round the inside wall, quivering and curious. Then out it came, out through the other socket, back through the reeds, over the stone flags, up the sheep-run, along your sleeping body and back into your open mouth.

You closed your mouth and opened your eyes. You saw me looking at you.

"It must be getting late," you said.

"It may be early and it may be late," I said. "I've just seen a wonder."

"You! You've seen a wonder," you said. "It's I who've seen the wonder. I dreamed I was heading down a fine wide road, flanked by waving trees and a rainbow of flowers. I came down to a broad river and a great stone bridge covered with rich carvings. After I'd crossed this bridge, I entered a marvellous forest – trees like blades. On and on! I went on until I reached a palace, glorious and abandoned. I passed from room to echoing room. Then I thought I might stay there, and with that I began to feel gloomy and strange and uneasy.

"So I left the palace. I came home the same way. And when I got in, I was very hungry. I was just about to settle to a meal when I woke up."

"Come with me," I said, "and I'll show you your dream kingdom."

I told you about the butterfly white as first-day snow. I showed you the sheep-run and the stepping stones, the clump of reeds, the skull of the old horse.

"This poor sheep-run," I said, "is your fine wide road flanked by waving trees and a rainbow of flowers. These stepping stones are your great stone bridge covered with rich carvings. This clump of reeds is the marvellous forest – trees like blades. And this skull," I said, "this is the glorious palace you walked round a little while ago."

"Wonders!" you said. "You and I, we've both seen wonders."

From *Between Worlds: Folktales of Britain and Ireland* (2018)
First published as *British Folk Tales* (1987)

ANGLO-SAXON POETRY

After coming down from Oxford in 1962 with a Poet's Third, I joined the publishing house of Macmillan and worked in the publicity department. But while my friends and contemporaries were entering into the spirit of the 1960s, I was dancing to another beat. Two, in fact. Early marriage, and raising two young sons. And, under the tutelage of my former teacher, Bruce Mitchell, the translation of Anglo-Saxon poetry.

I was attracted to this body of work for its staunch values, its emotional depth, its Englishness. Then and now I know it has brought me closer to understanding the Anglo-Saxons than any other aspect of their culture.

To begin with, I worked at the shorter poems, evening after evening. Then, with the encouragement of Macmillan, the British Council and Farrar, Straus in the USA, I addressed *Beowulf*.

By the end of the decade, when I served as Gregory Fellow in Poetry at the University of Leeds, my translation work was largely done. But I can well see what a seminal impact my involvement with Anglo-Saxon poetry has had on my own writing style and the great store I set by tradition – in G.K. Chesterton's words, "the democracy of the dead".

An Old House Packed with Memories

Each year I make a pilgrimage. I come back to the same, small, salt-wind-scoured, round-towered Norfolk church. I come back to a square eleventh-century font carved out of a massive hunk of Barnack stone.

On three sides this font is a kind of stone calendar. When I grasp the rough stone, it begins to warm to my touch. Here is a carving of January swigging ale from a horn, and February toasting his toes by the fire. March turns the earth with a curved spade, and April is pruning a vine. May is holding a banner and 'beating the bounds' – that is to say, walking the parish boundaries. June is mowing with his scythe; and July is busy raking. August binds a sheaf of corn, September threshes with a flail, and October is pouring ale into a vat. November is slaughtering a pig, and to illustrate December, there are four men sitting side by side, eating and drinking.

So here past and present meet. This wonderful font, sitting in a precious place that hasn't been 'discovered' or promoted as part of the heritage industry, records and celebrates the way most English people spent their hours and days and lives for century after century.

The poet – very likely an East Anglian – who composed the great epic *Beowulf*, tells us about a wonderful feasting-hall in which there are treasures and tapestries and "many a fine sight for those with eyes for such things". Britain itself is like this. The whole island, wrote the novelist Peter Vansittart, is "an old house packed with memories". We have only to open our eyes to see signposts all around us, pointing back through fifty generations and more to the age of the Anglo-Saxons.

Think of our coinage! Although we've set aside shillings and florins and half-crowns, we do still have pounds and pence; a few of them! Some of us don't greatly mind whether or not we trade them for euros; but others care very much, and one argument advanced for retaining pounds and pence is tradition. Well, the retentionists do have a point. Our pence originated in Anglo-Saxon England while our pounds derive from Roman times. The symbols £ and lb. both stand for *libra*, which is Latin for pound.

Another signpost is our legal system. British law has its origin, however distant, in the law codes laid out by Anglo-Saxon kings. The first of them was handed down by Æthelberht of Kent in about 602 AD. During the seventh century, too, rulers of English kingdoms began to succeed to the throne by virtue of primogeniture as opposed to 'tribal jostling'. The anointing of a successor and the ceremony of coronation with its Christian blessing: these procedures, too, were first enacted in Anglo-Saxon England. Indeed, 'Zadok the Priest' has been sung, first in Latin and now in English, at every coronation since that of King Edgar in 973 AD.

Of course we should visit museums and marvel at the tangible legacy of the Anglo-Saxons: glorious and glowing manuscripts, gold-and-garnet jewellery, and soaring stone crosses. Of course we should read their poetry: so proud, so shrewd, so full of longings, so humane, so lyrical, and so witty. But the Anglo-Saxons are not only to be found behind glass or on the page. Theirs is the culture that started to shape the very fabric of English society, the look of our land, and our language.

Henry James understood all this when he wrote, after visiting England, "You feel custom and tradition – another tone of things – pressing on you from every side... Morally and physically, it is a denser air than ours".

Signposts! Each time you or I use English words, half of them come from Anglo-Saxon. It's the good, tough, sharp, quick words that come from this root. Birth, child, meat, fish, man, woman, love, lust, earth, sea, plough, axe, sword, ship, old, year, death: all the words that tell us about the stuff of life here on middle-earth come from Anglo-Saxon while the polysyllabic language we employ to describe the abstract and conceptual derives from Latin and Greek.

So of course there may still be Anglo-Saxon strains within many of us. Is it true to say there is a dogged, stubborn strain in your make up? Do you relish the idea that when the going gets tough, the tough get going? Are you a fatalist? Are you inclined not to sentimentality but to melancholy? Do you have a strong feeling for the sea? Or a passion for ritual? I don't know whether it is useful or even possible to point to typical or enduring English characteristics. But if your answer to any of these questions is yes, then you share at least one quality with our Anglo-Saxon ancestors.

So I stand by my font, scribbling these words in the fading light. It is the eve of the summer solstice, and magic's in the air. So, too, are the seabirds, full of passion and hunger, screaming and wheeling round this round tower, just as they've done for the last one thousand years.

Word ond Andgiet

On Translating Anglo-Saxon Poetry

" *...ða ongan ic ongemang ðrum mislicum ond manigfealdum bisgum ðisses kynerices ða boc wendan on Englisc...*"

Well, that sounds familiar! "Then I began amongst other sundry and manifold troubles of this kingdom to translate the book into English..."

How reasoning, how committed, how diligent King Alfred sounds.

"... *hwilum word be worde, hwilum andgit of andgiete*"

"Sometimes word for word, sometimes sense for sense"!

Just so. The same issue that every translator has had to face before and since. How am I going to translate these foreign words (in Alfred's case, from Latin of course)? What do they mean? How do they mean? These and a host of ancillary nagging questions...

One of my early memories is of rushing (I seldom just walked) into my father's study, and seeing him and another man bending over a number of scrips and scraps of what looked like bark spread out on a table. The second man was Rupert Bruce-Mitford, sometime Keeper of Medieval and Later Antiquities at the British Museum, and what he and my father were inspecting were little pieces of the Sutton Hoo harp that Rupert had brought down in a bag from London! Their proposed reconstruction, as many of you will know, was later set aside in favour of a lyre, a stringed instrument without a soundbox – but I believe my father's suggestion that the strings were tuned to the pentatonic scale still holds good. If not, I will be glad to be corrected.

But this was more than seventy years ago – seventy! I can scarcely believe it. And the Anglo-Saxons meant little to me until I commandeered the garden shed a few years later and there set up my beloved museum. What wonders! Among them, a late fifth- or early sixth-century Anglian burial urn that once belonged to my grandfather, and had been 'lifted' from the Spon Hill dig in Norfolk during the thirties, let's say by penniless student volunteers!

May I risk a little more in this loose-limbed, biographical mode? I went up to Oxford in 1959, largely unaware or anyhow unabashed that the English course entailed a first year of reading Virgil in Latin, slabs of Milton, and learning Anglo-Saxon.

Well, I failed my Anglo-Saxon preliminary exams. At Oxford, one is allowed a second shot before being thrown out, or "sent down" as they decorously say. "Work hard", my college principal had advised me at that special kind of purgatory known as Collections, in which a student is confronted by a posse of a dozen or more dons. "Work hard, Mithter Crothley-Holland. We should be thorry to loothe you."

So I was sitting in a punt moored to the side of the Cherwell on an early May evening, eating a pork pie, listening to a piece of my father's music on a transistor radio, and trying to learn some Anglo-Saxon, when a swan sailed down the river. In short, it turned up its beak at the pie, disliked the music, hated the grammar, and attacked me.

I'd heard about Leda (via Yeats, I suppose) and wasn't in the least eager to suffer the fate she did. Fate, yes, that's the word! I leaped onto the bank, tore the cartilage in my right knee, and ended up in the Radcliffe in the days long before hydroscopic surgery.

There the college principal visited me and penned a verse still not on general release! But it began, "Kevin, the athlete-poet of our stair" and ended "His friends retrieved him from fair Cherwell's sward / And placed him, groaning, in a children's ward / There Ælfric and Old English verbs to con, / The victim of a music-hating swan."

What happened while I was in hospital was entirely unexpected, an experience that was one of the most formative of my life, and the beginning of a true *wunderreise*.

Attempting to read out the short Anglo-Saxon riddle about a swan with the correct stresses, for the first time I heard (or began to hear) the sound, the music of the language and verse form. I read it again. And again. And then I was able to sing it out.

> Hrægl min swigað,   þonne ic hrusan trede,
> oþþe þa wic buge,   oþþe wado drefe.
> Hwilum mec āhebbað   ofer hæleþa byht
> hyrste mine   and þeos hea lyft,
> and mec þonne wide   wolcna strengu
> ofer folc byreð.   Frætwe mine
> swogað hlude   and swinsiað,
> torhte singað.   þonne ic getenge ne beom
> flode and foldan   ferende gæst.

I've been reading that the great poet and artist David Jones' earliest recorded encounter with 'The Dream of the Rood' was an aural one, and how he was above all affected by "the strength of the sound".

It was the same for me. The sound; its drive-and-surge, and the way each non-syllabic four-stress line falls away in force and in meaning because the last of the stresses never alliterates with those preceding it. The accumulative strength of so many monosyllables and short words.

Listening to Anglo-Saxon verse, I sometimes imagine I'm sitting on a stony beach. Wave after wave gathers and breaks on the well-graded gravel, and as it runs up the beach, it loses its power. The swell, the breaking, and then the suck of the swash.

Not that the sound of Anglo-Saxon poetry is always stark or forceful. Not at all. It is of course many-tongued and various because of the subtle use of vowels, and soft rather than hard consonants, because of the synonyms, and the metrical alternatives. Think, for instance, of the soothing sound of the Lord's Prayer. Or of the lyrical, elegiac last lines of *Beowulf*:

> Cwædon þæt he wære   wyruld cyninga,
> manna mildust   ond mon-þwærust,
> leodum liðost   ond lof-geornost.

Enter Bruce Mitchell. Australian. A Fellow of St. Edmund Hall, University Reader in the English Language, and author of *A Guide to Old English*.

Bruce was my tutor and he was just not going to allow me to fail second time round. With a mixture of robust bonhomie, games of tennis and squash, gentle cudgelling and sheer persistence, he steered me through the rapids... and what happened during those spring weeks in 1960 is that I fell entirely under the spell of Anglo-Saxon poetry — not only the sound of it but its stateliness, its emotional force and integrity, and the 'otherness' not only of its high-flown language but its stirring themes: heroic, historical, saintly, allegorical, elegiac, and gnomic.

One afternoon, I was sitting at a capacious desk in the Radcliffe Camera between two acquaintances, Michael Alexander and John Fuller. And the three of us realised we were all at work, there and then, on translating Anglo-Saxon riddles. The first I'd translated, while still in hospital, was the one about the swan!

This aroused my competitive instincts, and almost at once I sent off a batch of my work to the BBC. At that time, George MacBeth was in charge of poetry on radio, and he commissioned me to put together a half-hour programme consisting of thirteen riddles. I'm dwelling for a moment on this because it was my bridge from an undergraduate life and the world beyond... That lovely weekly, *The Listener* (now defunct) printed my translations, and Sir Arthur Bliss, then Master of the Queen's Music, wrote to me to say he'd like to set some of them. When I went to listen to him play through his settings, he said, "Well, Kevin, I've changed these words... And these... just here and there. I'm sure you'll agree they'll sing better!" And when the settings were first performed, the *Observer* noted that Bliss had returned to his melodic best, but that "how he can have done so to such ghastly words is unimaginable!"

But the die was cast! I knew that whatever else I was going to do in my early twenties, I wanted to translate more Anglo-Saxon poetry. And this was the point at which Bruce Mitchell offered to help me.

At my viva, C. L. Wrenn had said in his squeaky voice, "Well, Mr Crossley-Holland, before you step out into the wide world and forget about Anglo-Saxon forever, can you just help us to tease out this crux in *Beowulf*?"

But within weeks, I was staying with Bruce and his wife Mollie, and discussing the principles that should underlie and guide my first efforts. What factors did I need to take into account? How was I best to convey the sense and word of the originals.

So, of course, we engaged with the metrical form and the vocabulary of Anglo-Saxon poetry. And I think we agreed at once that the non-syllabic four-stress line, governed by alliteration on two or three of the first three stresses, in either case including the 'head-stave' or third stress, was so distinctive that to set it aside entirely would result in translations that had little or none of the pulse and sound of their originals.

On the other hand, the nineteenth-century models we looked at were so stiff... on the other hand, Anglo-Saxon poetic diction was formal and highly-wrought... on the other hand... on the other hand...

Another keen discussion centred on the nature of the Anglo-Saxon word-hoard. Of the 60,000 or so words in modern English, I believe about one-half derive from Anglos-Saxon, and on the whole they're grounded and terse.

The more I translated, the more I wanted to reflect, to echo this word-hoard, and to eschew Latinates. Without becoming highly idiosyncratic like, say, William Barnes (who taught Thomas Hardy in Dorchester), I tried to root my translations rather than have them fly!

But translating from Anglo-Saxon is not at all like translating from a foreign language, let alone one that is not Indo-European, precisely because Anglo-Saxon and Modern English are blood-relatives.

There is, for example, a natural temptation to translate an Anglo-Saxon word into the word derived from it, but sometimes this has to be resisted because of the 'slippage' of meaning, and one has to look for the modern word that best reflects the original.

In what became quite regular weekend visits, (because Bruce was teaching and I was a young employee in publishing during the weekdays) Bruce and I often discussed the way in which I was translating highly-wrought and formulaic oral poetry into poetry for the page – from the oral to the literary. And, in parenthesis, what is more moving than the two riddles that describe the arduous making and binding of parchment pages, and the pen and fingers and the struggling arm (and wrist in my case!) inscribing 'black tracks' on the page?

Writing for the page, I was aware that I couldn't 'pitch' my poems as the scops (the old English bards) probably did. That phrase *singan ond secgan* is so fascinating, suggesting a manner of recitation that was perhaps partly pitched but not melodic. But I wanted my readers to *hear* my translations. I wanted them to hear the delightful shuffling repetition and variation essential to oral poetry; I wanted them to hear the powerful sound-effects achieved by the best of the Anglo-Saxon poets, just as much as I wanted them to see, see-and-hear, the memorable kennings. But above all I wanted to achieve versions that were recognisably poems, and recognisably the work of a living translator. I wanted to bring Anglo-Saxon poetry back mainstream. In the 1968 edition of my translation of *Beowulf*, I wrote:

I should perhaps note here the principles I have followed in attempting this translation. My staple diet has been a non-syllabic four-stress line, controlled by light alliteration. There are plenty of cases, though, where I have not conformed to this pattern; my concern has been to echo rather than slavishly to imitate the original. My diction inclines towards the formal, though it is certainly less formal than that of the Beowulf poet; it seemed to me important at this time to achieve a truly accessible version of the poem, that eschewed the use of archaisms, inverted word orders, and all 'poetic' language. I have not gone out of my way to avoid words that spring from Latin roots, but the emphasis has fallen naturally on words derived from Old English. This translation is, we believe, by and large faithful to the letter of the original, but it is the mood that I have been after. And if I have not caught anything of it, then I have not succeeded in my purpose.

Looking now at my first efforts — and I think *The Battle of Maldon* was *the* first — I see at once how lacking in confidence they are; how fumbling and inconsistent in their rhythm and choice of language. But I was learning, learning fast... and ambitious!

Just before my 24th birthday, in 1964, Macmillan published my translations of a selection of the shorter poems, edited by Bruce Mitchell. Later that year, my publisher hosted a dinner party (Muriel Spark was one of the guests) at which I met Roger Straus, co-founder of the American publishing house of Farrar, Straus and Giroux. I drove him and his wife back to their hotel — I remember it well because my bashed-up Beetle broke down on Lambeth Bridge! — and next morning he delivered a message to Macmillan to say that he'd like to commission me to translate *Beowulf*.

"In that case," said my English publisher, Alan Maclean, "so would we!"

Almost at once, Argo Records with the British Council decided that they would make an LP recording of about one-third of the translation, featuring Prunella Scales (as Wealtheow) and George Rylands. They were in a hurry (of course) so I began by selecting and translating the lines to be recorded…

Now and then I received blasts of encouragement – from J.R.R. Tolkien. From W.H. Auden. From Burton Raffel. From Gwyn Jones. And after Sir Arthur Bliss, William Mathias set more of my riddles (Naxos released his settings). But *Beowulf* was a long row to hoe…

Using publisher's dummies, I first ensured that I had an accurate prose translation of, say, thirty lines or so. Then I listened over again to the original, and began to piece together a draft translation, with pencilled alternatives and gaps and reminders and warnings… And then I took them to Bruce Mitchell, who for so long faithfully saved me from myself, and Anglo-Saxon from me! The fruit of these labours, that took three years and more, is now housed in the Brotherton Library (Special Collections) at Leeds University.

My work as a translator from Anglo-Saxon was to all intents and purposes *over* more than fifty years go! And I ended as I began by translating the remainder of the Exeter Book riddles, and was emboldened by Bruce Mitchell to do so on my own.

Someone sent Stephen Spender a copy of the Penguin Classics edition, and he wrote to me: "I have been trying to think why it is that these antique squibs – as I suppose they are – strike one as pure and beautiful poetry. I think the reason is that in *most* poetry which has as subject a concrete or animal thing – Shelley's skylark say – one begins with the object, the title, the thing, in mind, and then reads the poetry as relating back to the already-received idea. The Riddle is back to front. One gets the poetry emanating from the subject – thing – first and arrives – if one does ever arrive at it – at the subject last. The effect is something like pure poetry – a peculiar concentration on imagery – before one arrives at the actual image."

As my translating work diminished during the mid-60s, I was beginning to write more poems, and it's plain how much my intense engagement with Anglo-Saxon poetry influenced them. This is true of their subject matter (wild places, wild weather, endurance, suffering, choice and the lack of it, identity) and true of their prosody.

I wrote a short poem, 'Translation Workshop: Grit and Blood', in which I briefly reviewed one kind of problem facing the translator, before translating Byrhtwold's famous lines in 'The Battle of Maldon' into Modern English words derived only from Anglo-Saxon (except for 'spirit'):

> Hige sceal þe heardra, heorte þe cenre,
> mod sceal þe mare, þe ure mægen lytlað!
> Word-stand, locking shield-wall
> not to be broken down, nor even
> translated in its own bright coin.
> Courage, intention, resolve – won't do.
> Out with Latinates! I want earth-words,
> tough roots: grit and blood, grunt, gleam.
>
> Harder heads and hearts more keen,
> spirits on fire as our strength flags!
> Here lies our leader, axed and limp,
> the top dog in the dust. He who turns
> from this war-play now will mourn
> for ever. I am old. I'll stay put.
> I'll lay my pillow on the ground
> beside my dear man, my loved lord.

I'm sure, too, that my engagement with Anglo-Saxon has had a lasting (and I hope fruitful) impact on the way I've retold British traditional tales. Passed from generation to generation by people largely illiterate, folk tales demand simple language and speed. They busy themselves with action, not reflection, and move swiftly from A to Z.

My interest in early northwest European literature and culture broadened and deepened. And looking now over my shoulder, it's easy to see why. The ground had already been well sown, even partly harvested, and W. H. Auden's advice to me to "Look north!" led directly to my resigning from my position as Editorial Director of Victor Gollancz and departure with my two young sons on an extended visit to Iceland.

The punctuation points in this long journey range from the sublime to the... I don't know what! I see myself standing on Burial Mound One at Sutton Hoo on an October evening as the sun sets, surrounded by flaming brands, reciting to a great concourse passages from Beowulf, and I give thanks for it. I see myself in conversation with Seamus Heaney at the Oxford Literary Festival in front of an enthralled audience, packing the Sheldonian to the rafters, and I give thanks for it! I see myself reading a letter received only three days ago from a young boy in Derbyshire called Luca, suggesting that I should rewrite my children's version of Beowulf and "should leave out the arm chopping bit and give Grendel a chance to be good"! And I give thanks for that too, and the way in which the National Curriculum, for all its shortcomings, embraces the Anglo-Saxons. It was not always so.

Let me share a few lines in translation: that passionate first half of 'The Seafarer', culminating in the great declaration that is also a challenge, a challenge to try and try, and then try again:

> I can sing a true song about myself,
> tell of my travels, how in days of tribulation
> I often endure a time of hardship,
> how I have harboured bitter sorrow in my heart
> and often learned that ships are homes of sadness.
> Wild were the waves when I often took my turn,
> the arduous night-watch, standing at the prow

while the boat tossed near the rocks. My feet
were afflicted by cold, fettered in frost,
frozen chains; there I sighed out the sorrows
seething round my heart; a hunger within tore
at the mind of the sea-weary man. He who lives
most prosperously on land does not understand
how I, careworn and cut off from my kinsmen,
have as an exile endure a winter
on the icy sea...
hung round with icicles; hail showers flew.
I heard nothing there but the sea booming -
the ice-cold wave, at times the song of the swan.
The cry of the gannet was all my gladness,
the call of the curlew, not the laughter of men,
the mewing gull, not the sweetness of mead.
There, storms beat the rocky cliffs; the icy-feathered
tern answered them; and often the eagle,
dewy-winged, screeched overhead. No protector
could console the cheerless heart.
Wherefore he who is used to the comforts of life
and, proud and flushed with wine, suffers
little hardship living in the city,
will scarcely believe how I, weary,
have had to make the ocean paths my home.
The night-shadow grew long, it snowed from the north,
frost fettered the earth; hail fell on the ground,
coldest of grain. But now my blood
is stirred that I should make trial
of the mountainous streams, the tossing salt waves;
my heart's longings always urge me
to undertake a journey, to visit the country
of a foreign people far across the sea.
On earth there is no man so self-assured,

so generous with his gifts or so bold in his youth,
so daring in his deeds or with such a gracious lord,
that he harbours no fears about his seafaring
as to what the Lord will ordain for him.
He thinks not of the harp nor of receiving rings,
nor of rapture in a woman nor of worldly joy,
nor of anything but the rolling of the waves;
the seafarer will always feel longings.
The groves burst with blossom, towns become fair,
meadows grow green, the world revives;
all these things urge the heart of the eager man
to set out on a journey, he who means
to travel far over the ocean paths.
And the cuckoo, too, harbinger of summer,
sings in a mournful voice, boding bitter sorrow
to the heart. The prosperous man knows not
what some men endure who tread
the paths of exile to the end of the world.

Wherefore my heart leaps within me,
my mind roams with the waves
over the whale's domain, it wanders far and wide
across the face of the earth, returns again to me
eager and unsatisfied; the solitary bird screams,
irresistible, urges the heart to the whale's way
over the stretch of the seas.

The Anglo-Saxon Elegies

A man stands at the prow of a small boat tossing near the rocks.

Gannets and curlews circle and swoop around him, and a hailstorm dances on the deck. The man peers anxiously through the gloom... Again: a woman, earth-stained, living in a dug-out in the forest, suffers and seethes at the loss of her husband... And a court poet, a creaking, hurt old man, tries to come to terms with his abrupt dismissal by thinking of people who have had to endure worse...

Sometimes the clothing may seem rather strange, but the situations at the heart of the Anglo-Saxon elegiac poems are not unfamiliar. We have all experienced them, and their like. This is one reason why these poems, standing at the very head of the tradition of lyric poetry in the English language, speak so directly to us.

The designation of a small group of poems as elegies is no more than a modern convenience. It is the flag flying over seven or eight quite short poems concerned in different ways with grief and consolation. But the great critic C. L. Wrenn noted that in Anglo-Saxon poetry "the lyric mood is always the elegiac". This is almost true. Thus passages from some of the long religious poems and from the epic Beowulf, including the magnificent and mournful 'Lay of the Last Survivor', are very much of a piece with the elegies:

> The iron helmet
> adorned with gold shall lose its ornaments;
> men who should polish the battle-masks are sleeping;
> the coat of mail, too, that once withstood
> the bite of swords in battle, after shields were shattered,
> decays like the warriors; the linked mail may no longer

> range far and wide with the warrior,
> stand side by side with heroes. Gone is the pleasure
> of plucking the harp, no fierce hawk
> swoops about the hall, nor does the swift stallion
> strike sparks in the courtyard. Cruel death
> has claimed hundreds of this human race.

The elegiac poems are all to be found in the Exeter Book – the dog-eared manuscript used as a kind of a cutting-board at some point in the Middle Ages – that is one of only four great miscellanies of poetry to survive from the Anglo-Saxon period. Probably compiled during the last quarter of the tenth century, it was bequeathed by Leofric, first bishop of Exeter, to the cathedral library and has remained there to this day.

But of course most of the poems in the Exeter Book, originally composed for oral transmission, are of earlier, if uncertain date. It is impossible to nail down precisely where or when any of the elegies were first composed, and likewise impossible to establish how different the first version of a poem was from that which now survives. The very question would have baffled an Anglo-Saxon: the concept of a standard version is quite alien to an oral culture in which some words may differ from teller to teller.

Although our reading of the elegies is bound to be rendered more difficult by an inadequate frame of reference – uncertainty as to date of composition, and doubt as to the poet's intentions – we can nevertheless recognise the preoccupations and technical devices they share.

First of these is the matter of separation and exile. In 'The Wanderer', the speaker tells us how his lord's death has utterly changed his way of life. He has had to exchange the warmth of the feasting-hall, where voices were lifted in song and his lord often presented him with gifts of twisted gold, for a long and lonely journey in search of another man with whom he can enter into service; another lord who will take him in and secure him.

There is no easy way out for the wanderer. His lord's death and apparent lack of a successor entails for his follower serious social and physical hardship. He must dig and discover resources within himself to cope with the situation. This is just what the poet Deor, meaning 'dear' or 'beloved', has to do too. His position at court has been influential – in early Anglo-Saxon England, the poet carried in his head the stories of battles won and lost, the derring-do of individuals, the great love matches and confrontations that added up to a history, factual and fantastic, of the tribe; he was the warden of individual and corporate historical identity. But Deor has been ousted and he aches with the hurt of it. He begins to draw on his own memory-hoard: Wayland the Smith, hamstrung so cruelly by King Nithhad; Wayland's revenge on Nithhad's daughter; the suffering of the Goths under the tyrant Ermanaric… Deor summons up a succession of legendary Germanic figures, and his contemplation of their anguish helps him to come to terms with his own.

'The Wanderer' and 'Deor' advance two sets of circumstances that may lead to exile; and 'The Wife's Lament' suggests a third. The absent husband mourned by his wife has been forced overseas by his own kinsmen after becoming involved in a feud. His exile is not from a lord but from his wife and country.

The separation of man and woman, lover and beloved, is a theme shared by three of the elegies: 'The Wife's Lament', 'The Husband's Message', and 'Wulf'. It is rather tempting to see the first two poems as linked, perhaps constituting part of some longer, now forgotten story. Both are precisely the same length; and in both the husband has been driven overseas by a feud. If one does choose to pair the poems, the dramatic irony is obvious enough: the wife loves her husband and knows he loves her and longs for her – the word 'longing' is repeated several times in the poem – but, fearful of his fate, she seems to hold out no hope that they will ever be reunited:

> How often
> we swore that nothing but death should ever
> divide us; that is all changed now;
> our friendship is as if it had never been.

The husband, meanwhile, has done rather well for himself! He is well-off again, and well-established in his new home. His only worry, it seems, is whether or not his wife will have been faithful to her marriage vows, and will join him in exile.

While these two poems, one so passionate and tidal, and the other so calculating, invoke and affirm the marriage vow, the short love poem known as 'Wulf' flies in the face of it. It is thought very likely that this poem, too, forms part of a Germanic tale now lost, and that Wulf and Eadwacer and the speaker were characters known to the poem's original audience. The translator has some thorny decisions to make, since several readings of the poem are equally possible: I see Eadwacer as the speaker's husband and Wulf – by whom she has had a child – as her lover. But no matter what the argument, this is a quite remarkable poem. Passive and naked and passionate and defiant, all in nineteen lines, it is a distress signal that cuts straight through the darkness of a thousand years.

There is a third kind of separation explored in some of the elegies, and that is the separation of man from God. The speaker in 'The Seafarer' portrays "this dead life, ephemeral on earth" as a condition of exile from the kingdom of God, and argues that it is only by renouncing worldly pleasure and living a life of self-imposed hardship that man can be sure of a place amongst the heavenly host. The ascetic life, here exemplified by a strenuous and hazardous sea-journey, was very much part of early Irish and Anglo-Saxon monastic experience. If one travels through the north of England and Scotland, it sometimes seems as if there is scarcely a windy outcrop, let alone a wave-lapped islet, that was not once frequented by some solitary monk. The idea that voluntary exile from their own country would bring them safely to anchorage in heaven was, moreover, very much in the minds of the thousands of monk-missionaries who went out from the monasteries of seventh-century Northumbria, so full of faith and fire and the most touching piety, to work in continental Europe.

Provided one takes 'The Seafarer' to be of one piece, it seems clear that the convictions and lifestyles of generations of hermits and missionaries lie behind the poem. But it has also been argued – the argument is out of favour at the moment – that the memorable description of a life at sea is actually a pagan poem later appropriated and reworked by a Christian poet. The same argument applies to 'The Wanderer', the brief opening and closing sections being Christian, and here it seems to have much more force because the sense of fate governing the main body of the poem is so powerful that it overshadows the theme of Christian consolation. We need not be unduly surprised, however, at the way in which (at the beginning of the poem) the poet refers to the Lord and fate in the same lines. In 'The Fortunes of Men', God is shown as assigning different skills and fortunes to each human being, one of whom

> will have no choice but to chance
> remote roads, to carry his own food
> and leave dew tracks amongst foreign people
> in a dangerous land; he will find few
> prepared to entertain him; the exile
> is shunned everywhere because of his misfortune.

The tone of the whole poem is fatalistic, and the portrayal of an active Shaper is that of a poet trying to reconcile old ideas about immoveable fate (in Norse mythology fate takes the form of the three goddesses of destiny known as the Norns) to new ideas about Christ. "Fate", said the *Beowulf*-poet, "goes ever as it must"; but another later poet observed that "fate moves in the mind of Christ".

'The Seafarer' places in opposition present and future, life on earth and life in heaven, transience and eternity; but all the other elegiac poems (except for 'The Fortunes of Men') contrast present with past, immediate experience with memory.

For the wanderer and Deor, the passage of time has led to the break-up of a prized relationship. For the woman in 'The Wife's Lament' and the man in 'The Husband's Message', it has led to the dislocation of a happy marriage; and for the suffering speaker in 'Wulf', time brings no consolation but only greater bitterness and anguish. They and their relationships are all victims of time.

It is only in 'The Ruin' that we escape the terrible and personal sense of loss that informs these poems. The poet wanders around Roman Bath, noting how

> roofs have caved in, towers collapsed,
> barred gates are broken, hoarfrost clings to mortar,
> houses are gaping, tottering and fallen,
> undermined by age.

But all this, the poet seems to say, is only to be expected: what is born in time dies in time. The tone of the poem is not so much one of regret, let alone loss, as of admiration and celebration. The poet marvels at the stone buildings, so far beyond the skills of the early Anglo-Saxons who seldom built with stone and called the Romans 'giants' for being able to do so. He conjures up a sumptuous picture, more Germanic than Roman, of life in court and hall. He sees how the hot spring and scalding water were harnessed for the use of the inhabitants. The last few lines of 'The Ruin' are themselves in a ruinous condition but, as the poem peters out, the reader is left with a clear sense of the poet's excitement and, maybe, awe.

After contemplating the changes wrought by time, the wanderer consoles himself with the thought that:

> a man will not be wise
> before he has weathered his share of winters
> in the world

and he then launches into a string of aphorisms or maxims:

> A wise man must be patient,
> neither too passionate nor too hasty of speech,
> neither too irresolute nor too rash in battle,
> not too anxious, too content, nor too grasping,
> and never too eager to boast before he knows himself.

This kind of proverbial verse – folk-wisdom enshrined in pithy sayings – plays a significant part in Anglo-Saxon poetry. Poems like 'The Maxims and Solomon and Saturn' are expressly concerned with the revelation of wisdom while many other poems in the canon, like 'The Wanderer', are strewn with gnomic passages. In Anglo-Saxon England, it seems a poem was expected not only to instruct by pleasing but to please by instructing.

Seen in this light, the lines in 'The Wife's Lament' exhorting young men to "hide their heartaches" do not seem out of place but, rather, deductive. They contain the chill lesson to be learned from the situation of the luckless wife and her husband, and are thus an integral part of the poem. The maxims in the sermonising second part of 'The Seafarer' work in much the same manner, explaining how a man must conduct himself in this world. And what is interesting here is the way in which the Germanic eagerness for fame and a good name (the last word of *Beowulf* describes that hero as *lofgeornost*, 'most eager for fame') has been so easily adapted to Christian purposes:

> Wherefore each man should strive, before he leaves
> this world, to win the praise of those living
> after him, the greatest fame after death,
> with daring deeds on earth against the malice
> of the fiends, against the devil, so that
> the children of men may later honour him
> and his fame live afterwards with the angels
> for ever and ever…

Notions of originality for its own sake would have had little meaning for Anglo-Saxon poets. They refer regularly to the ideas and word-pictures of earlier poets and, working in an oral tradition, they also made use of a common word-and-phrase bank. 'The Husband's Message' also draws on the cryptic runic alphabet, which originated at the beginning of the Christian era and which consists entirely of vertical and diagonal strokes for ease of marking. The letters at the end of the poem are believed to stand for sun-path-ocean-joy-man: that is to say, travel south over the sea to your husband and happiness! The elegies are reflective poems designed to illustrate the price of wisdom and, naturally enough, their composers did not turn their backs on the past but made full use of it.

Anglo-Saxon poetry abounds with descriptions of the natural world – an environment seldom sympathetic and often wild and hostile. Sometimes, as in the light-hearted 'Riddles', these descriptions are an end in themselves; but more often they are used as a way of underlining the nature of a situation and emphasising a state of mind. Thus the images of falling sleet and freezing cold, the call of the curlew and the screech of the eagle, indicate that the exile of the seafarer and the wanderer, respectively voluntary and involuntary, are physically exacting. But they also say something about the sense of desolation of the two exiles, deprived of friendship and laughter lost or left behind in the mead hall.

In 'The Wife's Lament', the woman's wretched situation as a stranger in the country from which her husband has now been exiled seems to be epitomised by the unforgiving environment: steep-sided valleys, impenetrable woods, an earth-cave. And the tangle of briars is like an extension of her own tangled emotions – her longings and anxiety and indignation.

In 'Wulf', too, the thrice-repeated *iglond* immediately establishes the speaker's sense of isolation:

> Wulf is on one island, I on another,
> a fastness that island, a fen-prison.
> Fierce men roam there, on that island...

In the same poem, the speaker tells us that rain slaps the earth as she sits on her own and weeps. In no more than a few words and a few simple strokes, the natural world is shown to be sympathetic to her own condition.

In translating these poems, I have been guided by King Alfred's sensible method: "sometimes word for word, sometimes sense for sense". After all, the meaning of a poem is often to be found between the lines. The fierce clotted music of the originals is not at all easy to reproduce in readable modern verse, but I hope I have at least echoed it in inclining to a four-stress line controlled by light alliteration.

Of course these poems will present some difficulties for the reader as they do for the translator. After all, they were composed more than a thousand years ago. Some of these difficulties are of a general nature and tend to resolve themselves in proportion to the amount one learns about the sophisticated and sturdy English world that gave rise to them. Some, however, are local and specific, and it has only been possible to allude to the most obvious of them (such as the runes in 'The Husband's Message') in an introduction such as this.

But the elegiac poems can still challenge and move us – indeed, they can touch us to the quick, as they doubtless did the sorts and conditions of men so vividly described in 'The Fortunes of Men'. In mighty lines, the wanderer asks:

> Where has the horse gone? Where the man? Where the giver of gold?
> Where is the feasting-place? And where the pleasures of the hall?
> I mourn the gleaming cup, the warrior in his corselet,
> the glory of the prince. How that time has passed away,
> darkened under the shadow of night as if it had never been.

In the original, these words and those following them are like a long, magnificent dying blast on a trumpet: a literary Last Post from the Dark Ages. We do well to stop and listen. In them we hear the true tones of the Anglo-Saxon elegiac poems, by turns piercing and thoughtful and accepting and wise.

The Exeter Book Riddles

The nature of the riddle

The business of naming began with the Creation; the business of deceiving followed soon after, in the Garden of Eden. It is reasonable to suppose that as soon as men had wits they delighted in riddling. And they have delighted in it ever since: metaphor and simile, the detective story, the faked voice on the telephone, the crossword puzzle, the question in the cracker – they all hinge on recognition and, because they represent things as other than they are, they are all living members of the riddle family.

It was Aristotle who first put his finger on the similarity between riddle and metaphor. In his *Rhetoric*, he wrote:

> While metaphor is a very frequent instrument of clever sayings, another or an additional instrument is deception, as people are more clearly conscious of having learned something from their sense of surprise at the way in which the sentence ends and their soul seems to say, 'Quite true and I had missed the point.' This, too, is the result of pleasure afforded by clever riddles; they are instructive and metaphorical in their expression.

Just so, and many of Aristotle's fellow countrymen are reputed to have lost their lives for being unable to answer the semi-metaphorical riddle: 'What has one voice, and goes on four legs in the morning, two legs in the afternoon, and three legs in the evening?' This is, of course, the famous enigma that the Sphinx, that fabulous winged beast with the head of a woman and the body of a lion, put to each passer-by as she sat by the precipice outside Thebes. Those who were unable to answer she either devoured or hurled over the edge. And when Oedipus volunteered, "It is man, who goes on all fours as a baby, who walks upright in the prime of his life, and who hobbles with a stick in old age," the enraged Sphinx threw herself over the precipice.

We know that Egyptians, as well as Greeks, liked riddling, and there are riddles in the first sacred book of the Brahmans, the Rig Veda. One of them depicts the year as a twelve-spoked wheel upon which stand 720 sons of one birth (the days and nights); and a comparable riddle turns up in an early Persian collection which describes knights (the days of the month) riding before the Emperor. These Time-Riddles are one of a number of universal riddle motifs – which is why they are also called 'World-Riddles' – and find their counterpart in the twenty-second riddle of the Exeter Book, 'The Month of December'. There are riddles in the Koran, too, and in the Bible there is – *inter alia* – the impossibly difficult riddle that Samson asked the Philistines at Timnah: "Out of the eater came forth meat, and out of the strong came forth sweetness." Delilah seduced Samson into telling her the answer (a honeycomb in the carcass of a dead lion) and paid Samson out by passing it on to the Philistines.

The word 'riddle' derives from the Old English *rædan*, to advise, to counsel, to guide, to explain. And in a wide sense a riddle does teach: it presents the old in new ways. To men sitting at the mead bench, listening to the professional poet or taking the harp and themselves improvising, the riddle redefined the familiar. The Anglo-Saxon cast of mind and literary mode seems ideally suited to the metaphorical riddle when one considers that the entire body of Old English poetry is packed out with mini-riddles; they are known as 'kennings', and are in fact condensed metaphors. The sea is described as "the swan's riding-place", "the ship's road" and "the whale's path"; a sail is spoken of as "a sea-garment", a poet as "a laughter-smith" and a wife as "a peace-weaver". Setting aside puns and conundrums and catch-questions, of which there are only a handful in the Exeter Book, what is a riddle but an extended kenning?

The Exeter Book

The first bishop of Exeter was Leofric. He died in 1072 and amongst his bequeathals to the Cathedral Library was *i. mycel englisc boc be gehwilcum pingum on leoðwisan geworht*: 'one large book in English verse about various subjects'. This has always been taken to be the *Codex Exoniensis* or Exeter Book, one of the four great surviving miscellanies of Old English poetry.

Probably copied by one scribe during the last quarter of the tenth century, this manuscript consists of 131 leaves or folios and contains a great range of poetry. There are 'documentary' Christian poems, such as 'Christ', which relates the Nativity and the Ascension and anticipates the Day of Judgement; there are Christian allegories about 'The Panther' and 'The Whale', which turn up again in many medieval bestiaries, and 'The Phoenix' (a godsend of a bird because of its supposed miraculous resurrection); there are elegiac poems, such as 'The Wanderer' and 'The Seafarer' (memorably translated by Ezra Pound), that are ostensibly Christian in their comparison of the transient life on earth with the eternal life in heaven, but which celebrate the old Germanic qualities of endurance and resilience, tempered by melancholy; there are poems such as 'Widsith' and 'Deor' that draw on the traditions and stories of the pagan Germanic world, survivals of the time before the Angles, Saxons, Frisians and Jutes first came to England; and, of course, there are the riddles. The Exeter Book is a remarkable anthology and, had it not survived, we would have to suppose the range of Old English poetry to be much narrower than we know it to be.

That the manuscript has survived seems virtually accidental. It is possible to deduce from gaps in the text that at least seven folios are missing. At some time, it appears to have been used both as a cutting board – perhaps a sort of bread-and-cheese board – and as a beer-mat; there are scores and circular stains on the first folio. More seriously, the manuscript has also been damaged by fire. A long diagonal burn on the last fourteen folios has destroyed the text of some of the later riddles, the last group of which are the final entry in the manuscript.

The number, condition, authorship, date of composition, and sources of the riddles

There are 96 riddles in the Exeter Book and they have been copied into the manuscript in three groups: Riddles 1–59, Riddles 30b and 60, and Riddles 61–95. Because one folio is missing between Riddles 40 and 41, it is generally thought that, as with other earlier collections in Latin, there were originally one hundred riddles. It is the third group that has suffered because of the burn in the manuscript.

There is not, and is not likely to be, academic agreement over the authorship of the Exeter Book riddles. For a long time, the eighth-century poet Cynewulf was believed to have composed them all. Now, conversely, most commentators suppose that the collection is the work of many hands, and that Cynewulf's was not one of them. In the words of Krapp and Dobbie, editors of *The Anglo-Saxon Poetic Records*, "The question may, therefore, hardly be said to be definitely settled; but the burden of proof seems to be upon those who would demonstrate unity of authorship." The date of composition is similarly uncertain, and all the more so because of the likelihood of multiple authorship, although there is linguistic evidence that a handful of the riddles were composed in the first half of the eighth century. In this context, Krapp and Dobbie write: "It is of course very likely that a large number of the riddles date from the early eighth century, when Englishmen were most active in the composition of Latin riddles, but a more definite statement than this is hardly possible in the light of our present knowledge."

Who were these English riddlers writing in Latin, and what bearing do they have on the Exeter Book collection? The first question is easy to answer, the second less so. There are three surviving collections in Latin. They are ascribed to Aldhelm (c. 640–709), who was Abbot of Malmesbury and subsequently Bishop of Sherborne, and who wrote one hundred riddles or *Ænigmata*; to Tatwine (d. 734), who was an Archbishop of Canterbury; and to Eusebius (c. 680–c. 747), who is believed to be one and the same as Hwætberht, Abbot of Wearmouth and a friend of Bede. The riddles by Tatwine and Eusebius are preserved in the same manuscript and together number one hundred – Tatwine was responsible for forty and Eusebius sixty. Aldhelm acknowledges as his model Symphosius, whose collection of one hundred riddles also survives, and who is credited with originating the literary riddle in post-Classical times. He is thought to have lived in the late fourth or early fifth century.

Much valuable work has been done recently on the sources and analogues of the riddles, and it is clear that the three collections by Englishmen and the earlier collection by Symphosius were all known to the Exeter Book riddlers. In one or two cases, for example Riddle 40, the Anglo-Saxon riddler attempted a translation and elaboration of the Latin original; in several instances the correspondence between Old English and Latin is very close; while in a number of other cases either the Anglo-Saxon riddler borrowed and very freely developed an idea in one of the Latin riddles, or else both Anglo-Saxon and Latin riddles are analogues, referring to the same traditional material.

It should not be supposed, though, that the Exeter Book riddles are a collection of half-baked derivations. On the contrary they have great imaginative zest, great charm, and at times great subtlety; they are wonderfully attractive in their own right.

The elements of the collection

In many ways the riddles constitute a delightful and informative entrée into the Anglo-Saxon world. Some are folk-riddles (distinguished by their use of popular material, their shortness and simplicity), some are literary riddles (full of conscious poetic elaboration and attention to detail), and some combine both elements. Just as the tone and treatment varies from one riddle to the next, so does the subject-matter itself. As one turns from natural phenomena to animal and bird life, from the Christian concept of the Creation to humdrum domestic objects, from weaponry to the peaceful pursuits of writing and music, one wins glimpse after glimpse of the Anglo-Saxons and their attitudes.

It may be worth looking at the elements of the collection in a little more detail. Typically enough, more than a dozen riddles are concerned with weapons and war-gear, and contest – sword, for instance, shield, bow, and battering ram. This is what one would expect of a society caught up in almost endless turmoil – against the Romano-British, against each other, against the Vikings and, finally, against the Normans. It was a society whose values had changed very little despite migration from the European Continent, the advent of Christianity, and the passage of time. Describing the way of life of the German tribes living within the Roman Empire in the first century, Tacitus noted in his *Germania*: "As for leaving a battle alive after your chief has fallen, that means lifelong infamy and shame. To defend and protect him, to put down one's own acts of heroism to his credit – that is what they really mean by allegiance. The chiefs fight for victory, the companions for their chief." And again: "A man is bound to take up the feuds as well as the friendships of father or kinsman."

The bond between chief and followers, the emphasis on kinship, on physical and moral courage and on the blood-feud were just as important to the Anglo-Saxons at the Battle of Hastings as to their Germanic ancestors.

The deserter was condemned to live an unenviable life of exile, and the fundamental lord-retainer relationship is touched on in several of the riddles. So too is the overriding sense of *wyrd* – fate – and the need to struggle against it, which dogged the pagan tribes that first came to England and their descendants, the Anglo-Saxons. This was a society whose greatest ambition was for fame despite all; remember that the last word of *Beowulf* is *lofgeornost* – most eager for fame. One of the Old Norse sayings attributed to Odin very nicely sums up the pagan Anglo-Saxon's attitude to life: "One thing I know never dies or changes, the reputation of a dead man."

Just as some riddles in the Exeter Book reflect aspects of the Germanic heroic world, others describe objects, such as the Bible and chalice, associated with the new Christian faith that swept through England during the seventh century. One can visualise what hope Christian teaching must have brought, the hope of a life after death. Nothing exemplifies it quite as well as the much-quoted words of one of King Edwin's councillors (related by Bede), when that King was considering whether or not to adopt the new Christian faith:

> O King, imagine you are sitting at a banquet with your ealdormen and thanes in winter time; the fire is burning and the hall is warm, and outside the winter storms are raging; and there should come a sparrow flying swiftly through the hall, coming in through one door and out by another. While it is inside, it is safe from the winter storms; but after a few minutes of comfort, it soon returns from winter back to winter again, and is lost to sight. Likewise, this mortal life seems like a short interval; what may have come before, or what may come after it, we do not know. Therefore, O King, if this new Christian teaching brings any great certainty, it seems fitting that we should follow it.

King Edwin followed it!

During the seventh and eighth centuries, the scriptoria of the great Northumbrian monasteries produced a steady stream of manuscripts, for use at home and for missionary activity on the Continent. There are several riddles about the work of the scribe, the illumination of manuscripts, and the custody of books including a charming short poem about a book moth, while another group of riddles is concerned with musical instruments that would have been heard inside and outside the monastery: harp; horn, reed-flute and bagpipe.

Although the Exeter Book riddles reflect aspects of Germanic heroism and of Christianity, in either case quite formal and dignified, the foremost preoccupation of the collection is with the everyday life of working people, with household objects, and with aspects of the natural world. There are riddles about bucket and bellows, key and poker and loom, ale and mead, anchor and plough and seven of them (sometimes called the 'obscene' riddles) are double entendre, including onion/penis and churn/coition and helmet/vagina; riddles about badger and bullock, the swan, the jay, the swallow, the copulating cock and hen; riddles about the sun and moon, and sudden storms, and ice. They are informed by sharp observation, charm, an earthy sense of humour, above all by a sense of wonder – and they make us in turn recognise that every object around us has its distinctive attributes and a life of its own. Even if the riddlers were clerics (as they doubtless were), the majority of the riddles reflect the views of people who may have been aware of fate and of God, and struggled manfully to reconcile the two, but were in the end more concerned with crops than concepts. The Anglo-Saxons were above all an agricultural people and, more than any other literature that survives from the period, this riddle collection is the song of the unsung labourer.

In surveying the constituents of the Exeter Book collection, it only remains to mention the six runic riddles. 'Rune' means 'mystery' or 'secret', and the runic alphabet is thought to have originated at the beginning of the Christian era. It consisted of twenty-four letters (known as the futhark) and each letter had its name and meaning: the letter D, for instance, is represented by ᛗ in the runic alphabet, and its name was dag, 'day'. Since the letters consist entirely of vertical and diagonal strokes, and use no curves or horizontals, it is thought likely that the alphabet was originally designed for use on wood and metal. It was first used for magical purposes but was used more generally in Anglo-Saxon England, sometimes for protective purposes (runes engraved on a sword blade, for example), and sometimes for identification. The Exeter Book riddlers used runes instead of, or as well as, poetic ambiguity – a kind of additional conundrum.

It is with these runic riddles, and with the punning Riddle 30a, that the Exeter Book collection comes closest to the catch-question riddle that has doubtless prospered in every age, and that most children have up their sleeves today – the riddle more concerned with the value of words than with the object described. This kind of riddle must have reached its apogee with the Victorians: *Why is a good meerschaum like a water-colour artist? Because it draws and colours beautifully.* Why has the Dark Continent no terrors for Mr Stanley? *Because he 'makes light' of it.* What part of a fish is like the end of a book? Don't you know? *Why, the fin-is.* Teasers of this kind can be fun and they can be extremely boring. But either way they are devoid of poetry. The glory of the Exeter Book collection is that it consists of riddles which are, at their best, excellent enigmas and excellent poems.

The Cross Crucified

An Introduction to 'The Dream of the Rood'

The poem that we are going to look at begins with the injunction *Hwæt!* Listen!

> Hwæt, ic swefna cyst   secgan wylle,
> hwæt me gemætte   to midre nihte…

I translated those lines when I was 23, and there wasn't much left to learn!

> Listen! I will describe the best of dreams
> which I dreamed in the middle of the night
> when, far and wide, all men slept.

Many of the delightful Anglo-Saxon metaphorical riddles start *ic wiht geseah*. This means "I saw a creature…" The riddler then goes on to describe something in terms that seem at first strange – but then you see through them, see *into* them.

"Quite true," as we have seen Aristotle observe, in describing how a riddle works, "quite true, and I'd missed the point."

Just as, not very long ago, I borrowed – well, nicked actually – an apple from a headteacher's study and put it down on a table in front of a bunch of girls. "Tell me something new about this apple," I invited them.

"It will cry if you bite it," one girl said.

"It's speckled," said another.

And another: "It's freckled."

"It's like a sphere," said a fourth.

"What is a sphere?" I asked.

So she explained. And then a fifth girl volunteered, "Well, it's got these pips inside it."

"What are they like?"

"Hidden," she replied. "Hidden. Oh, I got it! They're like secrets."

So here was an apple on the table that wept when you bit it, was speckled and freckled, and like a sphere, and contained dark secrets. And this is the metaphorical way of working that poets make part of their profession.

While at Oxford, I started to translate some Anglo-Saxon riddles, and that was the beginning of my own involvement with the world of Anglo-Saxon poetry – anything rather than actually learn the grammar! There was one riddle that caught my eye which is actually a pun on the Anglo-Saxon word *beam* and can mean several different things – it can mean tree, it can mean ship, it can mean log, it can mean cup and it can mean The Tree, the Holy Cross. The riddle is just nine lines long: you can supply the meanings to the first six lines yourselves – tree, ship, log, cup...

> I'm surrounded by flames and sport with the wind,
> I'm clothed in finery and the storm's great friend,
> ready to travel, but troubled by fire,
> a glade in full bloom and a burning flame;
> friends often pass me from hand to hand,
> and I'm kissed by ladies and courteous men.

And then the last three lines are quite specifically about the Holy Cross:

> When I raise myself, many people
> bow before me; I bring
> their happiness to full maturity.

A riddle, then, in which quite shockingly, Christ's cross briefly speaks, and invites us to see the old in a new way. Let's just put that down as a marker.

*

The hoard of Anglo-Saxon poems was composed (I say that advisedly rather than written) for an oral culture between the sixth and eleventh centuries. Let me quickly categorise them.

Firstly, there are heroic poems, as early as the seventh-century 'Widsith' and 'Deor' which embody fragments and memories of the stories that the Angles and Saxons and Jutes brought over with them when they came into England in the fifth and sixth centuries. And there are poems as late as 'The Battle of Maldon', describing the fight between Anglo-Saxons and Vikings in 991 on a grey wet August day (it always seems to be raining in Anglo-Saxon poetry). Towards the end of the poem, there are lines that many readers may have come across in one place or another:

> Mind must be the firmer, heart the more fierce,
> courage the greater, as our strength grow less…
> … I mean to lie by the side of my lord,
> lie in the dust with the man I loved so dearly.

At the very heart of Anglo-Saxon poetry and society lies this binding relationship between a man and his follower – a leader and his retainer – and that is crucial as we draw near to 'The Dream of the Rood' – another marker to put down.

Then there are elegies – poems of exile, or of a first estate that has been lost and is longed for. Some readers will know 'The Wanderer', 'The Seafarer', 'The Husband's Message', 'The Wife's Lament', 'Wulf' – deeply relevant to our own age in which so many people are rootless and long to belong, people in transit camps, exiles, immigrants, an age in which the question of identity is a daily topic. These are poems of very great passion. Here are just seven lines from the middle of 'The Seafarer':

> Wherefore my heart leaps within me,
> my mind roams with the waves
> over the whale's domain, it wanders far and wide
> across the face of the earth, returns again to me
> eager and unsatisfied; the solitary bird screams,
> irresistible, urges the heart to the whale's way
> over the stretch of the seas.

The poet goes on to say that people living on land have got no idea of the rigour, the demands, the sacrifice endured by the seafarer. He then equates the life of the seafarer with the Christian life, and so this becomes a deeply moving Christian poem.

Then there are what I call the poems of law and learning. These include the maxims and the riddles, and these poems embody little pockets of learning and folk knowledge, as well as teaching us to look at old objects in new ways: household objects, animal and bird life, the elements and objects associated with the Christian faith.

Finally, there are the Christian poems. They form much the largest group surviving from this period, and they can be divided into six categories:

i) Free paraphrases of Genesis and Exodus
ii) Poems about Christ the Redeemer, including the Advent lyrics and 'The Dream of the Rood'
iii) Poems about the acts of the Apostles – for instance the very fine poem 'Andreas' (St Andrew)

iv) Poems quite specifically about Holy Cross, including 'Elena', which is about St Helena finding the True Cross
v) Allegories, like the 'Panther', 'Whale', and 'Phoenix'
vi) Poems about the second coming – such as 'Domesday' (*domes dæg* means the day of judgement)

*

The Anglo-Saxon Chronicle entry for 793 doesn't beat about the bush:

> In this year dire portents appeared over Northumbria and sorely frightened the people. They consisted of immense whirlwinds and flashes of lightning, and fiery dragons were seen flying in the air. A great famine immediately followed those signs, and a little after that in the same year, on 8 June, the ravages of heathen men miserably destroyed God's church on Lindisfarne, with plunder and slaughter.

Yes, the air-dragons were rapidly followed by salt-sea dragons, the dragon prows of Viking ships with their ominous crow-black square sails. Within a few years, the Danish Vikings were running riot through the monasteries of Northumbria, so many of them conveniently close to the shore – Lindisfarne, Jarrow, Whitby. They killed the monks, raped the nuns, stole the church plate, and promised to come back the following year.

Many years ago, I visited the tiny one-room museum on Holy Island, and found there a storytelling tombstone. On one side were seven rampaging Vikings waving axe and scramasax; on the other were two monks praying beneath the outstretched arms of Christ's cross, and beneath the sun and the crescent moon. I thought then of the monastery of Lindisfarne as a kind of hive:

Norsemen storm the cells:
The hive ablaze; sluice of blood
Garnet-bright, under sword and axe;
The golden comb iron reaps;
A knot of monks drones Pax Pax
By candles's light; wax weeps.
A furore Normanorum, libera nos, Domine.

Two monks crooked in prayer:
Cuthbert incorrupt and unscathed;
A good haul from Bee Hill;
Quick requital for slaughter;
Freedom from shadows still
Shrithing over the minds' water.
A furore Normanorum, libera nos, Domine.

On one side of the tombstone, then, piety; on the other, militarism. Let's keep sight of that.

This and the preceding seventh century were a time of conversion, religious ferment and extraordinary scholarship and artistic achievement in Northumbria. In their cells, and in their scriptoria and sculptoria, and other workshops, the monks and nuns of some thirty monasteries produced poetry, marvellously illuminated manuscripts (such as the Lindisfarne Gospels, with their well-nigh miraculous 'carpet' pages), texts about grammar, natural science, chronology, the lives of the saints, stone carvings, ivory casket lids, pendants, and brooches.

It was here that the alliterative technique of Germanic poetry is said to have been first harnessed to Christian purposes. In his glorious *History of the English Church and People*, Bede tells us that at the monastery of Whitby, the quite elderly cowherd Cædmon was visited in a dream by "a man who called him by name" and who told him to sing. Cædmon said he couldn't. He said he didn't know how.

He said that's why he sometimes left the feasting-hall as the harp was passed from hand to hand, and one person after another said-and-sang a poem. Cædmon's visitor wouldn't take no for an answer. He told the cowherd to "sing about the creation of all things". And Cædmon, singing in Northumbrian dialect, began:

Nu scylun hergan   hefænricæs Uard,
Metudæs mæcti   end his modgidanc…

Now we must praise the Ruler of Heaven,
the might of the Lord and His purpose of mind,
the work of the Glorious Father; for He,
God Eternal, established each wonder,
He, Holy Creator, first fashioned the heavens
as a roof for the children of earth…

One of the works of art produced in a monastery in Dumfriesshire in the north of Northumbria was an extraordinary, fine-grained, sandstone cross. It was almost eighteen feet high, and elaborately carved on all four sides with scenes from the Gospels, and vine scrolls inhabited with birds and little creatures, and on the margins of two sides with runes.

This cross, the Ruthwell Cross, was smashed in 1642 in conformity with the act passed against 'idolatrous monuments' – victim to the same dreadful tide that led to the appointment of William (Smasher) Dowsing as Cromwell's Iconoclast General, and the wholesale damaging or destruction of cherubim, rood screens, images of the Virgin, crucifixes, and church ornamentation of all kinds. In 1802, fragments of the cross were gathered together, and it became clear that there were four separate groups of runes, together totalling ten lines. A further nine lines were only fragmentary, or else wholly missing – become no more than sand grains once more.

I'm devoting time to these runes because the relationship between them and the wonderful passion poem, 'The Dream of the Rood', is tantalising and mysterious. One line of runes, translated into Anglo-Saxon, reads: *heafunæs hlaford hælda ic ni dorste*. And that, translated into modern English, means "I dared not hold Heaven's lord". Another line of runes reads, starkly, *Krist was on rode*: "Christ was on the cross". And a third: *Alegdun hiæ hinæ limwoerignæ*: "They laid him down limb-weary".

So how are we to explain that these same phrases, and more besides, carved in the eighth century in Northumbria, also lie at the heart of the poem known as 'The Dream of the Rood', which survives in a single manuscript, the Vercelli Book (now in the cathedral of Vercelli Library – and why that should be so is another mystery)?

While it's true that Anglo-Saxon poets, working in an oral tradition, set little premium on originality, and had recourse to a large common word-and-phrase bank, the correspondences between the inscriptions on the Ruthwell Cross and 'The Dream of the Rood' (it has no title in the manuscript and was first so called by Benjamin Thorpe in his 1836 edition of the Vercelli Book) are too substantial and striking to be explained away like that. It is possible that the poem was actually first composed in Northumbria at some time before the Ruthwell cross was carved, and that the carver took words directly from the poem and cut them into the Ruthwell Cross. And if this is the case, then we must suppose that the poem was passed by word of mouth (or maybe by way of manuscript now lost) through generations, and across the length of England, until it was entered in the late tenth-century Vercelli Book in West Saxon, the standard dialect in the south of England. But it is equally possible that some man or woman living in the eighth, ninth, or tenth centuries had seen and was deliberately quoting the Ruthwell Cross, inspired by it to compose the greatest religious poem of the age.

'The Dream of the Rood' is remarkable in being the oldest surviving dream or dream-vision poem in the English language. It is remarkable for its sustained use of the rhetorical device known as prosopopeia, in which an inanimate object (in this instance, the Cross on which Christ was crucified) is given a voice, and speaks from its own viewpoint. And it is remarkable for its mystical intensity and sheer voltage.

The poem is 156 lines long, and it falls into three parts. First a dreamer tells us how he saw the Cross and, showing us how it is both bejewelled and bloody, introduces us to the theme of triumphant suffering, suffering triumph, that is doctrinally at the heart of the poem. Then the Cross speaks, and what it has to say is firstly most vivid and excruciating description. The short, stabbing lines as the Cross describes the "God of Hosts" stretched on the rack are superbly dramatic not only in their brevity but in their cinematographic changes of scale — the way they juxtapose the single, solitary figure of Christ on the cross with a whole weeping universe: "All creation wept, wailed for the death of the King; Christ was on the cross." Having described the crucifixion and its aftermath, the Cross proceeds to homily. This is entirely typical of Anglo-Saxon poetry, that often moves from specific experience to the lesson to be drawn from it. In this third part of the poem, we hear from the dreamer again, now full of hope, awaiting the day when he will journey on from earth to heaven.

At the heart of Anglo-Saxon society lay the relationship of a leader and his followers, each bound by oaths and responsibilities, each depending on the other. In this poem, Christ is presented as a leader, and his disciples are in effect his warrior-band. Christ is an active hero, willingly advancing on the Cross, and 'stripping himself before battle'. He is victorious and yet willing, or victorious because he is willing, to suffer torment.

The Cross's description of the way in which the disciples took down Christ's body from the cross, and built him a sepulchre, and sang a dirge at dusk before they left him, reminds one at once of the end of the epic poem *Beowulf*:

> Then twelve brave warriors, sons of heroes,
> rode round the barrow, sorrowing;
> they mourned their king, chanted
> an elegy, spoke about that great man...
> They said that of all kings on earth
> he was the kindest, the most gentle,
> the most just to his people, the most eager for fame.
>
> Cwædon þæt he wære   weorold cyninga,
> manna mildost   ond mon-thwærust,
> leodum liðost   ond lof-geornost.

With breath-taking dramatic irony, the poet shows us that the cross (most faithful of Christ's followers) can only be loyal to Christ (its leader) by being disloyal to him (worst of all Anglo-Saxon crimes): it can only be loyal to Christ by crucifying him. This paradox must have made Anglo-Saxons shake their heads in wonder.

    Let me also draw attention to the way in which the poet carefully (and most strikingly) presents Christ as divine and yet wholly human. The way in which he does so, no fewer than ten times in quick succession after Christ has died, is by combining different attributes of God (such as his majesty or his omnipotence) with practical, common or garden, well-earthed verbs. Thus: "They took Almighty God away" and "They laid Him down, limb-weary" and "They laid therein the Lord of Victories". The cult of the Cross was, I believe, strong in northern and western Britain (influenced by Celtic Christianity) in the eighth century, and our poet was doubtless reflecting Christological disputes about the human-cum-divine nature of the Saviour, but the highly effective way in which he did so was – as far as we can tell – all his own.

One more point: towards the end of the poem, the reference to feasting in heaven (eagerly awaited by the dreamer) reminds me of nothing so much as the continuous round of feasting in Valhalla awaiting Viking heroes slain in battle. Have you seen in the British Museum the astonishing whalebone Franks Casket, made in Northumbria during the eighth century? The panel portraying the Adoration of the Magi rubs shoulders with another portraying the pre-Christian hero Wayland the Smith greeting his daughter. After all, Christians have always been very good as baptising what they could not suppress.

To my mind, then, 'The Dream of the Rood' is the place where for the first time theology and drama meet in English literature.

Earlier I described the Lindisfarne tombstone informed by piety on one side, militarism on the other. But as 'The Dream of the Rood' shows, the two were by no means mutually exclusive. On the contrary, they are but two sides of the same stone, two sides of the character of Christ Himself.

So the poem proceeds from fear and sorrow and sinful remorse to wonder and hope. To give hope: that is its purpose. So many roads lead us back to seventh- and eighth-century Northumbria, and that is where, I am at last persuaded, 'The Dream of the Rood' originated.

Remember how King Edwin's councillor (as reported by the Venerable Bede) won the day at Bamburgh Castle in 627 with his comparison of a man's lifetime to the lone sparrow's swift flight through the dining hall, and the 'certain knowledge' that a conversion to Christianity would afford?

There is an Anglo-Saxon half-line: *"lif is læne"* – "life is fleeting, life is transitory". And another: *"gæþ a wyrd swa hio scel"* – "fate goes ever as it must". Fierce and gentle, the new Christian faith offered above all hope – hope for the remission of our sins through the voluntary suffering and death of Christ, hope of an afterlife.

    and ic wene me
daga gehwylce   hwænne me Dryhtnes rod,
þe ic her on eorðan   ær sceawode,
of þysson lænan   life gefetige,
and me þonne gebringe   þær is blis micel,
dream on heofonum…

    Now I look day by day
for that time when the cross of the Lord,
which once I saw in a dream here on earth,
will fetch me away from this fleeting life
and lift me to the home of joy and happiness
where the people of God are seated at the feast
in eternal bliss…

From 'The Dream of the Rood'

Listen! I will describe the best of dreams
which I dreamed in the middle of the night
when, far and wide, all men slept.
It seemed that I saw wondrous tree
soaring into the air, surrounded by light,
the brightest of crosses; that emblem was entirely
cased in gold; beautiful jewels
were strewn around its foot, just as five
studded the cross-beam. All the angels of god,
fair creations, guarded it. That was no cross
of a criminal, but holy spirits and men on earth
watched it over there – the whole glorious universe.

Wondrous was the tree of victory, and I was stained
by sin, stricken by guilt. I saw this glorious tree
joyfully gleaming, adorned with garments,
decked in gold; the tree of the Ruler
was rightly adorned with rich stones;
yet through that gold I could see the agony
once suffered by wretches, for it had bled
down the right hand side. Then I was afflicted,
frightened at this sight; I saw that sign often change
its clothing and hue, at times dewy with moisture,
stained by flowing blood, at times adorned with treasure.
Yet I lay there for a long while
and gazed sadly at the Saviour's cross
until I heard it utter words;
the finest of trees began to speak:
"I remember the morning a long time ago
that I was felled at the edge of the forest

and severed from my roots. Strong enemies seized me,
bade me hold up their felons on high,
made me a spectacle. Men shifted me
on their shoulders and set me on a hill.
Many enemies fastened me there. I saw the Lord of Mankind
hasten with such courage to climb upon me.
I dared not bow or break there
against my Lord's wish, when I saw the surface
of the earth tremble. I could have felled
all my foes, yet I stood firm.
Then the young warrior, God Almighty,
stripped Himself, firm and unflinching. He climbed
upon the cross, brave before many, to redeem mankind.
I quivered when the hero clasped me,
yes I dared not bow to the ground,
fall to the earth. I had to stand firm.
A rood was I raised up; I bore aloft the might King,
the Lord of Heaven. I dared not stoop.
They drove dark nails into me; dire wounds are there to see,
the gaping gashes of malice; I dared not injure them.
They insulted us both together; I was drenched in the blood
that streamed from the Man's side after He set His spirit free.

"On that hill I endured many grievous trials;
I saw the God of Hosts stretched
on the rack; darkness covered the corpse
of the Ruler with clouds, His shining radiance.
Shadows swept across the land, dark shapes
under the clouds. All creation wept,
wailed for the death of the King; Christ was on the cross.
yet men hurried eagerly to the Prince
from afar; I witnessed all that too.

I was oppressed with sorrow, yet humbly bowed to the hands of
    men,
and willingly. There they lifted Him from His heavy torment,
they took Almighty God away. The warriors left me standing there,
stained with blood; sorely was I wounded with the sharpness of
    spear-shafts.
they laid Him down, limb-weary; they stood at the corpse's head,
They beheld there the Lord of Heaven; and there He rested for a
    while,
worn out after battle. And then they began to build a sepulchre;
under his slayer's eyes, they carved it from the gleaming stone,
and laid therein the Lord of Victories. Then, sorrowful at dusk,
they sang a dirge before they went, weary,
from their glorious Prince; He rested in the grave alone.
But we still stood there, weeping blood,
long after the song of the warriors
had soared to heaven; the corpse grew cold,
the fair human house of the soul. Then our enemies
began to fell us, that was a terrible fate.
They buried us in a deep pit; but friends
and followers of the Lord found me there
and girded me with gold and shimmering silver.

"Now, my loved man, you have heard
how I endured bitter anguish
at the hands of evil men. Now the time is come
when men far and wide in this world,
and all this bright creation, bow before me;
they pray to this sign. On me the Son of God
suffered for a time; wherefore now I stand on high,
glorious under heaven; and I can heal
all those who stand in awe of me.
Long ago I became the worst of tortures,

hated by men until I opened
to them the true way of life.
Lo! The Lord of Heaven, the Prince of Glory,
honoured me over any other tree
just as He, Almighty God, for the sake of mankind
honoured Mary, His own mother,
before all other women in the world."

From 'The Dream of the Rood' (first published in *The Battle of Maldon and Other Old English Poems*, 1965)

AUTHORS AND BOOKS

I progressed at Macmillan, publisher of Lewis Carroll and Rudyard Kipling, to become editor of the firm's children's books, which meant that I needed to become *au courant* with the world of children's literature; to be confident in my assessments; and to write courteous and encouraging words to authors young and old who submitted their work.

At the same time I was starting to write for children myself, and after winning the Carnegie Medal, (this for my pipsqueak *Storm* – the one and only time the Medal has been awarded to a book for primary school-aged children), I felt myself to be one of the great society of children's writers, quick and dead. But it was only after the publication of my *Arthur* trilogy and *Gatty's Tale* that my work began to be regularly translated.

In selecting from so very many candidates the pieces for this section, I recognise how they not only honour writers whose work I particularly admire for their style, but show how they helped me to discover different ways of engaging with character and theme, and to recognise and establish my own priorities – the relationship of people and place, and of past and present.

Rosemary Sutcliff

The Eagle of the Ninth

In many novels, most maybe, there is a moment of truth. With an image, an aphorism, an argument, the author reveals the very heart of the story.

Such a moment occurs in *The Eagle of the Ninth* when the young Roman centurion Marcus Aquila is talking to his British slave, Esca.

Esca contrasts the curves of life on a British shield-boss with Marcus's dagger-sheath, tightly patterned in Roman style, and observes that "You cannot expect the man who made this shield to live easily under the rule of the man who worked the sheath of this dagger." In fact, the dagger was made by a British craftsman but, Esca argues, "one who had lived so long under the wings of Rome… that he had forgotten the ways and the spirit of his own people." Later Marcus stares at the two objects:

> Esca had chosen his symbol well, he thought: between the formal pattern on his dagger-sheath and the formless yet potent beauty of the shield-boss lay all the that could lie between two worlds. And yet between individual people … the distance narrowed so that you could reach across it, one to another, so that it ceased to matter.

Rosemary Sutcliff was born in 1920. She suffered from the wasting Still's disease from the age of two, was educated at home until she was nine, and went to Bideford Art School at the age of fourteen to train as a painter. She was confined to a wheelchair for much of her life. So it is not, I suppose, in the least surprising that the central character in many of her novels is isolated by virtue of affliction or social circumstance.

The Eagle of the Ninth, published in 1954, was the first of Sutcliff's novels about a Roman family in Britain named Aquila, and their descendants, the next two in the sequence being *The Silver Branch* and *The Lantern Bearers*.

Marcus Flavius Aquila, aged eighteen, has asked for and been given a posting in England circa AD 126; he is eager to find out where and why his own father disappeared in AD 117 with an entire legion (the Ninth Hispana) and its bronze-and-silver Eagle, while trying to put down a rebellion among the northern tribes.

Marcus is open, eager, loyal, imaginative. And from the moment he is badly wounded while serving at Isca Dumnoniorum (Exeter) during a British chariot-raid, the reader is wholly on his side. Rosemary Sutcliff sees to that, with her ferocious descriptions of the pain Marcus suffers after smashing his thigh-bone and tearing the muscles to shreds, and the way his impatience to recover darkens into dignified acceptance of his condition:

> No need to be afraid now, not any more. He took it very quietly; but it meant the loss of almost everything he cared about. Life with the Eagles was the only kind of life he had ever thought of, the only kind that he had any training for; and now it was over.

An invalid with "a lame leg and no money and no prospects", wretched, homesick Marcus goes to stay with his engaging uncle, who lives with his elderly wolf-hound Procyon in the shadow of a watch-tower at Calleva (Silchester). For the past ten years, Uncle Aquila has been writing *The History of Siege Warfare*, a book one suspects he will never quite finish.

One day, Marcus is carried in a litter to watch the Saturnalia Games. This is the occasion at which he encounters two Britons who are to have a profound impact on his life. One is Cottia: "perhaps twelve or thirteen, with a sharply pointed face that seemed all golden eyes in the shadow of her dark hood", whose British aunt and uncle are "of the ultra-Roman kind", but who, herself, is utterly horrified by the killing in the arena and the bloodlust all around her. The other is Esca: a tattooed swordsman in the Games, the son of a Clan Chieftain of the Brigantes, too proud to beg for his life after being snared in his opponent's net in a fight to the death, until Marcus galvanises the crowd in the amphitheatre into granting him mercy.

Though Marcus's relationship with flame-haired Cottia, and with Esca, whom he buys as a personal slave, Rosemary Sutcliff explore the characteristics of the Roman and British cultures and the tensions as they interact.

Time and time again I found myself thinking 'Yes! This is how it was. This is how it must have been,' and there are good reasons for this. Sutcliff's heart may quicken to the Roman trumpet and drumbeat, but she is no less awake to Roman than to British shortcomings, and never in the least sentimental. Virtually every page is hallmarked by an unblinking realism and by concern to get the particulars right. Sutcliff's careful, sure-footed descriptions of chariot driving, day-to-day life in a frontier fort, making a sacrifice to Mithras, the clothing of the British Epidaii, a heron-tufted war spear, the family farm in the Etruscan hills, an abandoned broch and dozens of similar objects, places, activities, and ceremonies are evidence of meticulous research into Roman and British culture, leavened by vivid imagination. Her portrayal of bloody conflict, and there is plenty of it in *The Eagle of the Ninth*, is sensual, frank, and even meaty. In her fiction she faces up to the physical pain she experienced in fact. And yet she is also mistress of glancing detail and elusive atmosphere.

The dialectic between the Roman rule-book and British inspiration, between colonist and colonised, may lie at the heart of the novel, but what drives it forward is Marcus's quest for the lost Eagle of the Ninth. This gives him a new mission, a new sense of purpose:

a cloud of suspicion hangs over the mysterious disappearance of the entire Legion, and Marcus longs not only to exonerate his own father, but to redeem the honour of Rome.

While visiting Calleva, Uncle Aquila's old friend Claudius Hieronimianus, Legate of the Sixth Legion, reports a strong rumour that the Ninth Legion did indeed go down fighting against the Outland Tribes (also known as the Painted People), and that the Eagle itself has been seen, "receiving divine honours in some temple in the far north". Marcus at once volunteers to venture beyond Hadrian's Wall with Esca, to try to find out the truth of this rumour. His leg, he says, is serviceable enough now, provided he doesn't have to make a run for it, "but in strange country we should not stand a dog's chance on the run, anyway". From the moment the Legate gives Marcus his marching orders, and Marcus movingly gives Esca a slim papyrus roll declaring his manumission – his freedom – and then invites him to accompany him as a friend, the scene is set for the arduous, hazardous, surprising and often thrilling quest.

That Marcus leaves with desolate Cottia the gold military bracelet he has been awarded for loyalty and courage is evidence of the loving trust that has developed between him and the young British girl. "I cannot wear this where I am going," he says. "Will you keep it safe for me until I come back to claim it?"

> She took it from him without a word, and stood looking down at it in her hands. The light caught the Capricorn badge and the words beneath: 'Pia fidelis'. Very gently she wiped the raindrops from the gold, and stowed it under her mantle... She was standing very straight and still, very forlorn, and with the darkness of her mantle covering her bright hair as it had done when he first saw her ...
>
> "You must go now," he said. "The Light of the Sun be with you, Cottia."

"And with you," said Cottia. "And with you, Marcus. I shall be listening for you to come back – for you to come down here to the garden foot and whistle for me again, when the leaves are falling."

Away they go, Marcus and Esca, on what Esca characterises as their 'wild hunt', far beyond the bounds of the known, mapped, Roman world. And at once one is aware how much of Britain remained completely untouched by Rome, and that even in the Legionary cities, as Marcus has noted earlier while stationed at Isca Dumnoniorum, "Rome was a new slip grafted on to an old stock – and the graft had not yet taken."

Just the same was true of the Anglo-Saxons when they surged into Romano-British England during the sixth century, and of the Normans after they defeated the Anglo-Saxons at Hastings. It is one thing to conquer and occupy a country; altogether another to fuse with the old stock to the point at which cultural differences become a source of strength.

Throughout the summer season, Marcus, disguised as an oculist, and Esca wander through the abandoned province of Hadrian's Wall, unable to pick up the trail. "When there is nothing, nothing at all, to guide a man in his choice, then it is time to lay the choice on the gods," Marcus says rather grandly. He does not pray, though; he simply spins a coin. Then the two turn south again, towards Melrose (Trinomontium).

This is when, after sleeping in an abandoned fort, Marcus has the eerie experience of hearing someone whistling a song he knows well – a Legionary marching song:

Oh when I joined the Eagles,
(As it might be yesterday)
I kissed a girl at Clusium
Before I marched away.

Now the whistler begins to sing, and the singer is one of the Painted People, his upper body and arms tattooed, wearing nothing but an ochre-coloured kilt. He tells Marcus that his name is Guern. The carcass of a deer is slung over his pony's back.

Guern brings the two men back to his turf hut to meet his wife, Murna:

> ... clearly she was not a poor woman, or rather her husband was not a poor man, for there were bracelets of silver and copper and blue Egyptian glass on her arms, and the mass of dull-gold hair knotted up behind her head was held in place with amber-headed pins. Above all, she was the proud possessor of a large bronze cauldron...

So Marcus' suspicions are further aroused. And when Guern shaves and Marcus sees under his chin the unmistakable mark made by a chin-strap of a Roman helmet, those suspicions are confirmed.

It's a sign of Marcus' growing maturity – and this book, like most of Sutcliff's novels, is essentially concerned with rites of passage – that he doesn't immediately challenge Guern, and is subsequently more concerned to understand than to accuse.

Guern tells Marcus, "I have seen you before... I remember your face. In the Name of Light, who are you?" But the face Guern is remembering is that of Marcus' father, who was his own Cohort Commander in the Ninth Legion. Now Guern and Marcus both drop their guard, and Guern tells Marcus how, disastrously, the Legate of the Ninth refused to make terms with the Painted People despite being hopelessly exposed and outnumbered; how many of the Legionaries mutinied; how Marcus' father and a few survivors bravely made an attempt to carry the Eagle back to Eburacum and were hunted down.

Guern the Hunter is the most striking embodiment of the way in which *The Eagle of the Ninth* revolves around potent margins and crossing-places. In his character, Roman and British cultures actually meet. And what lies at the heart of his account of the fate of the Hispana? It is surely that the syndrome of victor and victim is a deadly one, only sowing the seed of the next conflict, and that nations and cultures must somehow accommodate one another. It is a powerful message for our own times.

Guern points Marcus and Esca north again in their search for the shining Eagle, symbol of Roman might, and directs them to the tribe of the Epidaii, who live in the mountains and beside the firths of western Caledonia. But even if they are able to find it, won't the Eagle be guarded by day and night? How will they ever be able to set it free to fly again?

Rosemary Sutcliff is a powerful and immensely skilful storyteller. Her language is quite stately and formal and yet it is vigorous, sometimes thrusting. She achieves magnificent descriptive passages, but knows when to dispense with unnecessary event and detail and cut to the quick. Her images, especially those relating to fire, mist, dogs, battle ("red work"), and the moon ("the pale curved feather") are striking, and she conjures up many singular compounds: "peat-reek", "mossy-faced", "sword-brethren", "ghost-ridden", "wave-lift", and "the run-honey evening light".

In a way, evening light is the colour of *The Eagle of the Ninth*: "run-honey", shot with gold-thread, but also grey-blue, and darkening. True, the novel celebrates friendship, nascent love (between Marcus and Cottia), moral courage, physical courage, honour, respect and the dignity of freedom. And true, it most interestingly explores the making of national identity. And yet Rosemary Sutcliff shows how glorious Rome has sown the seeds of its own decline and fall, and shows us a world in which men and women are born to sorrow. "Listen to me," Marcus tells Esca:

"Are you going to live all the rest of your life as though you had taken a whipping and could not forget it? Because if you are, I am sorry for you. You don't like being a freed-man, do you? Well, I don't like being lame. That makes two of us, and the only thing we can do about it, you and I, is to learn to carry the scars lightly."

Of the many dicta in this fine, moral novel, these last words – tempered and stoic, warm and forthright – sound most like the author's own credo.

The Eagle of the Ninth was published as a historical novel for young people but, in common with many of the finest children's books, it has always appealed to adults as well. To my mind, Rosemary Sutcliff is simply the best twentieth-century historical novelist to have written about early Britain. She won the Carnegie Medal for *The Lantern Bearers*, and was awarded the OBE in 1975. She died in 1992 at the age of seventy-two.

Floreat Aquila!

T. H. White

The Once and Future King

Of all King Arthur's many incarnations during the twentieth century, T. H. White's *The Once and Future King* is the most odd, the most innocent, the most entertaining, and most loved. Add to this that it is also one of the most learned, most wide-ranging and multi-form, and the pleasures and difficulties of writing about it become apparent.

In the last year of his life, T. H. White went on a lecture tour of the United States. In the course of one lecture, he said:

> My parents loathed each other and were separated; divorced when I was fourteen or so. This meant that my home and education collapsed about my ears; and ever since I have been arming myself against disaster. This is why I learn.

The theme of the armour of learning – learning with one's head, learning with one's body – underlies White's life and writing, and is seminal to an understanding of it.

"Do you think you have learned anything?" Merlyn asks the Wart (that is to say, the young Arthur) in *The Sword in the Stone*. "I have learned, and been happy," the Wart replies. "That's right, then," says Merlyn. "Try to remember what you learned."

Throughout *The Once and Future King*, T. H. White revels in knowledge – knowledge of the English language, knowledge of medieval Europe and the nature of chivalry, knowledge of the natural world, and more especially its wild birds – and shares it exuberantly with his readers.

But, of course, White's words about his parents also point

directly to the root of his unhappiness. Not only did his parents loathe one another but, worse, he loathed his domineering mother, Constance. "It was my love that she extracted," he wrote in his diary, "not hers that she gave... Anyway, she managed to bitch up my loving women... She had a way of grinding her teeth."

Terence (Tim or Timothy to all his friends) Hanbury White was an unhappy man. Born in Bombay on 29 May 1906, the only child of a hard-drinking police superintendent and a judge's daughter, he was – like Kipling – sent home to be schooled. It is rather too easy to cane preparatory and public school education, but it's clear that White had a miserable time at Cheltenham College, where for a couple of years he was beaten almost daily by prefects as well as masters. His studies at Cambridge were interrupted when he developed tuberculosis, though he made a full recovery and returned to become literary editor of *Granta* and take a first. Then, while teaching at Stowe under the leading headmaster of his generation, the liberal J. F. Roxburgh, he underwent psychoanalysis for his tendency to sadism and homosexuality.

His friend, John Moore, like White a writer and fisherman, noted:

> I think he was 75 per cent of his time unhappy and often very unhappy... Not always distraught, of course, sometimes gay, often wildly enthusiastic, tremendously moved, especially by natural beauty, then often quickly lapsing into melancholy because the beauty was so transient.

Self-tormented, repressed and often lonely, unfulfilled in his personal life: T. H. White was all these, though he gave great loyalty to his friends (and commanded theirs), and was generally charming in the company of children. Perhaps he was too damaged and too wary to love another human being unconditionally. The only time he really dared show his heart was when Brownie, his setter bitch, fell ill – and maybe that was because the animal asked nothing of him and yet depended crucially on him.

But what is so fascinating, so miraculous, is the way in which the driving forces and daily fabric of T. H. White's life fed into his breath-taking achievement in *The Once and Future King*. It is all there. The writer in him was like a powerful magnet, allowing nothing to go to waste, transforming everything.

White probably first came across King Arthur and Sir Thomas Malory's *Le Morte D'Arthur* while he was at Cheltenham. There, he said, he found "just one master who praised and encouraged me to be a writer. His name was C. F. Scott, and I shall be grateful to him till I die." In any case, White first wrote about Malory at Cambridge: an essay, according to T. R. Henn, an English don, "wild, violent, very funny; clearly the germ of *The Sword in the Stone*."

In the event, the Matter of Britain, that is to say Arthurian Romance, was to preoccupy White for the greater part of his writing life. So now then, a few bibliographical details. Of the four books that comprise this Folio edition of *The Once and Future King*, White published *The Sword in the Stone* in the UK and the US in 1938, *The Witch in the Wood* (later to be revised and retitled *The Queen of Air and Darkness*) in 1940 (US 1939), and *The Ill-Made Knight* in the following year (US 1940). He wrote the last part of the tetralogy, *The Candle in the Wind*, immediately afterwards, but it was not published until all four parts were revised for publication as *The Once and Future King* in 1958.

In addition to these four books, T. H. White wrote *The Book of Merlyn*, an appendage to the tetralogy which combines the fantasy of *The Sword in the Stone* (the aged king moves amongst birds once more) with fierce anti-war polemic. But although he wanted it to be published in one volume with the first four books, it was in fact only published posthumously in 1978. White, moreover, drew on two large sections of it in revising the text for *The Sword in the Stone*.

In taking the theme of Arthur's joyous childhood and apprenticeship for *The Sword in the Stone*, White was not only laying to rest his childhood ghosts and drawing on his teaching experience but also breaking new ground, since neither Malory nor any other medieval romance writers were much interested in the psychology of childhood or the years before Arthur became king. In the very first paragraph, White explains Arthur's nickname. "The Wart was called the Wart because it more or less rhymed with Art, which was short for his real name. Kay had given him the nickname." Logical and yet absurd! (In the same way, my own cheerless name at preparatory school was Morbus, inherited from a spotty boy called Holland who left the term before I came.)

Any synopsis of *The Sword in the Stone* is apt to make it sound ridiculous; rather like those opera synopses one never quite manages to absorb before the house lights go down. The Wart meets old Merlyn who lives his life backwards in time, and can thus foretell the future. Merlyn, wearing a flowing gown embroidered with the signs of the zodiac, and drawing water from a well, demands, "Why can't they get us the electric light and company's water?"... The Wart meets Archimedes, a tawny owl, who pretends the Wart doesn't exist... He becomes a merlin and takes to the air... He becomes an ant and takes to the earth... He becomes a badger and goes underground...
The Sword in the Stone is a picaresque and pastoral fantasy embodying an idealised portrayal of the Middle Ages. Its cousins are the novels of Richard Jefferies, Kenneth Grahame's *The Golden Age* and *Dream Days*, and, above all, John Masefield's *The Midnight Folk*, and its questing young hero, Kay Harker. Here and there, White has us believe that the Wart's experiences are a prolonged

dream, as when he finds himself lying under the grandstand, and hears the sergeant calling him from across the tilting-ground.

"Nah then, Master Art, nah then. You've been a-snoozing there long enough. Come aht into the sunlight 'ere with Master Kay, one-two, one-two, and see some real tilting."

But White's purpose wasn't dreamy and he wasn't an escapist. He was, as Moore noted, "a dead serious writer". In the Wart, he portrays a boy who has no mother and experiences an idyllic childhood. In Merlyn, he shows us a man committed to a system of education in which one learns from nature, not in theory but through experience. Merlyn is, indeed, the embodiment of the teaching–learning process. The Wart asks him, "Would you mind if I asked you a question?"; to which Merlyn replies: "It is what I am for."

Step by step, White and Merlyn and the birds and beasts he meets lead the Wart towards a tragic understanding that, unlike the rest of the animal kingdom, humans are consciously belligerent. They choose to wage war.

The young goose Lyo-lyok, who is "rather a blue-stocking", tells the Wart that when the Irish Children of Lir were turned into swans, "they were hopelessly nationalistic and religious"; and when the Wart says it would be fun to see two armies of geese fighting each other, Lyo-lyok protests, "Will you stop about it at once! What a horrible mind you must have!... What creature could be so low as to go about in bands, to murder others of its own blood?"

"I like fighting. It is knightly," the Wart tells her.
"Because you're a baby," Lyo-lyok retorts.

The truth is, of course, that there is much of T. H. White in the characters of both the Wart and Merlyn. His horror at the cruelty and stupidity of war increased from year to year and book to book, and his excitement at its trappings – reflected in his zestful technical descriptions of jousting and armour – never diminished:

> ... they retreated in the usual way, fewtered their spears, and charged together like thunder... The knights ducked and drew themselves together; the spears struck at the same moment; the horses, checked in mid-career, reared up and fell over backward; the spears burst and went sailing high in the air, turning over and over gracefully like the results of high explosive; and the lady on the palfrey looked away.

The Sword in the Stone is as much a book for children as adults – T. H. White's one true children's book is *Mistress Masham's Repose* – and the remaining three books of the tetralogy are not really for children at all. This is not so much because they swim in deep sexual and psychological waters as because they're often opinionated (though never as angry as *The Book of Merlyn* with its fierce diatribes against 'Homo Ferox' and war), because their narrative is punctuated by digression, and the central characters are not children.

The Queen of Air and Darkness relates the early part of King Arthur's reign, and the upbringing of Arthur's nephews, Gawaine and his brothers. T. H. White differs from his mentor, Sir Thomas Malory, in arguing that Camelot was fatally undermined not by the passionate affair of Sir Lancelot and Guenever but by the incestuous union of King Arthur and his sister, the vampish Morgause, and the subsequent birth of their son, Mordred. In his journal, White listed the people Morgause resembled, and they include "Clytemnestra... The matron at St. David's, whatever her name was... My mother. The witch in Snow White. A claw-padded, secret cat. Yes, and one who goes upon the tiles..."

White had great difficulty in finding the right tone for his book, above all because of "this nasty incest business", and he redrafted it four times. Even now, the farcical sometimes becomes facetious, while the scenes involving the killing of an innocent unicorn and the boiling of a cat are uncomfortably cruel.

The Ill-made Knight explores the relationship of Guenever and Lancelot. "He was a sort of Bradman," writes White, "top of the battling averages." Despite many sallies such as this, combining deliberate anachronism and wordplay, this book is much more realistic than the first two, generous in its understanding of the lovers, thoughtful in the way it charts their own growing self-knowledge. In her admirable biography of T. H. White, Sylvia Townsend Warner writes that "the narrative is barer, there are fewer flourishes, no farce, no extravaganzas. One feels one is reading a true story."

What is so moving, and so grand, about *The Candle in the Wind* is the way in which White portrays the ageing Arthur, Guenever and Lancelot as graceful, honourable and dignified for all their shortcomings; surrounded by the brash, intolerant, self-serving knights who betray Guenever to her king; stalked by the calculating and sadistic Mordred; trapped. In this portrait White is perhaps like Malory who – more than five hundred years before – suggested that King Arthur, his queen and his greatest knight were the victims of a personal and private tragedy, and castigated the jealous and salacious gossips surrounding them at court.

Lancelot brings Guenever back to Camelot after he has saved her from death by burning (her punishment for treasonable adultery), and White describes how the knight "pulled himself together with a sort of final care... With a lifted head he raised their tragedy to nobleness and gravity." The last three books may not have quite the Imaginative force of *The Sword in the Stone*, but it is still not too much to claim that White himself achieves that nobility and gravity for the whole legend of King Arthur.

T. H. White's style is a hotchpotch; a mixture of incongruous components. It is also *faux naïf* because White was extremely clever, always conscious of what he was doing, ready to draft and redraft to achieve the right balance. Caricature, parody, literary joke, medieval speak, modern idiom, pseudo-dialect, anachronism, verse, pure fantasy, psychological realism, polemic – they are all part of the mix.

White also had a wonderful eye for an absurd situation, and was able to tease it out with inventive and highly entertaining dialogue. Indeed, sustained scenes such as the joust between King Pellinore and Sir Grummore in *The Sword in the Stone* are as funny as anything written during the last hundred years. I have used them with American students bemused by their prep school terminology and indignant at their patronising (and sometimes racial) jokes, but still hooting at their absurdity.

T. H. White loved the English language. Wordplay and nonce words and archaisms – piseog, goleor, to-brast, vig, nigromant: his pages are peppered with them. He had, too, a marvellous ability to move from the idiomatic to the sonorous:

> "Bah!" cried King Pellinore.
> "Booh!" cried Sir Grummore...
> They met in the middle, breast to breast, with a noise of shipwreck and great bells tolling, and both, bouncing off, fell breathless on their backs.

"You should try to speak without assonances," Merlyn tells the Wart, and on every page it's plain how carefully White himself tuned in to the music of meaning.

Many artists have visited Camelot since Geoffrey of Monmouth thrilled early medieval readers with his account of King Arthur in his patriotic, quasi-historical *History of the Kings of Britain*, and each of us will have our own favourites. Above and beyond *The Once and*

Future King, my own include one of the most attractive of medieval romances, the genial, playful, and threatening *Sir Gawain and the Green Knight*, particularly appealing to contemporary readers for its subtle irony. This has been translated for The Folio Society by Keith Harrison, and was memorably reshaped by David Harsent and Sir Harrison Birtwistle into the opera *Gawain*. Dryden and Purcell combined to write potent words and succulent music for their semi-opera (combining music, drama and spectacle), *King Arthur*; and though it is overlong and in places too abstract, there are many passages in Tennyson's *Idylls of the King* which print themselves indelibly on the mind and heart. But if I had to pick one? Well, then, it might be the compelling work, both as artist and as poet, of David Jones (1895–1974), particularly his long poem – "this fragment", he calls it – 'The Sleeping Lord'.

The twentieth century was, of course, enormously rich in Arthurian reincarnations – poetry, fiction, painting, film – and, remarkably, *The Once and Future King* inspired perhaps the two most popular of all: Lerner and Loewe's musical, *Camelot* (Julie Andrews proved a loyal friend to T. H. White), and Walt Disney's cartoon, *The Sword in the Stone*.

Wealth at the end, then, and happiness? Yes, but no. Before his death in 1964, T. H. White certainly became rich; he was lionised in the United States and lectured to huge audiences; he went to live in Alderney; he fell uselessly in love with a young London boy, one of several on holiday and staying in his house; he was so lonely, "It has been my hideous fate", he wrote to a friend, "to be born with an infinite capacity for love and joy with no hope of using them."

What an energetic, difficult, demanding, argumentative, rude, eager, frustrated, funny, at times desperate man! A big man with brilliant blue, unhappy eyes. A man who somehow transcended his own deep disappointment to give lasting delight.

George Crabbe

'Peter Grimes'

The estuaries and creeks and saltmarshes of East Anglia are not pretty. They are flat. They want trees. They smell powerful and, at low tide, putrid. They taste of salt and tar and wiry samphire. They resound to the wild shrieks of seabirds and, just offstage, the muffed tom-tom of the North Sea or, as it used to be called, the German Ocean.

And yet this no-man's land, which never belongs to earth or sea entirely, is compulsive and enthralling. I'm not only thinking of the dramas unfolded in the huge turbulent skies, and the astonishing dry, defining light, and the creeks after sunset as they turn rose and lavender then pewter and zinc. I'm referring to the edgy wind, the yapping of the rigging, the abandoned jetties, the weed-ridden buoys, the marsh mud, the scurvy tideline—all those unlovely humdrum aspects of the place that barb locals and 'furriners' alike and never let them go.

The poet George Crabbe was hooked on the landscape around Aldeburgh in Suffolk. He didn't actually like it very much but, in common with his horrible, pitiable fisherman Peter Grimes, trudging along the Alde estuary, he was born part of it and it became part of him:

> Here dull and hopeless he'd lie down and trace
> How sidelong crabs had scrawled their crooked race;
> Or sadly listen to the tuneless cry
> Of fishing gull or clanging golden-eye;
> What time the sea-birds to the marsh would come,
> And the loud bittern, from the bull-rush home,

> Gone from the salt-ditch side the bellowing boom:
> He nursed the feelings these dull scenes produce,
> And loved to stop beside the opening sluice.

Crabbe was fascinated, too, by life in East Anglia's then-sordid little coastal towns and villages. He saw all around him poverty and degradation and suffering; and when he describes it, detail by detail, one can feel the strange way in which he is simultaneously drawn to, and repelled by, the squalor around him:

> Between the roadway and walls, offence
> Invades all eyes and strikes on every sense:
> There lie obscene at every open door
> Heaps from the hearth and sweepings from the floor,
> And day by day the mingled mosses grow
> As sinks are disembogued and kennels flow.
> There hungry dogs from hungry children steal,
> Three pigs and chickens quarrel for a meal:
> There dropsied infants wail without redress
> And all is want and woe and wretchedness.

*

George Crabbe was born on Christmas Eve, 1754. He was the eldest of six children and his father worked in Aldeburgh, first as a warehouse manager and then as saltmaster (that is to say, collector of salt-duties).

As a boy, Crabbe was unlike his extrovert and practical brothers, two of whom led remarkable lives, one as captain of a Liverpool slave-ship and the other, after being captured by the Spaniards, as a silversmith in Mexico and Honduras. George was bookish and inward. He liked sailing his own small boat. He liked listening to gossip, news, stories:

> To me the wives of seamen loved to tell
> What storms endangered men esteemed so well.

"He was cradled among the rough sons of ocean," wrote the poet's son, in his *Life of George Crabbe*, "a daily witness of unbridled passions, and manners remote from the sameness and artificial smoothness of polished society... Masculine and robust frames, rude manners, stormy passions, laborious days and, occasionally, boisterous nights of merriment – among such accompaniments was born and reared the Poet of the Poor."

No wonder, then, that when Crabbe addressed himself to the townsfolk he knew so well, struggling to win a livelihood from the sea and from barren sandy land, "with sullen woe displayed in every face", he was scornful of the kind of idealised pastoral poetry written by Oliver Goldsmith and Thomas Gray. He wanted to portray rural life as it really was. He wanted to –

> paint the cot
> As Truth will paint it, and as Bards will not.

Crabbe fondly recalled that, in his youth, he had spent "many an idle year", but in fact his childhood and early life were thoroughly uncomfortable. As a boy, he unwillingly helped his father hump around consignments of butter and cheese in the warehouse on the quay at Slaughden on the Alde estuary; and at the age of thirteen he was apprenticed to a doctor at Wickhambrook near Bury Saint Edmunds, but had to double up as a farm labourer, and share a bed with the ploughboy. He argued passionately with his father, who was turning into a violent drunkard, and after further enforced labour on the quay at Slaughden, further apprenticeships, and a spell as the town doctor in Aldeburgh, Crabbe decided that he wasn't cut out for the medical profession after all. His first poems had bred in him a longing. In his own words, he wanted to be a writer, and he "determined to go to London and venture all".

To begin with, Crabbe had a miserable time in London. His poems were disliked, he found no real friends, and he was all but overwhelmed by a sense of rejection. Threatened with prison because of his appalling debts, Crabbe sent some of his work to the statesman Edmund Burke, and appealed to him for help. Burke was impressed by Crabbe's work and moved by his misfortune; and he not only bailed out the young poet but took him under his wing. He introduced him to such luminaries as Samuel Johnson, and George Fox, and Sir Joshua Reynolds (with whom Crabbe got on particularly well), and sensibly arranged for his protégé to take Holy Orders.

In 1781, the Bishop of Norwich licensed George Crabbe as curate to the rector of Aldeburgh. But the young man felt desperately ill at ease when he looked out for the first time from the pulpit. The congregation had heard that his poems were disparaging of his home town and they resented them. "I had been unkindly received in the place – I saw unfriendly countenances about me and, I am sorry to say, I had too much indignation – though mingled, I hope, with better feelings – to care what they thought of me or my sermon."

Then Burke stepped in again. He found a job for Crabbe as Domestic Chaplain to the Duke of Rutland at Belvoir Castle. But even this sinecure was not a complete success. Crabbe and the duke got on well but the poet was rather a misfit at the castle; the servants insolently taunted him with being above his station, and made him feel uncomfortable.

Add to this melancholy litany the matter of George Crabbe's long courtship of pretty Sarah Elmy, only to see her decline into mental and physical instability soon after their marriage in 1783, and it is not difficult to understand why Crabbe formed a rather jaundiced view of life. The society in which he grew up was depressed, and his own early years were coloured by a fear of rejection and a sense of blighted promise. He concluded that the only consolation lay in meekly accepting harsh circumstances and putting one's trust in God.

*

When he was twenty-eight, George Crabbe published his long poem, 'The Village', an honest and gritty portrait of rural life. Although it was very warmly received, and won plaudits from Dr Johnson (who proposed some rather inferior revisions to it), Crabbe decided that his real vocation was as a novelist. During the following decade, he planned and drafted several novels but destroyed them all unpublished. He also wrote and then burned his *English Treatise on Botany* – a work devoted to the commoner lichens and weeds about which he wrote with such precision in his poems:

> There, fed by food they love, to rankest size,
> Around the dwellings docks and wormwood rise;
> Here the strong mallow strikes her slimy root,
> Here the dull night-shade hangs her deadly fruit;
> On hills of dust the henbane's faded green,
> And pencilled flower of sickly scent is seen;
> At the wall's base the fiery nettle springs,
> With fruit globose and fierce with poisoned stings;
> Above (the growth of many a year) is spread
> The yellow level of the stone-crop's bed;
> In every chink delights the fern to grow,
> With glossy leaf and tawny bloom below:
> These, with our sea-weeds, rolling up and down,
> Form the contracted Flora of the town.

Twenty-two years elapsed before Crabbe published poetry again: first a volume of shorter poems, *The Parish Register*; and then, in 1810, *The Borough*, a long poem in twenty-four 'letters' which is a brilliant anatomy of a country town, very largely based on Crabbe's knowledge of Aldeburgh. These 'letters' are story-poems revolving around village characters: the vicar, the curate, the lawyers and clerks, the physicians and quacks, the tradesmen and innkeepers, the schoolmasters and their students, the inhabitants of the almshouse, the hospital governors, the prisoners and the poor of the borough. In an unpublished notebook, Crabbe described the rationale for his selection:

> I have chiefly, if not exclusively, taken my subject and characters from that order of society where the least display of vanity is generally to be found, which is placed between the humble and the great. It is in this class of mankind that more originality of character, more variety of fortune, will be met with…

The four Borough Poor, who are fed and housed at the expense of the town, are all memorable characters. Jachin, the Parish Clerk, is self-important, over-zealous, quick to resent the success of others, and greedy. He brings about his own downfall when, during Mattins, he starts to steal coins from the offertory plate. Old Ellen Orford, stoic and kindly and blind in her "winter-calm of life", knows that "we should humbly take what Heaven bestows". Heaven has bestowed on *her* an unhappy childhood, an early seduction and a false promise of marriage, an idiot-daughter and five sons, one of whom has gone to the gallows and four of whom she has seen to the grave. Abel Keene, a simple and benign schoolmaster, getting on in years, is a tragic fool. He exchanges his job for more remunerative work in a merchant's office, falls in with a group of hedonistic lads, drinks too much, dresses like a beau, and lays aside his faith and habit of prayer.

> When youth is fallen, there's hope the young may rise,
> But fallen age for ever hopeless lies.

Abel loses his job, becomes more and more depressed, and finally hangs himself.

The fourth of the Borough Poor is the fearsome fisherman Peter Grimes. As a boy, Peter reviles and rages against his father, hits him over the head and precipitates his death. He grows up a lawless loner, animal and blunt and angry with the world, and savagely maltreats three apprentices in succession, all of whom die in suspicious circumstances. The Mayor bans Peter from hiring further apprentices and the fisherman falls prey to wild dreams. He gives up fishing and goes half-mad but, tortured by his guilt, he cannot escape the phantoms of his father and the pale boys:

> To hear and mark them daily was my doom,
> And 'come', they said, with weak, sad voices, 'come'.
> To row away with all my strength I tried,
> But there were they, hard by me in the tide,
> The three unbodied forms – and 'come', still 'come', they cried.

Even on his deathbed, Peter Grimes cannot shake off the spectres. He is one of the damned and they will accompany him beyond the grave.

These four portraits are commonly held to be among Crabbe's finest creations, and reading them again, I'm left in no doubt that his greatest strengths as a poet are precisely those we more often attribute to good novelists: a fascination with the workings of the human mind and heart, and with the relationship between an individual and society. Crabbe portrays Jachin and Ellen Orford and Abel Keene and Peter Grimes as fully human, ambivalent and complex, and susceptible to change; and he holds three of them up as in some ways representative of a careless, hypocritical and self-interested society. In 'Peter Grimes', for instance, the people of the Borough turn a blind eye to Peter's repeated beatings of his first apprentice,

> and some, on hearing cries,
> Said calmly, "Grimes is at his exercise."

Blow by blow, Crabbe builds up a formidable indictment not only of Grimes himself but of the Borough's negligent townsfolk, and of the sickening apprentice system – a system that survived and flourished in the early nineteenth century despite attacks on it almost a century earlier:

> A most unhappy practice prevails in most places to apprentice poor children, no matter to what master provided he lives out of the parish; if the child serves the first forty days we are rid of him for ever. The master may be a tiger in cruelty; he may beat, abuse, strip naked, starve, or do what he will to the poor innocent lad, few people take much notice, and the officers who put him out the least of anybody...
>
> (*Enquiry into the Case of the Increase of the Poor*, 1738)

Crabbe wrote of his descriptions of evil and misery in *The Borough* that they were intended to excite "that mingled pity and abhorrence, which, while it is not unpleasant to the feelings... binds us to all mankind by sensations common to us all, and in some degree connects us, without degradation, even to the most miserable and guilty of our fellow-men".

> On all a momentary silence came,
> A common softness, and a moral shame.

It is this profound sense of humanity that underlies the four portraits in this book. It's impossible to read them without thinking, at one point or another, 'There, but for the grace of God, go I.'

George Crabbe was a supremely good storyteller. When we read his tripping heroic couplets and hold our breath as Jachin has the audacity to line his pocket with bran, so that the coins he steals will not clink as he drops them into it, or suffer with poor old Ellen, still wild with grief at the memory of her beloved son Ned's death on the gallows, we may have the sense that we are watching unedited film or listening to unedited tape. It is not so, of course. These story-poems are small masterpieces of poetic realism: full of suggestion, detail and emphasis, their verisimilitude is the result of careful planning and careful selection by a highly skilled poet.

George Crabbe's strengths as a stylist, like his gifts as a storyteller, are essentially unobtrusive. He is not showy, like Byron, and he does not soar into the ether, like Wordsworth. He is not particularly elegant, though he is seldom inelegant; and he is not particularly witty, though he can be sardonic to good effect, as in the opening pages of *The Parish Clerk*. Rather, Crabbe has the virtues of simplicity and directness and doggedness, even ruggedness. His style (and he has a wonderful ear) is no more elevated than the people and places he writes about, and because of this, it has the supreme virtue of convincing you that he is telling the truth.

Crabbe's contemporaries were not of one mind about his powers and his truth-telling, though. Wordsworth went so far as to say, in a generous letter to the poet's son after Crabbe's death in 1832, that his father's poems would "last, from their combined merits as Poetry and Truth, full as long as anything that has been expressed in verse since they first made their appearance". And Byron thought Crabbe, with Coleridge, "the first of these times, in point of power and genius", and called him "Though Nature's sternest painter, yet the best". But Southey reckoned that Crabbe's relentless gloom was in the end just as untruthful to nature as Goldsmith's relentless sunshine, while Hazlitt wrote that

"He gives us discoloured paintings of things —helpless, repining, unprofitable, unedifying distress. He is not a philosopher, but a sophist, and misanthrope in verse."

Crabbe has never been fashionable. His characters are on the whole unappealing and they live in rural backwaters. His style is unadventurous and workmanlike. And the way in which he steps aside from penetration of a character or a situation in order to moralise can be frustrating. But there is no ignoring Crabbe's poems. They are highly readable. They are profound studies of human behaviour. They are strongly felt, even passionate. In their descriptions of landscape and seascape, they are sometimes hauntingly beautiful. And their use of the Augustan tradition of pastoral verse to present grim portraits of rural life is original and unique. There is about Crabbe's work an aura of permanence. It was made to last, and that is what it has done.

Footprints on the Grass

Of Gardens and Children's Books

Yesterday evening, I sauntered, I dawdled, I shuffled... ah! how rich in assonance, consonance, and alliteration the garden of our language is. Yesterday evening, I ambled and rambled, I padded, I pottered *between*.

Not between waking and sleep. Not between land and sea. Not across some tumbledown bridge, potent as all crossing-places are. No, I meandered between actuality and imagination in my own ever-changing garden.

Above me, the Milky Way, that astounding rash of stars never seen, not even once, by 42% of British children because of light pollution; below me, chalky earth, and the lifelines and layers of England; around me, such a depth of silence that any sound at all is singular and quick. A partridge, reshuffling its feathers; the hollow tom-tom of a distant owl; a cool breath of night wind; these, and that sense, indefinable, that sense of the green world growing.

No wonder our language teems with phrases, sayings and epithets relating to the world of the garden: "a tough row to hoe", "a rose by any other name"; "other men's flowers"; "our wills are gardeners" (that's Shakespeare in *Othello*): "Virtue! A fig! 'Tis in ourselves that we are thus, or thus. Our bodies are our gardens, to which our wills are gardeners"; "the grass withereth (the grath wizereth), the flower fadeth" (the verse I most dreaded when it was my turn to read the lesson at school); "in the gardens of the night..."

Indeed, each word in our language (there are well-over 60,000, virtually double the number of any other language, largely by virtue of modern English being derived from both Anglo-Saxon and Latin, via Norman-French), each word has its own *stem* and *root*. And other than the *OED* itself, the only book I use daily is the wonderful

Oxford Dictionary of English Etymology, edited by the felicitously named C. T. Onions. It may be short on silver bells and cockleshells, let alone rows of pretty maids; but, put simply, it makes my lexical garden grow.

And then, in my night-garden, I thought – I think I thought! – of how much the nature and purpose of a garden has changed, and how for our forebears in the Middle Ages it was essentially a place of order as opposed to the wilderness outside the walls or high hedges, a source of sustenance, a provider of healing.

"Get a garden!" writes Walafrid-Strabo in *De cultura Hortorum* in the ninth century:

> Get a garden! What kind you may get matters not,
> Though the soil be light, friable, sandy and hot,
> Or else heavy and rich with stiff clay;
> Let it lie on a hill, or slope gently away
> To the level, or sink in an overgrown dell –
> Don't despair, it will serve to grow vegetables well!

One of my pillow-books is Geoffrey Grigson's *The Englishman's Flora* (I used to publish Geoffrey's poems, and in Wiltshire, Jane once cooked me the most heavenly lunch while Geoffrey scattered rose petals over my VW Beetle!), and I've just opened the *Flora* entirely at random. Scarlet pimpernel! Almost every county has its own name for it (it's *Anagallis arvensis* in Latin) and I learn that it's been known for centuries as a combination of clock and weatherglass, and gives you second sight and hearing, and can be used for toothache, snake bite, and liver troubles, and also against melancholy. That's why it's known as Laughter Bringer, Shepherd's Joy, Shepherd's Delight.

This sort of knowledge, something we're now eagerly recovering, has never been lost to societies more 'primitive' than ours. Much of it is embedded and transmitted in quatrains and sayings; and a delight in plant names if not properties underlies a lot of rather 'weedy' verse as well as poems as charming as Robert Louis Stevenson's 'The Flowers':

> ALL the names I know from nurse:
> Gardener's garters, Shepherd's purse,
> Bachelor's buttons, Lady's smock,
> And the Lady Hollyhock.
>
> Fairy places, fairy things,
> Fairy woods where the wild bee wings,
> Tiny trees for tiny dames –
> These must all be fairy names!...

In classical Greece and Rome, and before as well as after the Renaissance, plant life and lore was the subject of academic study and a quarry for poets. But of course our sense of gardens being at the heart of the matter goes back much further. One can hazard a guess that ever since humans stopped being nomadic hunter-gatherers and began to cultivate, some of the plants they grew and protected were perceived as having crucial and magical powers.

For more than a couple of thousand years, Chinese gardens have been repositories of serenity, literary, artistic and philosophical meaning, and have been planted and tended so as to embody the interaction of Yin (the dark, passive, absorbing female force) and Yang (the light, active, penetrating male force) that underpins the natural world and human biology.

Water, Water! The source of life itself, replenishment, delight. Think of the Hanging Gardens of Babylon, just south of Baghdad, one of the seven wonders of the world – a series of terraces irrigated by water raised by means of a giant screw (this is in the days of Nebuchadnezzar, in the sixth century BC). Think of the glorious Moorish Alhambra in Granada with its "cuts and lodes and waterways", to steal a phrase from Philippa Pearce. The Koran describes paradise as a leafy garden where fountains play and running water courses, the place where the "fortunate ones" can take their rest. The word parádeisos was first used by Xenophon to describe the parks of Persian kings and nobles.

The most celebrated garden or orchard in Classical mythology, meanwhile, must be the one in North Africa containing the apple-tree guarded by a hundred-headed dragon – its apples belonging to the three Hesperides, daughters of Atlas. This myth has its Norse counterpart in the apples of youth that the goddess Idun picks and gives to all the gods and goddesses day by day – until they're stolen by the giant Thiazi, and after they've been recovered again by Odin!

And yes, I was coming to it! The Judaeo-Christian tradition has its Eden:

> And the Lord God planted a garden eastward in Eden; and there he put the man whom he had formed. And out of the ground made the Lord God grow every tree that is pleasant to the sight, and good for food; the tree of life also in the midst of the garden, and the tree of the knowledge of good and evil.

So here is the garden in which man and woman, called Eve "because she was the mother of all living", became conscious of themselves, conscious of right and wrong; in which, therefore (I suppose) they developed memory. Banished from it, at large in the wilderness of the world, this consciousness (as M. Scott-Peck has pointed out) brings them intense pain but also more joy than anything they could experience in paradise; an opportunity to grow into responsibility and commitment, and to shoulder the pain of others.

*

You'd not be wholly right if you expected to find many a garden – what's the collective name for gardens? – in the huge canon of folk tale European and Middle Eastern, but they're fairly plentiful in the Brothers Grimm.

Ashputtle is helped by little white doves in the dovecote and by the hazel and pear trees. Golden apples grow in a beautiful garden in 'The Golden Bird'. Rabbit eats all the cabbages in the highly erotic 'Bunny Rabbit's Bride'. There are two rosebushes in the garden in front of the hut where Snow White and Rose Red live with their widowed mother. And in one of the tales shared by the Grimms' with Perrault, 'Briar Rose' or 'The Sleeping Princess' or 'Sleeping Beauty', the briar hedge that grows round the garden and palace where the princess sleeps – a hedge teeming with "big beautiful flowers which opened of their own accord" – protects innocence. And of course one of the Grimms' most startling tales is also set in a garden: the grisly yet visionary sequence of events caused by the magic properties of a juniper tree...

But may I tell you a fifteenth century folk tale, beginning and ending, what, no more than fifty miles from my home?

> Long ago, and not so long, there was a pedlar and this pedlar had a dream that he must walk to London. London Bridge!
> London Bridge!
> He'd never been a tenth as far before. But he couldn't get this dream out of his head, and the next night he had the same dream again: a man was standing over him, dressed in a surcoat as red as blood, and urging him, "Go to London Bridge! Go, good will come of it."
> So that's what the pedlar did. He walked with his mastiff all the way to London Bridge. But when he got there, he didn't know why he'd come, or who to talk to. He felt completely lost.
> That night the pedlar stayed in a tavern.

Well! Three days went by. The pedlar admired a dancing bear. He saw a band of pilgrims set off for Walsingham, singing. But he was beginning to feel rather stupid.

"Why did we bother to come?" he asked his mastiff. "You tell me that."

This was when a shopkeeper waddled up to him. She looked more like a hen than a woman, she did.

"What are you up to?" she demanded. "Are you waiting for me to turn my back? I've been watching you loitering around for the past three days."

When the shopkeeper heard why the pedlar had walked all the way to London Bridge, she cackled with laughter. She nearly laid an egg!

"Only fools follow their dreams!" she exclaimed.

The pedlar looked at her so dismally. He was almost penniless, and very tired, and more than one hundred miles from home.

"We all have dreams," the shopkeeper told him. "Only last night I dreamed about a pedlar with a pot of gold at the bottom of his garden. I ask you! Nonsense!" She patted the pedlar on the shoulder and tutted. "Take my advice and go back home."

The pedlar went home.

He dug and he dug and right next to his gnarled hawthorn, the pedlar prised out of the clammy earth a very large metal pot.

Yes, and it was packed with gold coins.

He kept some, gave some away, and paid for the church to be rebuilt.

All because he followed his dream. The whole point of the pedlar's journey was to get back home again.

What is this folk tale saying? What does it mean? Follow your dreams? Be persistent, get stuck in? Give money to the church (not that medieval householders had any choice – they had to pay their tithe), give money and win a passport to heaven? All these things, no doubt. But surely the tale's primary meaning is that the greatest treasure in the world is to be found on our own doorsteps, in our own gardens, within the bosom of the family, if only we have the nous to recognise it; this, and that we may well have to go away first in order to come back and find the treasure.

It's really not so long since people in Britain accepted that we human beings were surrounded by thinking, feeling, two-legged beings, seldom or never seen – beings with whom, for the most part, it was perfectly possible to co-exist in harmony, but who exacted a price for disrespect.

Just over 400 years ago, Shakespeare wrote *Midsummer Night's Dream*. Those "hempen home-spuns", the illiterate, who saw a performance of the play, would certainly have not been wholly sceptical about the existence of fairy folk.

It was above all literacy that led to the decline of belief, or the willing suspension of disbelief: writing later in the seventeenth century, John Aubrey noted that the "divine art of Printing and Gunpowder have frighted away Robin-goodfellow and the Fayries."

Robin Goodfellow. In a felicitous phrase, John Rowe Townsend writes of him as "the symbol of old and continuing England", and that indeed is how Rudyard Kipling uses him in one of the most lovely and layered of novels, *Puck of Pook's Hill*.

More and more I find myself thinking that people may die but they do not go away:

> and, sometimes
> – times between times – when the fret
> lifts and the world grows wholly wonderful,
> we believe for a moment that we've levelled
> our gaze and are singing in unison,

> and only our own doubt
> and sense of difference dates us.
> Look! They have not gone away.
> Not one of them. It is we who leave them;
> and now all we can do is love and grieve them.

Given all this – the cultural significance of gardens and our human propensity to personalise the incomprehensible – it's scarcely surprising that gardens are a *leitmotif* in the story of children's books, and may well be inhabited not only by humans but all sorts of other beings.

Actual gardens! Gardens of the mind! Otherworldly, secure, threatening, contradictory, magical, paradisal, continuous, portals, places of growth and death, past, present and future. Timeless, and utterly, utterly alive.

*

Have you come across the goblin rather similar to Puck known variously as 'Lubberkin', and the 'lubber fiend', and 'Lob lie-by-the-Fire'? (Lob) In the north of England, he's called 'hob'. Hence, 'hobgoblin'. Edward Thomas wrote such a wonderful poem about him:

> He sounds like one I saw when I was a child.
> I could almost swear to him. The man was wild
> And wandered. His home was where he was free.
> Everybody has met one such man as he…
> He is English as this gate, these flowers, this mire.
> And when at eight years old Lob-lie-by-the-fire
> Came in my books, this was the man I saw.
> He has been in England as long as dove and daw,
> Calling the wild cherry tree the merry tree.
> The rose campion Bridget-in-her-bravery;
> And in a tender mood he, as I guess,
> Christened one flower Love-in-idleness.

Following in the footsteps of Edward Thomas, sundry folk tales, and of Mrs Ewing (author of *Lob Lie-by-the-Fire*), Linda Newbery makes this appealing creature the focus of her short novel *Lob*.

Lob lives at the bottom of grandpa's garden. He's old as old, and you can only see him sidelong, and only when he wants you to. When Lucy sees him on her own for the first time, her grandfather tells her, "You're learning to see". So we understand Lob to represent a way of seeing – a way of seeing that revolves around what he embodies and distils: green energy.

Lucy and Grandpa are gently laughed at, and often informed Lob is only make-believe, like the Green Man carvings in some churches...

And then green-fingered Grandpa dies; his cottage is pulled down; his lovely garden, Lob's home, is wrecked; the whole place is turned into a development site, and Lob becomes an exile, looking for another home, another garden nursed and reared by someone with green fingers.

Now the story becomes picaresque and an antiphon; an alternation between Lob on the road, walking and walking, sprinkling seeds as he goes, Lob on a canal barge with a floating garden, Lob entering a city, Lob "manhandled, kidnapped, imprisoned, buried, dunked and almost drowned" – between scenes such as these and Lucy at school, drawing green faces, Lucy derided for believing in fairy folk, Lucy missing her grandpa and his Lob stories, miserable when she thinks of the lost garden... until the day when Lucy's parents secure an allotment right next to blind Cornelius, who grows "tomatoes, and spinach, and callaloo... and peppers and squashes and eggplant."

This gentle, wise and very cleanly, lyrically written book fulfils T. S. Eliot's prescription of here and now and always. And in case you *haven't* read it, I'll do no more than anticipate the ending by saying that when Lucy meets Cornelius, "Each knew that the other knew Lob".

Linda Newbery is post-Arcadian in that she doesn't proclaim the superiority of country over city, but rather of green growth, wherever it may be, over concrete and whatever's stillborn. Her book is imbued with a deep sense of the passage of the seasons. It's a sort-of love song to imagining, understanding, and therefore breathing and living in the harmony with the natural world, and I wholeheartedly commend it.

*

It's many years now since Beverly Naidoo, Bali Rai and I (sitting round Julia Eccleshare's kitchen table in Hampstead) awarded the coveted Guardian Children's Fiction Prize to Sonya Hartnett for *Thursday's Child*, set during the 1930s Depression in the Outback.

The central character is Tin, a sort of human-dwarf-mole, the younger brother of Harper Flute, the now adult narrator. Born on a Thursday, Tin "has far to go", and where he goes is right under the garden-cum-yard and the foundations of the farmhouse!

After disappearing in a creek and surviving a mudslide by miraculously digging himself out of it, Tin often hides when he feels scared or vulnerable (the fortnight, for instance, when his little brother Caffy is dangerously ill), and where he hides is in the underground passages he keeps digging.

Worrying and upsetting his mother, Tin digs, and he digs, and he digs, until eventually the farmhouse collapses, and falls into Tin's network of underground tunnels and passageways. And yet the architect of this disaster, by now a kind of little earth wodewose, is also destined to be the family's (apparent) blessing... For Sonia Hartnett suggests that Tin is not only obsessive and a loner but, by digging, digging, may have been looking to find something, something that might help his impoverished family. Maybe he was prospecting, though the narrator Harper doesn't buy that. "That's cods, of course," she tartly says!

What a book this is: so superbly written as to make one elated; so firmly grounded not in imposed or manufactured events but in the rhythms of day-to-day life and the stillness of the Outback; so sensitive and yet unflinching in its handling of grief; so restrained in its use of metaphor; so poignant.

Plainly, this isn't a book about a garden in any conventional sense but it is a book about surfaces and interiors, a book about the landscape of the spirit. Let me reiterate: it's essentially on his own doorstep, in a kind of underground garden, that Tin finds consolation and works out his destiny and salvation. And in digging his own ground, he strikes treasures – just like the pedlar of Swaffham. One can press this line of thought too far, but the truth is that you simply cannot write about yards, orchards, gardens, without being conscious of (and having to take account of) their long story and significance.

Wreckage and healing. Well, of course they underlie the novel that (its author later allowed) was set in the house next to the one in which I was living.

First this author bombed it; then she curled up a little child against the square's garden railings; and then, she subtly portrayed the development during the Blitz of a relationship between two runaways sheltering and living in the basement of the house.

How is London to be mended? Well, in the longer run, with the building bricks of mutual respect and affection between individuals, nations and cultures. But in the first instance...

I remember my mother taking my sister and me to London, and sitting on the bleachers to witness the new Queen's progress to St Paul's, and being appalled by the devastation around me. And you'll recall, I know, the last and unforgettable words of Jill Paton Walsh's *Fireweed*:

I think of it now, leaning on a broken wall, looking at St Paul's. You can see it much better now that everything round it has been knocked down. All around me there are open acres, acres of ruined and desolate land, where the bombs fell. Over there the square tower of a gutted church survives as the only landmark, till the harmonious walls of the cathedral rise exposed in the background. It's quiet here, and beautiful, for into this wilderness the wild things have returned. Grass grows here, covering, healing, and russet sorrel in tall spikes, and goldenrod, swaying beside broken walls, full of butterflies, and purple loose-strife, and one plant, willow herb, that some people call fireweed, grows wild in this stony place as plentifully as grass, though it used to be rare enough to be searched out, and collected. It is a strange plant; it has its own rugged sort of loveliness, and it grows only on the scars of ruin and flame.

I suppose they will build on this again, some day: but I like it best like this; grown over; healed.

The garden of England: bombed, wrecked, grown over; healed. How can one not think at once of the early sixteenth century *Corpus Christi Carol?*

Lulli, lullay, lulli, lullay;
The falcon has carried my mate away.

He carried him up, he carried him down,
He carried him into an orchard brown.

In that orchard there was a bed,
Hung with gold shining red.
And in that bed there lies a knight,
His wounds bleeding day and night...

Here is the garden of the suffering Fisher King, the Guardian of the Holy Grail. He has been badly wounded, he is in agony. And only when one knight of the Round Table is so virtuous as to reach and see the Holy Grail can his garden, his orchard, his wasteland (it's described variously in different medieval Romances), become green and fertile again.

That rules out Sir Lancelot! Sir Gawain, too, because of his lack of charity and faith. Only the virgin knight Sir Galahad and innocent, child-like Sir Perceval, and plain, unpretentious Sir Bors, actually achieve the quest.

> Then they looked and saw a man rise out of the holy vessel, and his wounds were those of Christ on the cross, and they were bleeding openly. And he said: "My knights, and my servants and my true children, who have come out of dead material into spiritual life, I will no longer hide myself from you."

And in fact, gardens have an important part to play in my own Arthur trilogy. The first is the garden of the Fisher King at Corbenic, and the second is where Arthur de Caldicot learns that the secret and hidden must remain buried until it's time for them to see the light. The third shows the way in which experience (which we long for as teenagers) so quickly distances us from Eden, a garden where Arthur grasps how much the violence and pain he has witnessed during the Fourth Crusade have changed him.

While he's in Zara (now Zadar) in Croatia with the crusaders, Arthur de Caldicot steps into a garden after being involved in a terrible and tragic death, and it's a spirit-garden: not only a place of nourishing peace but one where Arthur can reach an understanding that everything that must die, as it does in a garden, but that God's children believe in the resurrection, just as the garden itself will be reborn.

By chance (or not by chance) I came upon a cloistered garden such as this while I was in Zadar, researching this book. It was behind a high wall and a locked door; and a nun, Sister Cika, who had the most engaging way of raising her eyes to heaven and slightly smiling, was working in it. I imagined at once that all her plants must have Biblical names: Jerusalem Cowslips, Mary's Milkdrops, Yellow Archangel, Ladder to Heaven, St. Johns Wort, Aaron's Rod, and spikenard – Steps of Christ.

> Sister Cika squeezed my hand softly. "Arthur," she said, "you care and think and feel, you are awake to the world; and the more awake we are, the more we hurt when those we love lie ill, or leave us. This is how God's children are. But He never allows us to hurt more than we can bear."
> "All will be well and all manner of things will be well," said Sister Cika. "Take my words on your way. Living we die, but dying we live, Arthur."
> Sister Cika half-smiled at me, and she lifted her eyes.

Guided by his experience, his joy and pain distilled in these gardens, Arthur de Caldicot comes to understand that, although he's no Grail knight, each one of us does make a difference. A crucial difference.

> Saracens and Jews believe a person who saves the life of another saves the whole world. I believe that too... It's people following each other like cattle, never questioning, never thinking for themselves, becoming numb to bloodshed and other people's pain, who turn our world into a wasteland.

When I 'replanted' Sister Cika's flower bed, I fondly supposed I was the first person to invent a spirit-garden. Not so, of course! Indeed, I visited one in Bamberg only a few months ago.

*

Minnow on the Say and *Tom's Midnight Garden* were Philippa Pearce's first two books, published in 1955 and 1958 respectively. And what they have in common, *inter alia*, are gardens, friendship, quest and a preoccupation with Time.

In *Minnow on the Say*, we learn that the garden where eleven-year-old David Moss and his family live in Jubilee Row is "something quite out of the ordinary", but this is largely because of its shape and the way in which it leads straight on to the shining thread of the River Say (which is the Cam). Though there are moments in the book when the garden becomes almost an extension of the river itself, because when the Say is in flood it advances up the garden-path, something thrilling for any child and the child in each of us.

But there's another garden of much greater significance. Adam is the orphan nephew of Miss Codling, and the Codlings have lived a little further up the river for centuries. Her garden is tousled and untidy and overgrown, and this is where Adam and David forge their friendship, often meet, and review what progress they've made in their search for treasure.

This treasure was hidden by one Jonathan Codling in 1588 after he was summoned to fight against the Spaniards and, paddling their canoe up and down the Say, David and Adam pursue their quest – trying to solve the puzzling clues left by Jonathan Codling (as narrated by his wife Judith), aware that adult rivals are threatening to find the treasure before they do, and up against Time itself.

In addition to the boys' awareness that time is against them, and that Adam may well have to return to Birmingham with the quest unresolved, and Miss Codling may even have to sell up because she can no longer afford to maintain the old house, Miss Codling's ancient father is caught up in time travel of his own. In his heyday, he was captain of the village cricket team, and played a pretty hand at bowls, but now he gets confused, and always thinks it's the time before his son, Adam's father, died.

It's in the Codling's garden – half-garden, half-wilderness – that Philippa Pearce allows David one of those moments of intense awareness, or raised consciousness, at which she so excels, so attentive to detail, and bringing the senses into play:

"He went out in the boat, secretly, with the treasure –"

"And hid it 'over the water' – somewhere on the far bank of the river!"

The boys gazed at each other, beaming mutual congratulations. David was stirred by so deep an excitement that he stood as in a trance of feeling: he felt the warmth of the sun on his neck; he heard the soft humming of the bees; he smelt the leaves of the apple-mint that had strayed over the neglected path and been trodden and crushed under foot. Adam stretched out his hand and took his, and began leading him, almost ceremoniously, towards the river. "This," he said, "is the beginning of our treasure-seeking."

Yes, a moment at which, *in* which, past, present, and future meet. But perhaps no less striking is the way in which Philippa Pearce characterises the limit of Miss Codling's aspirations when, at long last, the coveted treasure is found. Not for her the baubles or bling – of course not. The Tudor treasure may consist of "rings and chains of gold, and bracelets and other things, among them being the silver necklace, with pearls hanging thereby like tears, that was brought but lately from Italy", but, as Miss Codling tells David:

"I have to keep telling myself that we must go carefully. For example –" She hesitated, and then went on sadly but with firmness. "It would be folly, for example even to think of a greenhouse."

And when she discovers it would be "quite practicable and not too expensive after all to build just a small greenhouse", section-built, by the back-door, she whispers half to herself, happily, "And I shall stay here forever".

The two families celebrate together by drinking Flower Wine:

> Thimbleful by thimbleful, the wine was dropping into the glasses. It was a reddish-brown colour, that the last of the sunlight illuminated to a deep gold. From it rose a scent heavy, sweet, delicious.
> "No wonder they speak of the bouquet of wine," murmured Mr Moss.
> David, sniffing at his glass, tried to distinguish all the flowers of that summer bouquet: there was hawthorn, surely – and cowslips – mint – clary – roses, of course... His nose twitched, trying to remember where it had known that particular mingling of scents before.

This is such a lovely book, "scented with summer", steeped in summer. It's charming and kind and gently exciting. And in many ways it's a rehearsal for what was to follow.

Only a couple of years ago, Philip Pullman gave us a magisterial reading of *Tom's Midnight Garden*, so what follows are really no more than a few alternatives and addenda.

In *Minnow*, gardens are the means to an end. In *Tom's Midnight Garden*, the garden is an end in itself. It's a state, a condition, and that state is childhood. True, Philippa Pearce herself allowed that her walled garden represented the sheltered security of early childhood, and Tom certainly longs to remain there, but *Tom's* strengths are not in the least abstract or metaphorical but very firmly rooted. Let me just list and here and there illustrate them, straightforward as many of them are.

I know some children, and some parents too, who have been deterred from reading *Tom* by the extraordinary network of events, relationships and thoughts Philippa Pearce portrays in the first couple of chapters. And emotions too. Irritation, regret, hot tears, frustration, impatience, suspicion, petulance and wonder: they're all there.

But Philippa Pearce is a mistress of rapid establishing and swift characterisation and we know at once that we're in safe hands. How crucial this is. If it's not so, if even the author strikes a couple of false notes, the reader no longer so willingly suspends disbelief.

In touching on Philippa Pearce as a superb storyteller, let me simply draw attention to a couple of elements: construction and detail.

Tom's Midnight Garden is both shapely and artful. This has to do with pacing. We feel the lengths of each scene, and switches from scene to scene, to be right. Revelations (such as the bar in the window of Tom's room, once Hatty's room) are achieved by careful planning, and like little electric shocks in their impact on the reader; the many passages about time as experienced by Tom and Hatty, and the very nature of Time (I'll have more to say about these presently); and the visionary scene that goes outside the garden when Tom and Hatty skate to Ely, prepares the way for the end of the book, and is so appropriate in its timing as to seem to conform to the Golden Mean.

And now detail. The margins of my copy of *Tom* are littered with ticks and exclamation marks denoting my admiration of Philippa Pearce's brilliant attention to detail: what I call 'right' detail, which would better be called 'telling' detail. She never, never inundates us in the way that, say, Balzac does – indeed she seldom overwrites and is never self-conscious or pretty for prettiness' sake – and yet she engages all our senses, as well as bringing the sixth sense into play.

In addition to the felicitous instances one could pluck from every page, there are really beautiful set pieces, such as that describing how, in the grey, still hour before morning, Tom steps for the first time into the garden:

He had come down the stairs and along the hall to the garden door and stepped out into the garden, but time was much later. All night – moonlight or swathed in darkness – the garden had stayed awake; now, after that night-long vigil, it had dozed off.

The green of the garden was greyed over with dew; indeed, all its colours were gone until the touch of sunrise. The air was still, and the tree-shapes crouched down upon themselves. One bird spoke; and there was a movement when an awkward parcel of feathers dislodged itself from the tall fir-tree at the corner of the lawn, and seemed for a second to fall and then at once swept up and along, outspread, on a wind that new blew, to another, farther tree: an owl. It wore the ruffled, dazed appearance of one who has been up all night.

Tom began to walk round the garden, on tiptoe. At first he took the outermost paths, gravelled and box-edged, intending to map for himself their farthest extent. Then he broke away impatiently on a cross-path. It tunnelled through the gloom of yew-trees arching overhead from one side, and hazel nut stubs from the other: ahead was a grey-green triangle of light where the patch must come out into the open again. Underfoot the earth was soft with the humus of last year's rotten leaves. As he slipped along, like a ghost, Tom noticed, through gaps in the yew-trees on his right, the flick of a lighter colour than the yew: dark – light – dark – light – dark…

Ah! The reader is within a dream, even as Tom without knowing it, is within a dream – one of old Mrs Bartholomew's dreams – in which so much can happen, and does, within so few seconds. Or, one might say, in no time at all.

All this relates to the writer's craft: construction, timing, characterisation, language, and so on. But all this would count for little if *Tom* were not so warm, so wise, and tough-minded.

I vividly remember talking to a twelve-year-old girl about *Tom*, and she put her finger on the core strength of the book when she told me she loves the book because she can visualise the same things that happened to Tom happening to her. That's to say, its narrative and psychology are thoroughly sure-footed, thoroughly well-earthed. It contains no imposed and artificial flights of fancy – the bane of so many contemporary fantasies. On the contrary, *Tom* is organic, and, for all that it deals in dreams and spectral figures, quite commonsensical.

Despite the book's limited cast, Philippa Pearce shows us the full wheel of childhood: Tom alone, Tom as friend, as brother, as son, as nephew, Tom with other adults; and she offers us adult viewpoints as well, in particular those of Tom's uncle and aunt. In scene after scene, we follow the patterns of a child's thoughts and imagination, hear the cadences of a boy's voice, and recognise the voice of experience and the imaginative confidence behind them. So it's no surprise to learn that Philippa Pearce greatly enjoyed the company of children (as indeed do I).

I can only marvel at Philippa Pearce's way with *time* – with writing about time. Often using the grandfather clock in the house containing her uncle and aunt's flat as a point of departure, she punctuates the book with little interior monologues in which Tom wrestles to understand what's happening to him in the garden, and wrestles with the nature of Time itself. These are cunningly interwoven with earthfast action in such a way as never to lie heavy on the page, and are quite invariably written with lapidary clarity.

There's a "calm assumption of intelligence" – the words of a wise adult friend – in these passages, and it's something very many children recognise and rise to. Those who do so find awaiting for them acknowledgement that time is indeed a difficult as well as fascinating subject, for adults no less than children, and cannot be addressed without bringing memory and imagination into play:

> However long a time he [Tom] spent in the garden, the kitchen clock measured none of it. He spent time there, without spending a fraction of a second of ordinary time. That was perhaps what the grandfather clock had meant by striking a thirteenth hour: the hours after the twelfth do not exist in ordinary Time; they are not bound by the laws of ordinary Time; they are not over in sixty ordinary minutes; they are endless.

Tom's Midnight Garden is a book of many layers, just as our country is: our laws, our landscape, our language, our stories. In placing then-and-now-and-will-be at the centre of her novel, in allowing herself passages not apocalyptic but transcendent and visionary – everyday visionary; in the sensible, practical warning that we cannot hang on to our childhood, much as we would like to – and by its inference that those who do have to pay a heavy price for it; in these ways, and in setting the action within the stillness and flux of a garden that's always so much more than just a setting, this is a very English book. Herein may be found, as William Caxton might have said, the joy of childhood, the joy and the pain, lost and through memory and imagination partly regained.

"Nothing stands still," Hatty Bartholomew tells Tom, "nothing stands still, except in our memory".

*

Listen, if you will, to G. K Chesterton's wonderful words:

> Here it is that I differ, for instance, from Stevenson, who I so warmly admire; and who speaks of the child as moving with his head in a cloud. He talks of the child as normally in a dazed daydream, in which he cannot distinguish fancy from fact. Now children and adults are both fanciful at times; but that is not what, in my mind and memory, distinguishes adults from children. Mine is a memory of a sort of white light on everything, cutting things out very clearly,

and rather emphasising their solidity. The point is that the white light had a sort of wonder in it, as if the world were as new as myself; but not that the world was anything but a real world...

Ah! I must start now to set aside books, and lists: the garden of Oscar Wilde's selfish giant, the only place where it was still winter; Mr McGregor's garden; and David Almond's edgy, tender *Jackdaw Summer*, symbolically beginning and ending in a garden; the heartrending poems, so many of them turning on flowers and gardens, written by children in Terezin concentration camp and collected in *I Never Saw Another Butterfly*; the magic "moonflower" grown by crippled Dickie in Edith Nesbit's *Harding's Luck*; the kind-of garden at the beginning of Tove Jansson's very funny and glorious *The Summer Book*, set on the little Baltic island that it takes all of four and a half minutes to walk around (not a children's book but one with such a wise understanding of the relationship of child and grandparent); all these, and even Lucy Boston's wonderful *Green Knowe* novels, Tolkien's 'The Adventures of Tom Bombadil', and Elizabeth Goudge's *Linnets and Valerians*, and Frances Hodgson Burnett's *The Secret Garden*. Yes, all these and many, many more...

In the freezing early April of 2003 there was a memorable Federation of Children's Books conference at St Felix's School in Southwold, in Suffolk. Memorable on several counts. Because 45% of the delegates were lodged in seething hot rooms in which it was impossible to turn off the heating, and 45% in bone-cold rooms in which it was impossible to turn the heating on. 5% of the delegates decided to sleep in their cars, and 5% sought late-night accommodation elsewhere! Memorable because Philippa Pearce attended. And memorable because Morag Styles (still afflicted with jet-lag, if I remember rightly) gave an enthralling lecture on *Tom's Midnight Garden*.

I was at the conference to recite a bit of Anglo-Saxon from Burial Mound One at Sutton Hoo, and to give a talk about my own writing life and the process of writing. I went to Morag's lecture, and later wrote a few lines (there's a passing reference to Tiddy Mun, the little man who is the spirit of the Fens):

**On Listening to Morag Styles:
Skating to Ely**

And listening, we laced our skates
on a morning so porcelain
we could see clean
out of East Anglia
right across the German Ocean.

Each hissing edge scoring
the white-and-blue,
we were one fair fellowship
with the Fen Tigers,
and monks still at their orisons,
yes, and Tiddy Mun,

skating to Ely with Morag
and Tom...

I made so bold as to send this cameo to Morag – and to Philippa.

"Dear Kevin..." After acknowledging the verses in over-generous terms, Philippa soon got down to brass tacks, with an assessment of my own talk. "The second [part] was a getting down to the nitty-gritty of your writing and books (and after all that's why you and not someone else had been invited). And I know you won't mind my saying as one pro to another, that this second part was indeed interesting, but not enthralling..."!

Philippa also spoke of the first part of my talk – an evocation of place-names and people-names in East Anglia – and because I treasure her words so dearly, please allow me to indulge myself and repeat them here: "what you said *glowed*," she wrote. "I could have listened to you much, much longer. I was transported…"

Philippa's response suggests much about herself: how collegiate she was (and to tell the truth, many writers are, much more so in my experience than artists, let alone composers) – Gillian McClure has told me that she and Philippa Pearce were not only good friends but that Philippa Pearce was "a very good literary friend" and read and commented on Gillian's writing; how Philippa generously served her time on committees (she and I, and Jan Mark were all on the East Anglian Arts Association literature panel together); how direct she was and how she didn't mince words; how quickly and lightly she responded to any attempt to step between then and now, and between childhood and adulthood.

For my own part, I've disinterred my Southwold talk, and as an homage to Philippa I recast the first few paragraphs here for the reader:

> In East Anglia, we're in the presence of great writers: John Skelton, rector at Diss; George Crabbe at Aldeburgh, the finest poet ever to live on this coast; William Cowper; W. H. Auden, at school in Gresham's – where my daughters studied for their A-Levels; Edward Fitzgerald, translator of Omar Khayyam; George Borrow, at home with the Romany; the Charles Dickens of *David Copperfield*; P. G. Wodehouse at Hunstanton; the much-underrated Mary Mann, author of splendid, grim, Hardyesque short stories; Lilias Rider Haggard; Edmund Blunden; Adrian Bell, Sir John Betjeman on regular raids; Ronald Blythe.
>
> And in East Anglia we're in the presence, more specifically, of memorable writers and illustrators for children: Anna Sewell, author of Black Beauty, was born in Great Yarmouth; H. Rider Haggard, whose King Solomon's Mines and She thrilled me to bits as a boy; Mary Sewell, who wrote ballads for children; the Arthur Ransome of Coot Club, set on the Broads; Rachel Anderson; Jan

Mark; twice Carnegie Medallist, who lived at Ingham in Norfolk for 15 years; another Carnegie Medalist, Mal Peet; Malcolm Saville and Redshanks Warning (do you remember – the light in the pencil tower at Blakeney church?); Lucy Boston and John Rowe Townsend and Jill Paton Walsh (there are many who hold Goldengrove and Unleaving to be the two finest children's novels written during the last fifty years). All these, and then there's what one might admiringly call the Cantebrigensian Brigade: some Cambridge born and bred, some more recent arrivals: Althea Braithwaite, Adèle Geras, Pippa Goodhart, Mick Gowar, the great John Lawrence and Gillian McClure (with both of whom I've shared books), Tony Mitton, Jan Ormerod, Victor Watson, all of them underpinned by the truly valuable and exciting work being done here at Homerton and at Anglia Ruskin. All these and at Shelford, and in everyone's hearts, everywhere, our Philippa.

Who is there amongst us here – writers, illustrators, storytellers, publishers, librarians, teachers, booksellers, parents, grandparents, godparents, disciples and apostles of fine writing for children – who has not been influenced by one or more of these authors?

Like so much of our country, East Anglia is – to use the words of the brilliant Suffolk historical novelist, Peter Vansittart – "an old house packed with memories". It's a place instinct with its own history. And to live here is to live in one layer of time, conscious of what's gone before, responsible for what's to come.

"Footprints on the grass: they were still plainly visible, although the warmth of the rising sun was beginning to blur their edges"…

Michael Longley

Breathing on the Embers

It's little wonder that, *faute de* Faber, Michael Longley elected to offer his poems to the House of Macmillan. He was following in the footsteps of a succession of brilliant Anglo-Irish writers: in batting order, Æ (George William Russell) and James Stephens, and then W.B. Yeats (only after being turned down sixteen years earlier) in 1916. They were succeeded by Padraic Colum – once upon a time he and I drank coffee together at the back of Bewley's – and, *inter alia*, Sean O'Casey, F. R. Higgins, Katharine Tynan, and Frank O'Connor.

I was the Macmillan poetry editor in 1967, and to my everlasting shame I turned Michael's poems down. Not long afterwards, I received an evening phone call. "You won't know me from Adam", said a rich, warm voice. "I think you made a mistake with my friend. *Maykle!* Will you have another look?"

I did; and I was persuaded that my caller, Seamus Heaney, was right and that I had indeed made a horrible mistake. Somewhere or other, Herbert Read wrote that the poetry editor in a large trade publishing house must be akin to a fifth columnist, and that is what Macmillan allowed me to be throughout the sixties. So Michael soon found himself in the company of Philip Hobsbaum and David Wevill, Alan Brownjohn, Patricia Beer and Ruth Fainlight and, in due course, R. S. Thomas, Charles Causley, Gavin Ewart, and our mutual friend Eavan Boland – more than twenty poets in all.

From the first, I saw that while Michael refused to take himself too seriously, he took his own poetry very seriously indeed. And he and I embarked on a correspondence that was, at least on Michael's part, exceptionally spirited and eclectic: self-aware, trusting, generous and invariably appreciative of generosity in others. I have on my desk a clutch of letters in Michael's open, sometimes loping, sometimes thrusting, often hurried hand; and in the earliest, penned from "my slovenly bed in my troubled city" immediately after the publication of *No Continuing City* forty years ago, Michael writes gladly and gratefully about (the "Old Tiger") Geoffrey Grigson's readiness to espouse his cause and "to praise a first volume of poems for the first time in God knows how many years".

The generous cast of Michael's mind is apparent from the way in which his letters, like his poems, engage so eagerly with the lives and work of other artists. The very first poem in his 1965 Festival Publications pamphlet was about Emily Dickinson, while the letters busy themselves not only with his Irish peers but also Sophocles, Edward Thomas (then as now the subject of his wife Edna's fine scrutiny), Geoffrey Hill, Louis MacNeice, and many others.

When I became editorial director at Victor Gollancz, after returning to London from Leeds where I had been Gregory Fellow in Poetry, Michael bravely chose to come with me – and there, I published his second and third full collections, an *Exploded View* and *Man Lying on a Wall*.

Michael's letters of the seventies are those of a friend. They tangle with personal relationships (his and mine) and with our children (of his son, "Daniel is very handsome and sociable, with two teeth now and charming bangles of fat"; and of his daughter Rebecca, "she's a secret manic like me, registering everything deep down in her gut"); they are accompanied by new poems "for your personal not professional perusal" and they contain little confidences ("'For Marie' is a secret until the third teeney Heaney arrives – until the unveiling"); they go in for a bit of literary gun-slinging, and enquire after my own poems ("What is the news of your collection? You're playing possum, you naughty boy."); they engage with the natural world (including a splendid 'scholarly note' about fulmars, petrels and shearwaters, nightfliers all); they revel in gossip ("Do write and give me the news in scandalous detail"); ruefully they recognise the presence and problem of *post vinum triste*; and of course they keep coming back to politics: "The whole province is sick. We're all just sitting around, bemused, waiting for the worst to happen, the crunch to come – half dread and, after six weary years, half desire."

But what these letters reveal above all is Michael's unwavering sense of vocation, and view of himself as a poet; by turns acute, on fire, self-mocking, 'sour grapey' and immediately reproachful of himself for being so, collegiate, anxious, unashamedly ambitious. And, of course, they're letters of a man in love with language, playful, full of phrase-making, rapid and graceful. I only and devoutly wish I had those letters in which Michael and I actually discussed (and sometimes, I think, tussled) over the contents of each collection. Where are they? In the Macmillan archive, I hope.

How quick and kicking and crucial all this was – and is. And all of it in the name of fine poems, all of it subject to the rapids of publication. True, our interdependence came to an end after I left Gollancz in 1977, but from time to time we've met and breathed on the embers. "With love, friendship and thanks for so much" says the unaffected inscription in my copy of *No Continuing City*.

Sláinte! The same to you, Michael.

Annie's Wonderland

On receiving the Carnegie Medal for *Storm*

Annie's wonderland is a heavenly squelch stretching in front of the sea's claws and white applause – a huge, almost empty theatre of salt-marsh and sand-dune and shingle-ridge and shining creek. Flickering ribbon formations of pink-footed geese and greylags and Brent geese tie it up and untie it. This land smells of iodine. It's lit from within, each filament and follicle. It's pink and violet and indigo and pewter and oyster and grey. The north wind often blusters all day and at night he cups his rough hands and bellows down chimneys.

In this land – I call it Waterslain – there lives a woman called Miss Disney, who catches her breakfast with her webbed feet. Her great-great grandmother was a seal (many readers will know the legends of sealwomen, and -men). But no less miraculous, my webbed woman, Miss Disney, also claims to be related to the great Walt. Walt Disney!

Here too lives a beachcomber who is always returning from the strand with a shoe bag swinging from his broad belt, stuffed with treasures; here's a huge black dog – a relative of the Warwickshire Hooter and the Lancashire Skriker – whose eyes are large as marsh-pools (pulks, they're called), and whose blood is silver-black as the arteries and veins filtering through the marsh in the moonlight. In this land, there are the shouts of children and the laughter of children...

We've all known places similar to Annie's wonderland – which is, of course, my wonderland too.

We've all known them during the most colourful and interesting and sharply distinctive time of our lives: the first ten years or so of our existence. Students of autobiography will know that the first chapter of an autobiography is almost invariably the most singular and most fascinating. It may seem rather regrettable, but the fact is as the years pass, most of us grow more like one another! We start wild and dissimilar and grow (and are trained) towards similarity.

Wonderlands are to be found partly on a map and partly in the mind – the very existence of which is a graft, a fusion of place and imagination – because in a young child's mind, as we all know, the actual and fantastic walk quite easily, quite naturally, hand in hand.

Only this morning, I asked my young daughter to bring me a couple of eggs from the larder. As it happened, there was only one egg left for her to bring. Out she came, bringing me *two* eggs, an actual one in her right hand, an imaginary one in her left, confident that like her, I would be able in my imagination to compensate for the actual world's defects!

In a sense, the whole world is a child's wonderland: he or she will make magic wherever she – I'll say she, I think – wherever she is! A mucky strip of no-man's land; a backyard. But of course some places are especially conducive to magic: a deserted quarry, maybe, or a tree beside a laughing stream, an attic, a cave, a lakeside... The shouts of children, the laughter of children: the place soon grows tall with folk tales and legends and mythologies.

At home, at school, and in libraries, children soon begin to learn truths about a place: how it has shaped the lives of people who have lived in it, and how has in turn been shaped by passing generations. This is a process we must all continue in our adult lives. If the wonderland of place is not to be lost to us, we should ask questions of 'our' place. We should peel away its layers of history. So, for instance, here in Annie's Waterslain: the dykes first built by Dutchmen, the great banks of grit and mud piled up to fend off the sea rampant, the dark groynes, the cockle-path with its crazy paving of dried mud, the village itself with its little brick-and-flint-and-chalk cottages and Dutch gables – the marks of man and woman. As we grow older, we mustn't close our eyes, we mustn't become blasé, we mustn't lose our precious sense of curiosity. We must ask questions of our places. And we must have them ask questions of us.

This concern with the relationship of person and place, and the relationship of present and past, has been central to my writing. I see my poems, my books for children, my work on mythology, my translations from Old English, and some of my broadcasts, as being somewhat like spokes radiating from the same hub, bound by the same concerns, and – I hope – a deepening search. This search has to do with a sense of belonging. It has to do with roots and anchorages and continuities.

Let me return to *Storm*. The way in which this little ghost-story broaches the relationships of person-and-place and present-and-past is probably self-evident. Annie's days, for instance, are largely shaped by her solitary life on the edge of the apparently empty but in fact teeming marsh. And Annie's mother, she puts down her aches and pains to the marsh. "Every day her mother complained that she felt as stiff as a whingeing hinge. 'It's that marsh,' she kept saying. 'The damp gets into my bones.'"

Then again, it's the relationship of present and past that lies at the very heart of the tale. The past, an earlier layer of the place, presents itself to Annie in the form of a ghostly horseman, a local farmer who has been killed by highwaymen. And by facing up to him, Annie is of course the more able to face up to herself.

In common with all of my writing, this tale – every syllable of it, every piece of punctuation, and silence – was subjected to the most intense scrutiny. To be sure, it all came tumbling out to begin with: I wrote it in well under a week, sitting in my converted garden shed, looking out over a blond Suffolk cornfield. But then I put it through draft after draft. Our first thoughts are seldom our best.

Language defines – it actually defines – thought and feeling. Imprecise and sloppy language blurs what it is trying to express. A really good piece of writing is always, *always* distinguished by precise and vibrant use of language. The specific words used may be as conventional as, say, in a poem by Emily Dickinson. Or they may be glittering and unexpected. But there are certain basic rules that, as I write, I'm always conscious of. Why use a long word when a short one will do? (Far too many people use far too many Latinate words.) Secondly, is the sound right? (Why, for instance, is "whingeing hinge" preferable to "whining hinge"?) And thirdly, is the rhythm right? In so far as sound and rhythm are both part of the meaning, a good writer must also be something of a musician. Fourthly, show a little daring, take chances, let go, at all costs avoid the language of the advertisers – the language of mob-meaning.

Remember Dryden's recognition that "Great wits to madness sure are near allied". This going out on a limb, the necessary small madness, are what and only what enable the writer to produce the words that stick. You have all now and then experienced that marvellous sensation, when you know that content, form and language have melded for a moment to say what and precisely what you mean: something that is inspired and is original only because it represents exactly what you think, what you feel, who you are.

To be the recipient of the Carnegie Medal is certainly a great honour, and I feel more part of the children's book world than ever before – part of a huge community of children assisted by librarians, teachers, parents, publishers, and booksellers – whose common cause is good writing for children. We all thrive on reciprocity, we all need to nourish and be nourished. So thank you all – thank you for your utterly invaluable work, and thank you for my medal.

The King Within Each of Us

Some years ago, I reached two reluctant conclusions:

i) I would no longer frustrate myself by attempting and failing to retell Arthurian legend
ii) I was not capable of writing a novel

But maybe the very act of relinquishing long-held ambition sometimes enables one to approach it in a different manner. At all events, innocent again, I soon got down to work. *Sic vita*!

I had a charmed childhood. A country childhood in the Chiltern Hills, between London and Oxford. My parents long concealed from me and my sister the crack in their own teacup, and it was my father who introduced us to a wealth of myths, legends, and folk tales, above all stories of the Celtic fairy folk. With his Welsh harp he would sing-and-say stories with half-closed eyes until we could stay awake no longer. "While you charmed babeldom, I slept," I wrote in a poem recalling that time.

One of the stories my father told us was about a Welsh king who did not die when he died but still lay sleeping with his warriors under a hill, awaiting the day when he would wake and lead them out and rid Britain of all those nasty Anglo-Saxon-Frisian-Jutish invaders we now call by the generic name of Anglo-Saxons. I didn't doubt for a moment that the hill in question was the hill rising to high heaven behind our little cottage, and from time to time I went in search of a hidden entrance to it. It may not escape readers of *King of the Middle March* that Arthur de Caldicot identifies his beloved Tumber Hill as King Arthur's sleeping-place:

> First I walked round the bottom of the hill, keeping my eyes open for any sign of an opening. That took a long time. Maybe it's higher up. There must have been a lake here once. I'll go on searching...

I'm sorry to report that I read little – to be truthful, precious little – as a boy. I adored T. H. White's *The Sword in the Stone*, but, really, the only genre that stirred me was historical fiction: I read *Our Island Story* – a compendium of fictionalised episodes from British history – until it fell apart in my hands; and I read Baroness Orczy, Cynthia Harnett, early Rosemary Sutcliff, Geoffrey Trease, and, later, Thomas Hardy. Now, of course, I reckon I'm well aware of how, because story ignites imagination, fiction is an absolutely crucial way to develop child's sense of history, but my own historical sense derives rather from the landscape and from objects: truths in the lie of the land, ancient hedgerows, coinage in my pocket newly-minted yet descended from a system more than one thousand years old; potsherds; arrowheads; and fossils.

At the top end of our little garden, next to the gooseberry bushes ("goosegogs", we used to say), there was a small shed I commandeered as my 'museum'. Here I spent my days amongst my own small artefacts, some found, some donated, arranging and rearranging, listing, dreaming... One day, my grandfather bought for a song an old rusty shield, and he gave it to me for my museum. I scoured it, and out of it appeared, as if by magic, scimitars and stars. When my father and I took it to the Armoury, then at the Tower of London (and now in Leeds), we were told that it was a twelfth century Muslim shield, perhaps captured and brought home by an English crusader. I was electrified! Who and what and how and why and when and where? Look long enough and one begins to see: the object tells you its story.

Always an opportunist, I realised I could supplement the pittance of my pocket money by charging entry to the museum. Until my parents realised what I was up to and stopped me, I duplicitously put up a large sign on the main road a few hundred yards from our house, announcing MUSEUM – ENTRANCE FREE. And then I attached a much smaller sign on our cottage gate, saying ENTRANCE – ONE PENNY. My generous first visitors were Rumer Godden and Jacob Bronowski, both family friends! But the museum's benefits long outlasted my childhood. It helped me to understand that adage of the novelist Peter Vansittart, that "England is an old house packed with memories," and that, moreover, we need to look back the better to look forward. History can be a dead hand, or it can be an energising and directing force.

Like any English undergraduate, I read dollops of Malory and the sly, saucy, wise *Sir Gawain and the Green Knight*, now best translated by Keith Harrison. I flirted with Chrétien de Troyes, felt sledgehammered by Wolfram von Eschenbach, and thrilled to bits by Gottfried von Strassburg's wild, white passion:

Tristan, Isolde: Isolde, Tristan:
A man, a woman; a woman, a man.

But when, in my twenties and thirties, I began to write and to engage with northwest-European traditional tale, for a long time my involvement lay elsewhere: first with the British folk tales that illustrate the whole gamut of non-religious human experience – all the longings and rewards and sorrows and frustrations and hazards and absurdities of our lives; then, encouraged by J.R.R. Tolkien, with the sturdy, passionate, and wise canon of Anglo-Saxon poetry; then with the racy, ice-bright Norse myths and the wild, richly imaginative tales of the Welsh *Mabinogion*. But as I tried to unlock these shining word-hoards, I was aware always – to mix my metaphors – of the Himalayan range of Arthurian legend: hugely attractive and utterly perilous. I looked at all the doomed versions of Arthurian legend strewn through the decades and couldn't figure out how to map my own new route.

I did try! First Faber commissioned me to retell little known Arthurian legends. But my versions seemed to me little better than précis, as extinct as dodos. Over four years, I repaid my advance. Then I stepped into prison with Sir Thomas Malory and attempted to write a novel incorporating Arthurian legends. For three years I laboured before setting the novel aside – or, rather, mining it for a series of six quite attractive BBC radio plays. Then I entertained the idea of writing simple, straightforward retellings of Arthurian legends grouped according to topic (magic, kingship, love, and so on), and accepted a commission to do so. For twelve years, I tried to find my way into the high mountains...

*

During the early 1990s I was given a Fulbright to teach at St. Olaf College, and was then offered an Endowed Chair in the Humanities at the University of St. Thomas, both in Minnesota. My love of Arthurian legend deepened as I taught courses examining Arthur in literature, art, and music, and I renewed my vows! Then, in 1997, I had a simple idea. In retrospect, it seems to have been accidental, but perhaps such things are never quite so.

Dissatisfied with my commission to write simple retellings, because I wanted to challenge myself and grow or perish in the attempt, I picked up the lovely hunk of obsidian on my desk that has long served as a paperweight. I held it in the palm of my hand:

"Take it!" said Merlin.
    When I stared at the stone, I could see myself inside it. It was black of black, and deep, and very still. Like an eye of deep water...
    "It is made of ice and fire," Merlin said. "Its name is obsidian...
    The stone is not what I say it is. It's what you see in it."

What if, I thought. What if... What if I were to write two stories in tandem? One would be a historical novel, in which a boy, eager to serve as a squire and to go on crusade, is given this piece of obsidian; and one would be the stories, the Arthurian legends, that this boy sees in the obsidian. These legends, I thought, would anticipate and reflect his own eagerness and ideals and anxieties and passions and sorrows. His own rites of passage. After all, as William Caxton (the first printer of Malory) wrote of *Le Morte d'Arthur* in the fifteenth century, "Herein may be seen noble chivalry, courtesy, humanity, friendliness, hardiness, love, friendship, cowardice, murder, hate, virtue, and sin. Do after the good and leave the evil..."

So what, I wondered, should I call this boy. Arthur? Yes, let my Arthur discover his namesake in the stone. So when and where should the historical strand be set? At the end of the twelfth and beginning of the thirteenth centuries, I thought, because this is precisely when King Arthur was about to enter the literary mainstream and become the pan- European hero; and in some potent borderland, because my young Arthur will be crossing from childhood into adulthood, and because there will be a continuous interplay between the world (rough, gruff, tough, early medieval England) and the imaginative world of Arthurian legend. I didn't have to think twice: I knew the setting should be the magical Welsh Marches so rich in Arthurian association, here secretive, there expansive, looking east to plainspoken England, looking west to dreaming Wales.

My long-time friend and editor, Judith Elliott encouraged me to set aside the simple retellings that she had commissioned in favour of this more ambitious scheme, and I shall always be grateful to her for doing so. So I began to research and to plan. I immersed myself in books not only about the fabric of medieval life but also, so much more difficult to get at, the temper and imagination of the medieval world.

I read the domestic advice of Le Ménagier de Paris to his young wife and contemporary accounts of the crusades not only by Villehardouin and Robert of Clari but also by Islamic writers. I read and reread Geoffrey of Monmouth, Sir Thomas Malory, Chrétien de Troyes, the *lais* of Marie de France, *Perlesvaus*, 'Culhwch and Olwen', the Vulgate Version, the anonymous 'Alliterative *Morte Arthure*', ranging further and further afield in search of likely candidates. But I also read historical fiction for children by living writers, and if there is one book that set me on fire and emboldened me to write in the first person, it is Karen Cushman's wonderful *Catherine, Called Birdy*.

I visited museums, national and local, sometimes haphazard and dusty. I talked to medievalists, especially my generous friend (and Arthurian scholar) Richard Barber – author of *The Holy Grail*. I visited and revisited places in the Marches, in particular Stokesay Castle, the fortified manor I adopted as my Caldicot, as well as Venice, and Zadar in Croatia where – in one of the most disgraceful episodes of the disastrous Fourth Crusade – Christian crusaders laid siege to a Christian city. Zadar (once known as Zara) is the theatre for much of the action in *King of the Middle March*.

As I began to get to know my Arthur de Caldicot and to think about the legends he would see in his obsidian, it soon became clear that I was letting myself in (and my publisher, Orion) not for one book but a trilogy. Frankly, this scared me. I had only recently concluded that I wasn't capable of writing a novel, and now here I was proposing to write three. But I also saw there was no way round this if I were to explore in some detail the fabric and temper of medieval life and to engage full-bloodedly with the three phases of Arthurian legend: that is to say, Arthur's childhood, the glory of Camelot, and Camelot's decline and fall.

*

All these preliminaries may make it sound as if I beat the life out of my trilogy before beginning it. But, in practise, I'm like my Arthur who says, "I need to see what I write to know what I think." Just so. No sooner do I begin to commit words to paper (yes, with my old Waterman, black ink on white paper) than my plans begin to change and, before long, my characters lead the way.

Authors often write about this. In my experience, here is a moment at which I get to know my characters really well because they and I have kept each other company day in, day out, for season after season. Their lives seem scarcely to depend on me or my novel. Within the trilogy, there's a village girl, Gatty: illiterate, brave, tender-hearted, salt of the earth. For two years I accompanied her on a pilgrimage to Jerusalem, during which she learnt to read and write and to see at first hand some of the cultural and trading contracts between Christians, Muslims, and Jews that existed before, during, and after the Crusades. But what if Gatty were to walk through the door now, pink-cheeked and freckled, with her tempest of golden curls and river eyes? I know what she'd say: "Cor! I never seen a place like this. It's more books than walls. Look at your candles, then! They're orange like them oranges in Sir Faramond's courtyard…" And so on and so on. That's to say, my characters themselves soon suggest responses, ideas, and incidents.

Unlike some authors so good at conceptualising that they need to revise very little, I put down an approximation and then get to work on it – to simplify; to deepen; to make music. When I began to write poems in my teens, the first person to whom I showed them was my father:

> You thinned my words like seedlings. And avoid
> long words where short suffice. (Work; will do.)
> For vogue and buzz and all-too-commonplace
> you wrote in almost timeless substitutes
> (ex-Yeats, ex-Graves). Revise and then revise.
> Our second thoughts strike deeper than the first.
>
> Sometimes you mused aloud, or asked me how
> my craft related to the science of sound –

> abstract in this, its power akin to music.
> And sound, you told me then, includes silence.
> One part of the performance, integral...
> I hear myself. Hear all that's left unsaid.

I think that the trilogy's short chapters owe much to my experience of writing libretti. In opera, aria and ensemble often anticipate or reiterate an intention or a situation, whereas recitative carries the action forward. I was very eager to avoid all-action novels. I wanted to give Arthur de Caldicot time to think and feel and anticipate and reflect. So in broad terms, the very short chapters are akin to arias, written in somewhat intensified prose, whereas the longer ones are akin to recitative.

*

It sounds obvious enough to say that in writing my Arthur trilogy I tried to research thoroughly and yet give free rein to the imagination, but it isn't, entirely. What it means is that I've aimed to be so well-steeped, so immersed in a time and place that my own ideas are truly consistent with it.

Here's an instance of this. The garden is a regular presence in medieval literature, not only as a place of pleasure and repose, a place in which to grow flowers and herbs and vegetables, but a secret meeting-place, a place of passion, a prison, a magical enclosure. I thought that I could perhaps play a number of variations on this theme. In an herb-garden in *The Seeing Stone*, Arthur de Caldicot learns about the hidden, the secret that must remain buried until it's time for it to come to light; and from his mentor Merlin, effectively the trilogy's impresario, he learns that he himself must become the good earth, ready to receive knowledge and grow. My Merlin never answers Arthur de Caldicot's questions directly. Rather, he responds with another question, challenging Arthur to answer it for himself. "Many questions," he tells Arthur, "are like nutshells – with their nuts still inside them."

At last on crusade, Arthur de Caldicot is shocked by the mindless brutality of so many of the crusaders. One day, he strays as if by chance into a garden cultivated by a Croatian nun:

She led me to a little fountain, its water splashing into a stone basin. Oh! I sank my face into it. My whole head. I tried to wash away everything.
"Thank you," I said. "God go with you!"
The nun looked puzzled. "*Govorite li engleski?*"
"What? Is that..."
"Slavonic, yes. You speak English?"
"I am English," I said eagerly.
She gazed at me, eyes shining; then she raised her eyes to heaven again, and smiled blissfully.
"I have never meet English," she said. "I studied English. You know Oxford."
"Well, I know about Oxford," I replied. "Schoolmen."
The nun clapped her hands, then took my right arm, and we walked through the cloister into a little garden protected by high walls...
"This is the garden of spiritual love," she told me. She shook her head. "Not in bloom yet. Not in December. Look!" she said, stooping to a plant with white-spotted leaves. Jerusalem Cowslips Or you say Mary's Milkdrops?"
"I don't know," I said. "Lady Alice would. She's my stepmother. In England."
"Here is a passion dock," the nun said. "Yellow Archangel. Ladder to Heaven..."
"Where do they all come from? These holy flowers?"
"I grow them. I send for them."
"Send?"

"From other *samostan*." She screwed up her eyes and smiled. "Slavonic!" she said. "Monastery! I send for them from other monastery and nunnery. Other country."

"How can you send plants? They'd arrive more dead than alive."

"Like you," said the nun.

I groaned. "It's so peaceful here. My head!"

The nun smiled like the sun in the earliest spring.

"I could stay here forever," I said.

"You wrap them in waxed cloth, and sew the cloth and smear it with honey," the nun said in her light bright voice. "Then powder it with flour. You can send plants wherever you like."

Here, then, Arthur is in a place not only of nourishing peace but also of deeper understanding – of himself, and of the world around him; a place where he comes to terms with the way in which everything that is born must die, but that God's children believe in the resurrection, just as the garden dies and is reborn.

When Arthur returns from the crusade, he first sees flame-haired Winnie, to whom he is betrothed, and his cousin Tom beekeeping in a kind of Eden: a manor garden from which he is now distanced because of the violence and pain he has seen at first hand, and because he has won the knowledge of good and evil. And the bees (the Pandora's box, I suppose) which do not touch playful Winnie or Tom, still innocent in their white clothing, promptly sting poor Arthur.

In counterpoint to these gardens – the herb garden, the spirit garden, the garden of Eden – I have also used one of the gardens that appears in Arthurian legend: the garden of the Grail King at the Castle of Corbenic.

Many of King Arthur's knights have quested for the Holy Grail and failed; but until one succeeds, the Grail King, King Pellam, must lie in his garden writhing in agony, bleeding day and night, wounded by the spear the Roman soldier Longinus used to pierce Jesus in the side when He hung on the cross. Around the Grail King, the ground is not green lawn but parched yellow grass; on the trellises, the vine leaves are shrivelled, and the grapes are wrinkled grey pebbles. This courtyard garden is a microcosm. Around it, the whole world is a wasteland.

Men fight, kingdoms crumble, crops fail, people starve, babies are bloated with hunger, and nothing will change until one of King Arthur's knights is able (by virtue of his virtue!) to see the Grail and remembers to ask the critical question.

Sir Gawain fails because, despite his virtues, his fame is written in other men's blood; Sir Lancelot fails because, in his heart of hearts, he will not repent of his passion for Guinevere; but in the final event three knights do achieve the quest:

> Sir Perceval and Sir Galahad and Sir Bors: three men, speaking as one.
> "Whom does the Grail serve?" they ask.
> "The Grail serves me," Jesus replies. "The Grail serves you." Jesus lifts his voice. "My body and blood live within you and each of you becomes the living Grail. You are knights-of-the-head-and-heart. Vessels of the spirit."

So the garden which represents the world's loss and sorrow and suffering, and has been unable to heal and grow again, is redeemed by the individual:

> The earth itself sighs and begins to breathe.
> The wasteland lies waste no more...
> "So many of us have quested," Sir Perceval says. "Many of us have come close. Each of us must have a dream."

*

In writing my Arthur trilogy, beginning with Arthur's innocent, often merry childhood in the Welsh Marches and culminating in the barbarity of the Fourth Crusade, I was well aware I was engaging with extremely serious issues:

    i) The umbrella presence of a fundamentalist Church preaching that the Muslims were vile pagans who should be driven out of Jerusalem and exterminated, and offering pardon without penance to any man who took the Cross and joined the crusades for one year
    ii) Hatred of Jews
    iii) Social inequality and the lack of social mobility
    iv) Dislike and distrust of women
    v) The legitimised and glorified violence in Arthurian legend

It would be untrue to say I saw parallels between then and now at every single turn; but of course I could see much common ground.

Certain recurring and highly topical values helped me to shape the story inside and outside the stone: leadership, or the lack of it; loyalty, or the lack of it; a sense of duty or responsibility, or the lack of it; compassion, or the lack of it.

Helped by episodes inside the stone, so often anticipating or echoing his own experience, Arthur de Caldicot thinks about these values and remembers the way in which not an army but an individual has redeemed the wasteland. Then he remembers the Croatian nun telling him that Muslims and Jews both believe a person who saves the life of another saves the whole world…

I had no wish for my Arthur to give away any intellectual or emotional currency by being an absolutist or fundamentalist. Rather, I tried to create a character who, without stepping outside the boundaries of his own time, questions and keeps questioning (as Merlin has encouraged him to do) and never accepts the easy hand-me-down:

It's people... following each other like cattle, never questioning, never thinking for themselves, becoming numb to bloodshed and other people's pain, who turn the world into a wasteland.

In a world scarcely less divided and scarred than our own, my Christian Arthur recognises that "we all need each other"; and, like Muslims and Jews, he concludes that "each one of us makes a difference". In his own anagrammatic manor of Catmole, eager and idealistic despite all, Arthur dreams of establishing a place in which, to be sure, each individual has his or her own duties, but in which there is one fellowship. One ring of trust:

Catmole, Catmole, I kept saying the word to myself over and again, and the letters began to seethe like the stars in my seeing stone; the stars in the night sky when I try to count them.

Cometale... mot... malecot, elmcoat... comelat!

That was when I realised. I sat up, I filled my lungs with cool October air, and I yelled!

Catmole. I'll remake it. My pillar. My cloud of dust and, within it, a grail of sunlight. After Venice, after the crusade: my own March Camelot.

The king in oneself! Maybe this is the deeper meaning of the old promise: *Rex quondam, Rexque futurus.* That King Arthur lies sleeping within each of us, each child, each woman, each man, and that each of us can in turn awaken him. He embodies an idea, a dream, and that greater part of you and me that longs for the better – that longs for the best – must always hear and respond to him.

A Sort of Song of Everything

Gatty's Tale and Music

Our language is an instrument, and many but not all of our better writers have been able to play it to great good effect, so that the music of their words is part of their meaning.

While it's no guarantee of success, it can scarcely hurt to become aware of pulse and sound and some of the subtleties of language at an early age. This was true in my own case. My witty mother often read me light verse, and my father – composer and musicologist – 'said-and-sang' stories to us.

Throughout my childhood, too, I attempted to play the piano and viola and to sing, in general without the least distinction. Nevertheless, my musical background must have sharpened my ear, although I'm no great linguist and learn languages other than my own only with difficulty.

Perhaps there's a compensatory element in the way that much of my writing has involved working with composers (including Bliss, Mathias, Chilcott, Hughes and McDowall), or expressly reflecting an interest in music. I don't know, but it's certainly true that I've regularly written carols, cantatas, and even libretti for opera over a number of decades, and no less true that music matters very greatly to some of the characters central to my fiction.

In this short piece, I want to concentrate on my own favourite character, Gatty, and the way in which her book approaches sound and music along different spokes. But first let me just waltz through a few earlier items.

In *Wordhoard*, co-authored with Jill Paton Walsh, I wrote about the tone-deaf cowherd, Cædmon and his vision – and throughout my twenties I translated verses from Anglo-Saxon, an oral tradition in which the poet accompanied himself on his lyre. My little trilogy, brought together as *Wulf*, is full of the music of the monastic offices; for BBC radio, I assembled programmes of Worksongs and Initiation Songs. And collaborating with the composer Nicola LeFanu on our two operas, 'The Green Children' and 'The Wildman', I began to learn some of the skills of writing libretti.

And so on! Traditional song goes hand in hand with folk tale; many kinds of music animate my Arthur trilogy; and halfway-to-heaven songs are instrumental to the discovery of the *Waterslain angels*! And then there is *Heartsong*, set in the Ospedale della Pietà in Venice, where Vivaldi taught the violin and brought together his renowned orphan choir and orchestra. Jane Ray's and my central character, Laura, is fulfilled despite her inability to speak by her divine playing of the oboe. This story hints at the power of music in pre-natal memory – and turns on the gentle rocking tune that Laura almost thinks she almost knows, and that Vivaldi subsequently used in his Gloria.

I'm not sure that there is much point in pitching one art form against another, but will say that unlike almost every writer I know, music matters even more greatly to me than the word. My sense of the world around me is as much a matter of sound as of sight, and the 'organised' sound of classical music, ancient and modern, puts me more deeply in touch with my own head and heart, and offers me more ecstasy and consolation, than any other art form.

But now – Gatty! In preparation for writing this short piece, I've reread my novel – the first time I've ever revisited a book of mine except to quote from it during some talk – and have been quite startled by just how much musical reference there is in it.

Music was very much part of medieval life, sacred and secular. Most people, illiterate, were nonetheless able to join in chanted responses at church services; incantations were used by medicine women as a way of healing or protecting people, though by no means everyone believed in them ("God in heaven," exclaimed Sir John. "Armed men keep people safe – not singing."). There was community singing at festivals such as Easter and Harvest Supper and Christmas. And of course song also formed part of the language of love, chaste and erotic.

Gatty has a rather disarming way of crooning or humming to herself as she works, and then putting words to her tune. At Caldicot, where she is growing up, the priest Oliver often hears her singing (her voice is a lovely, red-gold contralto) and he tells Sir John that she has the voice of "an apprentice angel". Sir John rubs his nose thoughtfully. "I wouldn't know," he says.

It's not surprising, then, that when Gatty reaches Ewloe before setting off on her momentous pilgrimage to Jerusalem, the choirmaster Everard (who is joining the pilgrimage) starts to teach her to sing.

"Me and my voice are friends," Gatty tells Everard. "It keeps me company." And then she confides in him that her father didn't like her to sing, because it reminded him of his dead wife...

"Sing me a scale."

"A what?"

Everard plucked one string of the psaltery and, making an open purse of his lips, sang "Uuuuu-t..." Then, waving his delicate white hands, he signalled to Gatty to join in.

"Uuuuu-t," sang Gatty, a whole octave lower than Everard.

Everard plucked the next string and half-opened his mouth. "Re," he sang.

"Re," sang Gatty.

Now Everard covered his upper teeth with his top lip, like a horse. "Mi," he sang.

"Mi," sang Gatty.

"Good," sang Everard. "Very good. Very rich," he sang. "All on the same note. Keep it steady." And then, plucking the next strings. "Fa... Sol... La"

"La-a-a-a-a..." sang Gatty.

"Go on," sang Everard, "and on and on and on and on..."

"a-a-a-a-a-a."

"On!"

Gatty coughed. "Can't" she said. Her eyes were bright with excitement. "I haven't got no more breath."

Gatty responds to this first lesson by telling Everard to close his eyes, and then singing him the sound of the wind kissing the horn-windows, and the soft *cu-ic, cu-ic* of the nightjar, and the *p'weet, p'weet* of a lapwing; and then, right behind him, the sound of a mare, loudly neighing!

That's to say, Gatty is a girl who hears and sings the music of the green world – a girl who translates what she hears and learns into song. And more besides, as we shall see...

There's a point when, talking to a Muslim astronomer aboard a boat heading from Venice to Jaffa, Gatty says that her eyes and ears get mixed up, and her nose as well:

I can touch what I smell
And smell what I hear
And hear what I see.
Mongrel-and-jumbled-and-scrambled-and tangled.
That's me!

So Gatty has a kind of synæsthesia, I suppose – and it enables her, inter alia, to believe she can actually hear the sound of sunlight, and of the wind, and of the stars.

When you or I hear a solo singing voice of great beauty, more especially an upper voice, it can cut us to the quick, and induce hot tears. Why? What is its power? I think it has something to do with innocence. And with memory, perhaps.

When Gatty is stranded in Cyprus, she sings in the half-built monastery of Bellapais in a refectory packed with monks.

"I don't know no song about Mary Magdalen," she called out, "but I know that one about all the saints, flourishing like the lilies, hidden in the clouds."

"Alleluia," Gatty began to sing. "Alleluia. Alleluia."

In the refectory, there was a great stillness. Gatty's voice was like a scalpel, cutting away the monks' sins, and it was a balm, healing their wounds.

Time passed outside the door.

Gatty looked around her. She could tell the monks all wanted her to sing more.

"Audi filia," she sang, as Everard had taught her. "Listen, my daughter, look..."

The holy men listened, and they looked. One remembered his mother and one fingered his rosary; one thought of the girl he had kissed from top to toe under an olive tree, and one tried to think about God.

The abbot rose to his feet. "You have given us fine gifts," he said. "In your voice, Gatty, we hear the grace of God. Never have I heard a voice as beautiful as yours. I only wish you could stay here. It's a pity you're not a boy!"

So Gatty loves melody and she loves song; and in writing her tale, I afforded myself the most wonderful opportunity to show off my own love of language!

The wordplay in the first eleven words of the book point the way, and from there on I did all I could to make the lexicon, and the pulse, and the silences, and the speech rhythms, and the varying tones, of the book musical.

At times I went clean over the top, I know! When Gatty reaches the Holy City, for instance, she hears it and sees it not only from A to Z but from Z to A!

Absolving and blessing, caterwauling, dancing, elbowing, fiddling, gawping, haggling, insisting, jeering, kissing, limping, mourning, neighing, ogling, pick-pocketing, questioning, rosary-telling, sweating, taunting, ululating, vowing, wailing, exclaiming, yelling, zither-plucking; zit-picking, yawning, explaining, whistling, vandalising, uttering, tale-telling, showing, rabbiting, quaffing, pleading, oat-eating, nagging, money-changing, laughing, kneeling, jostling, hugging, gossiping, flagellating, entreating, doddering, chanting, breast-beating and arguing.

Well, why not? What I was trying to do was to capture not only the energy and excitement of the scene, but the way Gatty engaged with it.

I've been describing how Gatty translates what she hears and sees into song. But there is a moment when Gatty becomes more than an interpreter. She becomes a maker.

For a long night, she is alone in the heart of the church of Holy Sepulchre – a little Saracen boy has let her stay there against all the rules – and Gatty knows she is blessed. "I don't deserve this. I done nothing in my life. I'll make it different because of this, all my life, each day of it."

During the night, Gatty sings. As she tells her solitary companion, Snout the cook, when they are reunited the next day:

"I sang psalms and that" she told him. "And songs without words. And a new song."

"New?"

"I can't explain. A sort of song of everything. I mean, I made rock solid and gritty."

"Rock is!" said Snout.

"I know, but it might not be, if I hadn't sung it so."

Snout frowned.

"I made steps climb and passages twist, I made darkness blind, and candles waxen. I made light shine. In my song, I created them."

Snout shook his head.

"With my head and heart, my flesh and blood, I made air breathe. I made air sing."

"You and your notions," Snout said fondly. "You are a one."

So there it is. Gatty sings to pitch her world. And I write words to tune mine.

From *Storm*

When Mrs Carter opened the cottage door, the wind snatched it out of her hands and slammed the door against the wall.

"Blast!" said Mr Carter. "That's a rough old night!"

The four of them stood just inside the door, huddled together, staring out, getting used
to the storm and the darkness.

There was a slice of moon well up in the sky. It seemed to be speeding behind grey lumpy clouds, running away from something that was chasing it. The Carters' little garden looked ashen and the marsh looked ashen and Mr Elkin's fields looked ashen.

They all heard it then: the sound of hooves, galloping.

"Blast!" said Mr Carter. "Who can that be, then?"

"In this storm!" cried Annie's mother.

"At midnight." said Mr Carter.

Annie slipped one hand inside her mother's hand. The hooves drummed louder and louder, almost on top of them, and round the corner of the cottage galloped a horseman on a fine chestnut mare.

"Whoa!" shouted the rider when he saw Annie and her family standing at the cottage door.

"That's not Elkins, then," said Mr Carter, hauling himself in front of his wife and daughters. "That's not his horse."

The horseman stopped just outside the pool of light streaming through the open door, and none of them recognised him. He was tall and unsmiling.

"That's a rough old night," Mr Carter called out.

The horseman nodded and said not a word.

"Are you going into Waterslain?"

"Waterslain?" said the horseman. "Not in particular."

"Blast!" said Mr Carter in a thoughtful kind of way.

"I could go," said the horseman in a dark voice, "if there was a need."

Then Annie's mother loosed her daughter's hand and stepped out into the storm and soon explained the need, and Mr Carter went out and asked the horseman his name. The wind gave a shriek and Annie was unable to catch his reply. "So you see," said Annie's mother, "there's no time to be lost."

"Come on up", Annie, said the horseman.

"It's all right," said Annie, shaking her head.

"I'll take you," said the horseman.

"You'll be fine," said Mrs Carter.

"I can walk," insisted Annie.

But the horseman quickly bent down and put a hand under one of Annie's shoulders and swung her up on to the saddle in front of him as if she were light as thistledown.

Annie's heart was beating fearfully. She bit hard on her lower lip. Then the horseman raised one hand and spurred his horse. Mr and Mrs Carter stood and watched as Annie turned away the full white moon on her face and then she and the horseman were swallowed in the stormy darkness.

From *Storm* (1985)

IN TANDEM

My mother was a renowned potter, and my father a composer and musicologist; my sister Sally danced and studied at the Ballet Rambert School. So there was a decent likelihood that I would be creative. Moreover, I've long enjoyed being a team-player: a doubles partner in tennis, a co-teacher for university courses, and joining forces with artists working in other disciplines.

In collaborating on the immensely time-consuming writing of opera, there is so very much that can go wrong: the dovetailing of word and music, the alternation of recitative (narrative) and emotional aria, set-design, choreography, costumes... pacing. Only once have I been caught in a *furore*, and that was because of personal tensions, not artistic considerations.

The Girl from Aleppo directly addresses political issues, violence and especially the matter of children caught in conflict. These same concerns underlie my *Arthur* trilogy, and *Waterslain Angels* with its focus on Cromwell's outrageous destruction of church statuary.

Two of my own grandchildren, Miriam and Danylo, are Ukrainian... Refugees, matters of language, identity, memory – those will be my waymarkers now.

Collaborations with Artists

Throughout my writing life, I have collaborated with many visual artists – painters, etchers, wood-engravers, lino-cutters, watercolourists, photographers, even a stonecarver. Thirty-seven of them, if my arithmetic is right, without taking account of occasional exchanges with illustrators of foreign editions of my books. But this is the first time I have written about the nature of any of these partnerships, or more generally about relationships between words and images. And confronted with this *embarras de richesse*, I've chosen six artists to represent very different ways of working together.

It's not easy to set aside, for the moment at least, Brian Wildsmith, who had just won the Kate Greenaway Award when he illustrated my first novel, *Havelok the Dane* (1964). Some of his spirited, meticulous line drawings, with their replacement characters and glue and whiteout as Brian improved on his first thoughts, hang here on my walls.

Indeed, he and I thought about collaborating on a picture book about the life of the Anglo-Saxon cowherd Cædmon, and I went to see the legendary Mabel George at Oxford University Press to discuss it. Actually, it was more like an interview! She was the soul of courtesy, and then showed me the door!

It's not easy to omit Margaret Gordon either. She and I made three picture books together, one of which, *The Green Children* (1966) won the Arts Council Award for the Best Book for Young Children 1966–8. We each received £500, more than half my annual salary as a young editor at Macmillan. Margaret's watercolours are wonderfully innocent and appealing and had she not died desperately young of cancer, we would have worked on more books together.

The *Guardian* journalist who interviewed us *chez* Gordon after we had won the prize wrote:

The scene is so domestic, the way they talk together, and the way he has slight agonies when she says something wild. In fact for half an hour, Peter Johns, who took the pictures, thought that they were married. But no, in fact, they are not. Or at least they are both married happily to other people...

"You have to be child-like – not childish, but child-like – to write a children's book." Kevin Crossley-Holland says. Both he and Margaret Gordon, you can see, are very child-like, sometimes bursting with excitement, sometimes wonderfully solemn.

Their prize book, *The Green Children*, and a newer and more sombre one, *The Callow Pit Coffer*, are seriously done, with no sense of writing down or jollying along. Children have their dignity, and this they both respect.

Margaret finds that she gets quite far into his mind while working on his book. "I feel I know you better," she said to him, "through working on the books than I ever do by seeing you." They obviously enjoy it, all the plans and all the meetings, all the quarrels and the makings up that working together means.

No, it's downright difficult... John Hedgecoe, great photographer, and biographer of Henry Moore. When I worked with him on my *Norfolk Poems* (1970), he somehow persuaded me to wade fully clothed up and down muddy back-creeks, with strings of seaweed around my neck. Cussed, determined, imaginative, immensely talented, and generous. Did you know that the image of the Queen on British postal stamps is based on one of John's photographs?

Embarras de richesse – Alan Marks, whose first commission was to illustrate my ghost-story *Storm* (1985), winner of the Carnegie Medal... Susan Varley... Shirley Felts... Hannah Firmin... Peter Melnyczuk... Gillian McClure (we worked side by side as she realised her memorable images of the Norse gods and lumpen giants)... Meilo So... Peter Malone... Emma Chichester Clark...

Stéphane Jorisch, three-times winner of the Governor General's Award in Canada... Frances Castle...

But after some deliberation – and not least in the interests of representing a range of text (children's books, landscape history and poetry) as well as image – the six visual artists I've chosen to write about are: Charles Keeping, John Lawrence, Andrew Rafferty, Norman Ackroyd, Jane Ray, and Jeffrey Alan Love.

John Lawrence

One summer afternoon in 1987, John Lawrence drove over from Cambridge to our house, The Old Vicarage in Walsham-le-Willows. For a couple of hours he followed my three-year-old daughter Oenone around, chatting and taking snaps which captured much of her spirit – her unbridled curiosity and gaiety, her studiousness and sweet affection, as well as her untrammelled red hair, wellington boots, and complete command of Tempest, our retriever.

These moments John combined into a miraculous panel of twelve detailed tiny wood-carvings (each measuring about 4x2 centimetres). I think he called this "a detachable frontispiece" and he then used each image on its own within our limited edition book, *Oenone in January*. He first used this economical method in *The Road to Canterbury* (1979), and it's one that he has successfully repeated, including the splendidly energetic, entertaining, and gruesome images for my collection of East Anglian tales, *The Old Stories*. But nowhere has it seemed more appropriate than in the Old Stile's very small (18x13 centimetres) book about a very small person!

From the first, sometimes wood-engraving, sometimes lino-cutting or using line-and-wash, John Lawrence has illustrated in a way that children respond to. He may work in the same tradition as Thomas Bewick and the Victorian engravers and, amongst modern masters, Richard Shirley-Smith, but his delightful quirky, wit reminds one most of Edward Ardizzone, while his 'busyness' is all his own.

"What I'm looking for," he says, "is the excitement of metal going through wood and coming out with interesting marks – I hope it isn't just fireworks – but a way of drawing."

Anyone interested in just how he effects such a wealth of detail with his burin and other tools – working in an area as circumscribed as Hillier's miniatures – should consult Douglas Martin's masterly essay in *The Telling Line*.

I've never known John well and only once visited his Cambridge studio. And yet in a way, I feel I've never not known him – perhaps because of our shared interest in traditional tale and belief, and in the medieval. Sometimes he has sent me roughs to comment on, but for the most part he reads my text, and we then talk and correspond; without more ado, he then gets on with it, and I'm confident for him to do so. Trust is certainly a necessary part of the chemistry between author and illustrator, and there is no one I have trusted more.

I wrote the foreword and John provided the engravings for the Folio Society edition of T. H. White's *The Sword in the Stone*. And then we joined forces for their marvellous edition of my Arthur trilogy (*The Seeing Stone*, *At the Crossing-Places*, and *King of the Middle March*).

John's lively illustrations are linocuts with added wash, and at once we enter a rustic world with cattle chewing the cud and a boy slithering into a sloppy pool of first-day dung; a tiny figure trooping out to work with a heavy scythe, and a charging bull; all of this below an impossible, completely conical hill: a combination of the actual and the fanciful. Always *alive*, always inventive, often witty, often touching, I think his large body of illustrations are the perfect complement to my portrayal of the medieval world of Arthur de Caldicot, and hope I've told him so. We have tended to take each other's work for granted.

I try to address and use language in the way John addresses wood – with a toothpick, with an eye for grain, with an ear for music. Attention to detail: this too we have in common. I remember Jane Ray telling me that she was finding it increasingly difficult to produce her miniatures because of the strain on her eyes, and it's a wonder John – always working with such care and precision – can still see at all! *Multum in parvo.* That's the epithet, of course, that suggests itself when one looks at his work. But so does *festina lente.* During the last sixty years John Lawrence has produced a very large amount of wonderful illustrations

Andrew Rafferty

My collaboration with the photographer Andrew Rafferty has been akin to a two-act drama with an intermission lasting thirty years.

One of three artistic brothers and a closely-knit Cumbrian family, Andy (as everyone calls him) was until 2018 the headteacher of Roman Catholic state primary schools in Hertfordshire and Middlesex, and then parachuted in by ILEA to rescue failing schools in London. We first met in the late 1980s when he invited me as a children's author to one of his schools.

At that time, Andy was keenly interested in the Neolithic and Bronze Age sites in Britain – their standing stones and chambered barrows – and when he showed me some of his brilliant black-and-white photographs of places such as Avebury, and Callanish, and Stenness, they quickened my own interest in them: as stepping-stones to understanding more about the men and women who created them, and why they did so – questions that of course ultimately bring us back to ourselves.

After finding a publisher interested in his work, Andy invited me to write a text reflecting on these dramatic sites, and I readily agreed to do so. But I'd just been awarded a Fulbright and was leaving with my family to teach for a year at the liberal arts college of St. Olaf in Minnesota.

As soon as the summer semester ended I took myself off to a silent two-room forest cabin – and there in the course of seven days, surrounded by Andy's images pinned to the wooden walls and laid out on the floor, I wrote not only fifteen thousand words – the first half of the text for our book, *The Stones Remain* – but also seven of the better poems I've written in my life. What days!

> Left the log house with a weight on by back:
> the old world, the whole world, slung in a sack
> that rocked me from side to side. Couldn't stop
> thinking, stop think-thinking, muttering shop
> for a mile or so down the shining track.
>
> Large as a flittermouse a butterfly
> steered past me, steered and waved, sailed on the dry
> thyme-rich ocean. Stepped over a beetle,
> an aged scarab hammered from metal
> emerald and black. The how, when and why
>
> never bothered them. They followed their bliss…

After the well-received publication of *The Stones Remain*, Andy was eager to collaborate again. Up to my eyes with several commissioned writing projects, and with teaching and speaking and the like, I was less so.

During years that added up to decades, he put to me many ideas and showed me many images to ignite my interest – on ancient carved stones, for instance, with their inscriptions and arcane markings – and many times we met, by now very good friends, to discuss them. But it wasn't until Andy, very recently retired and an immensely assured technophile, returned to *The Stones Remain* with a plan to develop it into an all-moving, all-dancing, all-everything book that the situation changed.

Andy rightly thought that Seahenge, the prehistoric oak circle now dated to 2047 BC should be included in any revised edition, and he asked me to write a poem to accompany his images. I happily agreed. (When Seahenge was first revealed by shifting sands on a North Norfolk beach in 1999, I had covered the event for the BBC World Service.) Then something happened. I wrote nine poems!

I began my sequence of poems where I had grown up, under Whiteleaf Cross in the Chiltern Hills. After following the Neolithic Icknield Way and Peddars Way that run north to the Wash near Holme, I adopted the persona of a young woman helping to build the timber circle and to lay the body of her father within it.

Andy at once saw this sequence as something he could publish in its own right with his own small Kailpot Press. I was happy for him to do this and almost at once there followed the most intense months of collaboration I have ever experienced. Time and time again Andy appeared on the doorstep or sent me bulky packets of the astonishing photographs he was taking of Seahenge and as responses to my journey.

"All the images", Andy wrote, "are single-frame photographs, not composites, taken at a moment in time – albeit that a 'moment' may range from a fraction of a second to several seconds. Many images are the result of intentional camera movement performed during the opening of the shutter, some are the result of subject movement."

These are immensely daring photographs that translate elements of the natural world into something beyond themselves. Not wholly unlike the paintings of Howard Hodgkin. Look! The flight of birds becomes extended into elegant single strands weaving across a whole page, or into threatening Vorticist shapes, dark and delta-winged; a scarecrow becomes an ethereal dancer; poppies catch fire and blaze; and the treasures in my childhood museum in Whiteleaf become emblems, solid and yet misty, of then, now and forever.

Never has any artist paid such attention to the substance and music of my writing, and I'll always be deeply grateful to Andy for doing so. And the price? Well, I realised that I was working with an artist well-nigh obsessive. For each image in the book, Andy discarded upwards of one hundred; and he told me that he'd taken more than fifteen hundred photographs of one arrangement of objects from my museum. Fifteen hundred! I saw too many of them.

Andy was no less particular about every single aspect of the book's production, dismissing the first proofs printed in Poland, and flying off to Cyprus to superintend work at another printer. There was no element of the book he didn't consider and reconsider: the paper, the layout, the typeface, the endpapers, the binding... everything. When it came to distribution, Andy ran into precisely the same challenges as every small press, but by combining two wholesalers with personal hand-to-hand sales, he made some headway. Meanwhile, I recorded the sequence, and Andy made two masterful and highly atmospheric DVDs of his images and a little music (one with my voice and one without).

Proudly, I sent complimentary copies to my family and a few friends, and the response that mattered most to me was from the finest storyteller in this country, Hugh Lupton:

> Setting the boyhood and age of your own lifeline as a movement along the Ridgeway from the Chilterns to Holme alongside the (perfectly pitched) voice of the daughter of the elder who was committed at the Henge touched me very deeply.
>
> Having been one of the 32 that cold January morning in 1999, having walked the Peddars Way several times, and also walked large chunks of the Ridgeway, having been obsessed for years by henges, tumps, stones etc., having also had a museum when I was a boy, having struggled to find a voice for our remote ancestors in several performances... in short having (like you) been engaged with the

Matter for a good number of years... I am in awe of so few words conjuring so much.

It is also a very beautiful book... the combination of word and image work so well together (always a delicate balancing act). It's up there with [Ted Hughes' and Leonard Baskin's] *Cave Birds*, [Hughes' and Fay Godwin's] *Ruins of Elmet*, the Kinsella and Louis le Brocquy's *Tain* and Heaney and Rachel Giese's *Sweeney's Flight* as a perfect combination of text and image.

Jeffrey Alan Love

Judith Elliott was recognised as one of the most outstanding children's books editors in London for more than forty years. I worked with her at Heinemann, then at Orchard Books and at Orion where, in each case, she founded the lists and was editorial director. Judith and I have long been close friends, but some years after she retired, my literary agent Hilary Delamere suggested that Denise Johnstone-Burt at Walker Books would welcome me and be an ideal editor for me. She was right.

Walker wanted me to retell a group of Arthurian legends. I agreed to do so but, sensing the very strong following wind behind the Vikings – not least because of the Marvel films and *Game of Thrones* – I said I'd prefer to write a completely new version of the Norse Myths first.

When we met for the first time, and lunched together, I fainted into my soup. A few days later, I had a stroke. Denise later told me that she didn't think I would be able to write either book! A month or two later, and while we were at something of an impasse, Walker's quite outstanding art editor, Ben Norland (the son-in-law, as it happens, of Philippa Pearce) stepped in. He showed Denise and me the work of a brilliant young American, Jeffrey Alan Love – and before long he was writing to him to say that he thought he had been born to illustrate the Norse myths.

Then Neil Gaiman stepped up to the plate, telling Jeff that so far as Norse mythology was concerned, "Kevin Crossley-Holland is the master". So that was that!

Jeff is a young American now living in California who has been nominated for a fistful of international awards and won a gold medal from the Society of Illustrators, and he is an obliging, rapid, and appreciative collaborator. The way in which we work is that he sends over roughs, in three different colours, and Ben, Denise and I write brief or detailed comments all over them, before returning them to him.

And this is how Jeff produces his dramatic, often fearsome roughs:

> I work digitally for sketches in Photoshop, as for me sketches are not about drawing ability but composition. I'm only interested in value, shape, and edges and whether or not the image is reading and telling the story I want it to tell. In general, I use only black and white, and Photoshop allows me to copy/paste the sketch over and over, so I can make Thor tiny in one version, and see what happens if I make him GIGANTIC in another without having to redraw him – I just lasso, copy and paste and I can see if it works within seconds. That efficiency with time was always important with previous jobs, but it was invaluable this time around – I was doing thousands of sketches for a 230-page book, with paintings on every single page.
>
> I print out the digital sketch and lightbox it onto Stonehenge paper. I paint the silhouette with black paint or ink, depending upon how much surface texture I want at this stage, and then I coat various brayers, paint rollers, socks, petrified sticks I found on the beach, sponges, brushes, old shoes, my fingers, etc. with paint and start distressing the image. Just about anything can leave an interesting mark, and I try to have fun and leave myself open to happy accidents at this stage.

I intentionally relinquish control of the piece to the materials and let them do what they want. I used to cringe when something happened on a painting that I thought was a mistake or weird – now I love when that happens, when something surprises me in the process. The pieces begin to resemble a Rorschach ink blot, and I start to see things within them. Using white and black ink and paint and coloured pencils I go back into them and try to bring out a little further the things I see within the silhouettes so that the viewer will see them too.

Then it's just the simple matter of painting day after day, piece by piece, until it's done and you look back and wish it really was a thousand-page book and that it didn't have to end and you could keep painting it forever, because this truly was a dream job for me.

Simple you see! No problem.

Jeff's illustrations for our *Norse Myths* were hailed here and in the USA. And Amanda Craig's comments in the *Times Literary Supplement* helpfully contextualised his work:

> It is the humour, moral ambiguity and inescapable impetus towards tragedy that makes Norse myth so unusual. There is an obsession with tricking the enemy into doing your own work, and with capture and humiliation. Odin loses an eye for wisdom. Tyr sacrifices his hand, and ultimately all the major gods die when flood and fire, monsters and chaos over-whelm armies of the living and the dead. Rebirth is promised, with a few surviving minor gods and a mortal man and woman hiding in the World Tree, but it is overshadowed by a vision of almost total annihilation. As we destroy our own planet, it is no wonder these themes resonate.
>
> To this, Jeffrey Alan Love's pictures add a monumental grandeur. Chris Riddell's elegant illustrations for Neil Gaiman's version of the myths emphasised the stories' beauty and mischief; the d'Aulaires

gave them an appealingly colourful naivety; Brian Wildsmith conveyed character and emotion through a delicate web of pen and ink in the Lancelyn Green version. By contrast, Love's craggy black silhouettes stamp a graphic power, mystery and dynamism on every page. All the gods are instantly recognisable, from Thor with his crude hammer to Loki, whose curling head-piece seems part jester's cap and part grasshopper's antennae as he crouches, leaps and persuades.

Jeff and I have now worked together in the same way on a second book in which gods and humans interact (*Five Norse Tales: Stories from Across the Rainbow Bridge*). The way in which he deliberately "relinquishes control" of a piece and allows the materials "to do what they want", is not altogether unlike the latitude Andy Rafferty allows his camera when he takes his single frame images; and in each case, their work skilfully combines freedom and control.

Jeff has a young family – his wife is Gwyneth and their two sons, Arthur and Owain. I think that when they first come to Britain, a visit to Wales with them will be in order. Maybe to where King Arthur still sleeps, and waits.

Jane Ray

On the face of it, Jane Ray's renowned illustrations and my writing for children have little in common, but for many years I've found her portraiture extremely appealing (those wistful faces, often almond-eyed with dark pupils, so expressive of their inner as well as their outer lives) and I've liked, too, her vivid and detailed scene-setting.

In particular, I admired her illustrations for the very ancient Lugulbanda poems, and was taken by her ability to portray 'wist', if there is such a word: her sense of drama, and her use of chiaroscuro, here and there portraying the natural world as if it were no more than a misty memory.

From time to time we met and talked at festivals and conferences, and when we found ourselves together at a Carnegie/Greenaway event in 2005, (she should have won the Kate Greenaway Award long since, and likewise the international Hans Andersen Award), I told Jane that I'd long had an instinct, and harboured a hope, that we might work on a book together. She looked – well – slightly bemused, perhaps quite touched, and said she'd have a think about it.

So here was a different kind of collaboration-in-the-making: an author and illustrator in search of a story.

When we met a few months later to discuss various ideas, I arrived bristling with possibilities, including a book about the Green Man, a book of carols, and the retelling of a particularly haunting folk tale. For her part, Jane arrived with just one.

She told me how, in the Vivaldi Museum in Venice, she had found in a great ledger the names of all the foundling babies left at the Ospedale della Pietà. "I came to the bottom of the page: *Laura*... no: 3170, born 1724. Next to the open page with Laura's name were tokens left by tragic mothers... my head swam with pictures and a story..."

Jane said that although she could see all the elements of what would be a profoundly emotional story – set in that watery city filled with birds, winged lions, ancient buildings, narrow passageways – and although she could even see exactly what Laura looked like, she couldn't fathom how to write her story. "Laura's story," she said, "kept slipping from my grasp like a dream on waking."

So she asked me whether I thought I could write it. And only a little while later, she sent me a single sketch. I see that on the back of the envelope I wrote "Extremely appealing – wistful – eager – gave me a lump in the throat – *retroussé* nose – a touch of Cinderella but lovely loose strands of hair – and something appropriately awkward about her mouth (just slightly twisted)."

This is how we worked. Jane and her conductor husband David Temple doubled back to Venice where she filled an entire notebook with superb sketches, and she was also engaged in work with the Foundling Hospital, the Coram Foundation in London; I researched the history of the Ospedale, and Vivaldi's teaching there (he was born only two hundred metres away), and listened to much of his choral music, and then my teacher wife Linda and I returned to Venice too (it plays no small part in my *King of the Middle March* and *Gatty's Tale*) and I listened to and almost imbibed the plashing, misty, mysterious, breathing city. And from then on we exchanged a series, a torrent almost, of Jane's sketches and little bits of my text.

I suggested that our Laura should tell her own story of life in the noisy Ospedale that housed some eight hundred children, the great majority of them girls; we agreed that Laura should be mute; we agreed that she should be taught by the young Vivaldi and join his choir and orchestra, "the daughters of music", because she could play the flute *á bec* (a flute with a beak played in the same way as a recorder). How she could play! So Laura's music-making, and ability to hear music in everything, became her way of communicating, expressing her longings, and summoning half-memories.

I suggested... she suggested... we agreed... It wasn't as seamless as that, of course, but it was mutual and it was organic. It was also inclusive. While David commented on Jane's paintings, my wife Linda and a close friend, Lynda Edwardes-Evans, both of whom regularly read and improve my writing, commented on my text. "The final score," wrote Lynda, "is achingly beautiful and carries such an emotional charge for the reader as well as Laura that perhaps we don't need such an emphasis on Laura's physical responses: the lump in her throat, swallowing, saliva swilling. These details will engross a younger reader and detract from the most important things, her heartsong... I'm not sure it's as necessary as her music itself. This is the moment when the angels are stopping to listen to her, after all."

How fortunate, how very fortunate I have been, to have had two such fierce and tender critics at my side, my own guardian angels.

There was one piece of music, a lullaby, that became absolutely central to our book: a movement from Vivaldi's 'Gloria in D'. One day, Jane rang to tell me that she had resumed singing lessons after a long lay-off, and that she was learning to sing this piece. When *Heartsong* was published, and we travelled around to talk about it, we showed a PowerPoint illuminated by Jane's radiant soprano voice: *Domine Deus, Rex ceolestis, Deus pater omnipotens.*

Norman Ackroyd

One of the very few publishers of Artists' Books in the British Isles is Enitharmon Editions, directed by Stephen Stuart-Smith. Its books are in the tradition of the *livre d'artiste*: limited edition collaborations between artists and writers, containing original artwork. During the last twenty years, Stephen has published a series of virtuoso and significant editions, including collaborations between Jim Dine and Robert Creeley, Christopher le Brun and Ted Hughes, Hughie O'Donoghue and Seamus Heaney, David Hockney with Marco Livingstone, and Gilbert and George.

Stephen and I have been good friends since the early 1980s, and Enitharmon published my volumes of poetry between 1996 and 2015, so I was overjoyed when he suggested that we might approach Norman Ackroyd with a view to his collaborating on my new north Norfolk sequence of poems, *Moored Man*.

Not only has Norman had many one-man shows in Britain and throughout the world, and fulfilled many important public commissions, and not only is he a Royal Academician but – most significantly from my point of view – his superb series of etchings of the British archipelago portray our coastline, wild and misty, often inaccessible, home to monks and seals, screeching gulls and guillemots, in a more compelling way than anyone has done before. It's no wonder that many people regard him as our finest etcher since Turner.

When she was Director of the Oxford Gallery, my mother Joan Crossley-Holland mounted art shows to complement her groundbreaking exhibitions by leading craftsmen and craftswomen. One of them included Norman's etchings and, I think, paintings, and it was there in the 1970s that I first met him. He is a Leeds man and studied there at the College of Art, while I had just completed my term as Gregory Fellow in Poetry at the University of Leeds (1967–9). We had plenty to talk about, agreed to keep in touch, and failed to do so.

Moored Man is the spirit of the wild north Norfolk coast with its mesh of saltmarshes, tidal creeks, sand dunes, sand flats and shingle ridges, and he embodies its warring elements. He is virile, he keeps shape-changing (among his forms is that of the trickster), he suffers, he endures, and he has a fierce beauty. He moulds the dykes, and sorts and carts gravel; he tricks and cuts off the unwary; he drowns children, howls like the wind and dances like the sea.

Norman took kindly to Stephen's suggestion, and wrote to me "I like the pewter-dove-oyster-charcoal references: my image of that coastline is of 1000 greys – even the fields are grey-green in winter... I am imagining an extended landscape format... The poems have a great abstract imagery which is really the only way to approach that coast. Look up some of my more abstract collections [of etchings]... Meanwhile, I will look you up in Burnham Market... My feeling is we have a real possibility here."

Going on to invite me to his London studio, and telling me about his show "along with Turner's engravings" (!) about to open at the Academy, inviting me to meet him there "and have lunch. Whatever!", this is Norman all over. He is Yorkshire through and through; quite cautious to begin with; then forthright and decided; 'in for a penny, in for a pound'. The first words he wrote to me were: "Dear Kevin – thank you for the poems. I can see what you're getting at."

Norman, Stephen and I decided that our book should include both etchings and watercolours, and before long Norman was making repeated visits to the north Norfolk coast (on one of these, he was delighted to run into an old friend, the poet Kit Wright, whom I had invited to give a reading at the Poetry-next-the-Sea Festival; the two of them had both played for the Private Eye cricket team, captained by Harold Pinter). Then he began to send me photocopies of the liquid images in his sketchbooks – most of them stretching across complete openings with the margin marks down the middle. I blue-tacked them to the walls until I was adrift in Moored Man's world. This led to my writing more poems to add to the sequence, and I can point to many images that directly took their lead from Norman's work ("sheen-eyed and unblinking, quick / to the creek's sudden lurches and quivers", "once again the ruckled beds and lays go under, and the soft mound, silver and grey, around the freshwater spring", "effortless his water / swans down midstream, softly/ it backheels in the margins").

Likewise, Norman pinned up my poems all over his studio in Bermondsey, and told me that they were points and guides and that certain passages had a direct bearing on his work. These he asked me to write out in my own hand, with a view to exploring whether it would be practicable to embody them within his etchings. We tried several methods (including typeset passages), but none of them really meshed, and we abandoned this approach. Each of us, I should add, made his own choice which images and poems to include, which to omit.

Norman's etchings! The brilliant singularity and specificity of his reeds and rushes, down to the last seed-head, rising from twisting watercourses; the way the light is at one moment icy sharp, the next misty, as if the whole world were dissolving – as if earth, and water were all one lung. They are wondrous, and the whole is greater than the sum of the parts.

Of the people who wrote about the sequence, Ronald Blythe came closest to describing what, in Norman's words, I was 'getting at':

> What enthrals us when we arrive at the coast is neither land nor sea but that narrow flux of both of them called the shore. It is the shore which does most of the talking, which utters, which we listen to. At first it seems to say the same things over and over again, and is mesmeric. Then it becomes both soothing and threatening, musical and dissonant, inspiring and wretched, easy to understand and complex as it articulates things which cannot be heard in any other place. *Moored Man* interprets this watery voice in a wonderful manner. In a sequence of wild, desperate, beautiful and original statements the seashore tells how it can never get away, now it has struggled in its liquid chains, and how it is both captive and yet free. *Moored Man* may be tied to the edge but he is never stationary. He is all movement. He may be mud-dull but yet he is a marvellous orator. Although below the rocks, he is a visionary. This is a fine poem. There is a tragic loneliness in it reminiscent of that in Ted Hughes's *Crow*.

Moored Man was launched in great splendour in the Fine Rooms at the Royal Academy of Arts – and the President, Norman, Stephen, and I all spoke briefly about it. In addition to the deluxe limited edition designed at the Libanus Press and slipcased by the Fine Bindery, numbered 1 to 90, Enitharmon also published a regular trade edition of 1500 hardback copies. Both editions sold out.

Thereafter, Norman and I with our partners made a number of festival visits. Audiences invariably like to hear about process, and Norman is exceptionally good at describing the journey from dream to finished article. Not long ago, indeed he presented a very well-received BBC2 programme on the elaborate, messy process of making an engraving.

I greatly enjoyed these public sessions with this quite gruff and gravelly, plainspoken, generous man, who once cheerfully announced, "From what I can tell, Moored Man was a miserable old sod". And I won't forget the visceral relish with which, while we were in Ilkley, he attacked a three-tiered silver platter piled with shellfish of every kind – lobster and crab and cockles and mussels and winkles and shrimps and prawns and langoustines…

"There was an old man of the sea…" I thought. And perhaps there has never been a finer explorer of the place where water and earth meet, argue over and over again, and reshape one another.

Charles Keeping

In approaching Charles Keeping to illustrate my second book, a retelling of the medieval romance of *King Horn*, I was taking a step with far greater consequences than I could have imagined at the time.

Charles was already very well known and highly regarded for his illustrations of fiction by Rosemary Sutcliff (and also her retelling of *Beowulf*) Barbara Leonie Picard, E.M. Amedingen, Alan Garner, and the brilliant, terse Viking novels of Henry Treece; he was the court illustrator, as it were, to the guardians of the hoard, the historical novelists and retellers of folk tale in whose footsteps I have tried to follow for well over fifty years.

Buoyed by the relative success of *Havelok the Dane* and my partnership with Brian Wildsmith – and also, I think, with the confidence that a public school education may bring – I sent Charles a copy of *King Horn*…

In his *Charles Keeping: An Illustrator's Life*, Douglas Martin has written in vivid detail about Charles' Cockney childhood – the seething streets, costermongers, working horses, dilapidated houses and squalor. From the start, Charles learned to look, look again and again, and became a master of finely drawn and pointed portraiture.

"What matters is feeling and understanding, and any images must reflect this," he wrote. "That is what makes a good illustration, and if the drawings derived from this type of concentration... are put or a wall or in a book, it makes little difference to their artistic merit."

But vigorous as his early work was, it was also somewhat static. Not so *King Horn*. His characters and horses leap all over the page, charging and cutting and thrusting. The illustrations are properly described as line drawings; but what they do is combine the most delicate fine line with jabs and splatters and blazing slashes, made perhaps with a black marker pen. The *Times Literary Supplement* commented that my story, "especially in its tougher episodes, is reinforced powerfully by Charles Keeping's illustrations. These are startling in their power and vigour." In the *Listener*, meanwhile, Charles Causley wrote that Charles Keeping's "fairly hurtle along with the text".

More than a decade passed before I turned to Charles again – this time to illustrate my elaboration of a terse entry in Ralph of Coggeshall's early thirteenth century *Chronicon Anglicanum* describing how a merman was caught at Orford in Suffolk during the reign of Henry II, imprisoned in the newly-built castle, did not recognise the Cross, did not talk despite torture, returned voluntarily into captivity having eluded three rows of nets, and then disappeared never to be seen again.

Charles and I met to talk about the draft of my text: a fluid monologue as much poem as prose, in which the Wildman describes his life at sea, the cruelty of his captors, and the way in which he is nevertheless drawn to them. "There were so many of them almost like me, and I've never seen anyone in the sea like me." The sheer intensity of the Wildman's story, his confusion, his sorrow, his stubbornness and powers of endurance, greatly appealed to Charles, and for this little book he produced fourteen line-and-tone drawings of quite extraordinary fluidity and sensitivity. Waves rise and fall, the Wildman's long hair drifts, only the constraints of ropes and hawsers and nets are sharply drawn; and in contradistinction to his captors' cruel expressions, the Wildman's eyes are saucers of pain, appealing and agonised, luminous and unforgettable.

Looking at these drawings again now, I'm plunged back into the intense making with Nicola LeFanu of the opera based on the story of the Wildman, commissioned by the Aldeburgh Festival in 1999, in which the part of the agonised Wildman was sung by Gwion Thomas. And I see in the drawings too, the expressions of so many refugees, at once hopeful and hopeless, and in great pain. They are pictures of great and lasting power, and for them Charles was awarded the coveted Francis Williams Prize in 1977.

With this work, he was taking the first step – at a time when so many artists were rioting with full colour – towards four of his most famous books, all illustrated in the same manner with line-and-tone drawings: in order of their publication, *The Highwayman*, *Beowulf*, *The Wedding Ghost*, and *The Lady of Shalott*.

Early one evening in 1981, while I was living in Greenwich, the telephone rang. It was Charles. "Do you want to write a version of *Beowulf* for me?" he asked. "Leon says you're the person to do it."

"Why not him?" I asked. "You did *The God Beneath the Sea* together, and the *Golden Shadow*."

"He rates your translation," Charles replied, "So do I. And you and I have worked together before haven't we? You never replied to my letter asking if you had any more stories around like your *Wildman*."

"Let's talk about it," I said.

"Can I come round?"

"Of course. I'm in Greenwich."

"I live in Bromley. I'll be there in about half-an-hour."

"What? Now, you mean?"

Charles duly arrived, we drank a beer, and he showed me the little paper concertina he had made containing his first ideas for our children's version of *Beowulf*.

Briskly, he marched me through it. "I'll have this first spread... and you can have a bit of text here... and then I want another spread..." That sort of thing.

Then Charles began to spring surprises on me. The first was that he rather pitied the monster Grendel, and saw him not as unredeemable but as a human gone wrong, with a properly vengeful mother. There is, I think, some justification for this, as the Anglo-Saxon text describes Grendel as "one of the seed of Cain". Then Charles told me that he viewed the superman Beowulf's companions as a bunch of lookalike thugs, akin to helmeted trainee policemen. And by the time we'd reached the aged Beowulf's fight with the fire-breathing dragon, I was up in arms.

"Just a couple of pages" Charles announced, "Two openings at the most."

"But the dragon's quite different to Grendel and his mother," I protested. "Quite different. The dragon is *time*. You may win a reputation that outlasts time but you can never defeat time, because you're human."

"Well, you write the story," said Charles over another beer, enjoying what became a quite sustained punch and counter-punch. "You write it, and I'll see."

Long after dark, he departed – it had been one of the most febrile evenings of my writing life.

So I drafted the text for *Beowulf*. Charles told me he liked it, and suggested no alterations whatsoever.

Some months later, Ron Heapy admitted me to his office at the Oxford University Press. Charles' complete set of twenty-two line-and-tone illustrations, with a couple of further illustrations in black and brown, were hanging round the walls. The impact of seeing them like that, all around us, was stunning and unforgettable – the only comparable experience I can think of was on entering the Rothko Chapel in Houston. For a while, neither of us said anything at all.

Some of the ways in which Charles and I agreed and disagreed about *Beowulf*, already made plain in our Greenwich meeting, were at once apparent; although he did gracefully grant much more space to the dragon of time, and to the loyalty of his nephew Wiglaf in coming to Beowulf's rescue. But it's not necessary for author and artist to agree all the way down the line; and sometimes it's important for the writer to draw back and allow space for the artist to imagine, not imitate or repeat, though children are always quick to spot any discrepancy between text and image.

What I recognised, recognised at once, was that Charles had thought deeply about this great Anglo-Saxon poem that I had translated into verse during the 1960s, and entered into the principles, the morals, the obligations, the dangers, and passions underlying it. And in doing this, he had produced the images for one of his greatest books – one that has been continuously in print for more than forty years.

Charles' and my collaboration on *Beowulf* has been well explored not only in Douglas Martin's biography but also in his essays on fifteen contemporary book illustrators, *The Telling Line*. This book also includes chapters on artists I like very greatly, including Brian Wildsmith, John Lawrence, Shirley Hughes, and Raymond Briggs, as well as artists I think overrated.

Charles and I talked together about *Beowulf* to a large audience at the Cheltenham Festival; and a month or two later we spent a day together in a primary school in Herefordshire. As he drove me back to Greenwich, we chatted and laughed and argued all the way.

That's all. Or not all, really. The last words in my children's version of *Beowulf* speak of a loving obligation:

> Then twelve warriors rode round the barrow, grave guardians, brave
> Geats. They chanted a death-song, they talked as men should about

their dead and living king. Round and round. They praised his daring deeds, warm words for a breathing name. Round. They said that of all kings on earth, he was the kindest, the most gentle, the most just to his people, the most eager for fame.

'Tump' and 'Altar' from *Seahenge*

The cycle consists of nine poems. In 'Tump' I approach Seahenge along the Icknield Way from my childhood home in the Chilterns. I then adopt the persona of a woman who, in 2049 BC, helps to build a timber circle and lay the body of her father within it.

Tump
Back again! Back
and up to that oval tump above the chalk cross
to search for a thumbnail of pottery,
a single sherd.
When I launched myself into the trench beside it,
packed with crackling beech-leaves,
I believed I was an inmate of the barrow.

Commentator, diplomat, viola player, priest
– all four beached on my limitations
and quickening sense of myself.
But why did I not train to be an archaeologist?
That riddled oak lectern,
and the scarabs and beads from Ur,
a nacreous perfume bottle lifted
from some settlement south of Alexandria...
Asking, deducing, dovetailing
past and present, matter and spirit:

my heart quickens
to Whiteleaf and my childhood museum,
that shed growing into the ground,

and with one eye on the threatening sky,
one on a molehill,
I brighten at the little finds
I'm still adding to it.

Altar
I closed your lids
with this right thumb.
Then we fashioned your death-cradle.
The elders and the lame
with chains of song unbroken,
and the young splashing, delving, squeezing out,
then heaping up your island,
all the men and women with their singing axes.
With honeysuckle ropes we snared the posts
and set them up in trenches side by side.
Past the hazels and alders
we hauled the huge oak-stump
with its horn roots to the bog.
We chipped all the bark
from your cradle.

    Your white altar.

    Your shining altar.

From where sun dies the wind blew,
tides gulped and shunted
behind our dunes for many days.
But at last we lifted you
on thick green trusses and silver wormwood
we carried you out from the dead-house.

    You wore flowers.

    You wore flowers.

Sun-cups, silken cottongrass,

threaded and twisted,
starlight, marsh-mallow.
Your choker wreathen sea-pink.
So gently we laid you
on the crush of chalk and clay
between the roots
of the upturned tree.
    Our death-baby.
    Our death-baby.

Each of us sipped three sips
of the sweet water, the sweet water
lapping you.
And I, blood of your blood,
placed your death-gifts around you.

The sea-eagles and harriers heard our cries.
They cried with us.
Then each of us sang.
I sang I felt the darkness knotting
inside you.
I sang you were the setting sun.
I sang until I closed the lids
over your eyes
with this right thumb
sky always always shone in them.

From *Seahenge: A Journey* by Kevin Crossley-Holland and Andrew Rafferty (2019)

Collaborations with Composers

The accidental discovery of English language papers while abroad ranks high in my list of life's small pleasures, and on a blistering afternoon in Izmir during July 1963, I spied a copy of *The Times* on a newspaper stall.

Somewhere in its bowels, and much to my own surprise, I came across my own name. "No doubt Thane and Ealdorman knitted shaggy eyebrows over these riddles when they were new-minted, but little of their poetry or magic has survived Mr. Kevin Crossley-Holland's pedestrian modernisation."

As I later discovered, *The Observer* went one step further. Peter Heyworth wrote of my translations as "a rather ghastly sort of modern 'poesy'", while allowing that Sir Arthur Bliss' *A Knot of Riddles* for baritone and chamber orchestra, first performed at the Cheltenham Festival, was "one of the most engaging things he has written in recent years" and that "the instrumental writing is handled with a mellifluous assurance that recalls late Richard Strauss with strong French overtones."

Shortly after coming down from Oxford I'd made my first broadcast in 1962 (on the Third Programme): translations of thirteen Anglo-Saxon riddles. When they were printed in *The Listener*, the Master of the Queen's Music – yes, even then! – at once wrote to me to say that he would like to set them.

Before he orchestrated them, Sir Arthur invited me to his St. John's Wood studio for a play-through, and he cannot possibly have expected anyone so green and musically untutored, the more as my own father was a composer and musicologist.

"This riddle", I said, "the one about a bookworm, you've dedicated it to Ravel."

Sir Arthur nodded. "I studied with him," he said. "Learned a lot from him."

"Oh!" I exclaimed.

"Sounds a bit like him, doesn't it? Now, Kevin, I've changed your text a little bit here... and here. Sings better, don't you think?"

"Er..." I didn't know what to think.

Of course Sir Arthur's small adjustments did help the text to sing better, but this was my first direct experience of the utterly crucial relationship of words and music; my first steps in a long journey towards understanding why a text will or won't set well.

When I got home from Izmir, I telephoned the great man to ask him about the performance and reviews.

"Oh, Kevin," said Lady Bliss, "Sir Arthur has just gone to his study." I've often smiled, remembering this courteous, absolute and enviable reply. Concentration and interruption may live together in the shallows, but never in deep water.

*

My father was certainly eager to help me develop my own musical skills, perhaps more so because his own authoritarian father had resisted his own passionate wish to study music, at least before he had secured an Oxford degree in physiology, and the prospects of 'proper' employment. In the event, he then studied at the Royal College of Music, won the Folio Composition Prize (now the Rathbone's Folio Prize) and studied under John Ireland.

So it was that he rehearsed me in the singing of various hymns including the dismal 'There is a Green Hill Far Away' (until I was, according my tone-deaf mother, "white in the face") before I took the choral scholarship to St. George's Chapel, Windsor. The school telephoned to say that I had courteously shaken each judge by the hand, and wished them all a happy Christmas, but they had wondered whether perhaps I had a sore throat.

Between the ages of ten and thirteen I studied the viola with Philip Cannon. To no avail. Never really able to read music, never rising above the Second Orchestra at Bryanston School, I still cannot understand why not. I loved classical music. I still do, with a great passion – and above all, as my father predicted, the music of Bach. Was it simply that I was trying to please him much too hard?

Because of my father's compositions and his work in the Music Department of the BBC, I met many distinguished musicians during my teens, among them Vaughan Williams – when his 'Hodie' was premiered alongside my father's 'Sacred Dance' at a Three Choirs Festival Concert in Worcester Cathedral, he dandled my sister on his knee and offered to adopt her. Herbert Howells and Gerald Finzi and Rudolf Schwarz and Larry Adler and Sir Adrian Boult and Sir Malcolm Sargent and Edmund Rubbra (a close friend of my father's) and Villa Lobos and the many Indian musicians who were in and out of the house were generous to me. But I knew I was not of their tribe, much as I longed to be, and could not talk music with them.

But I was beginning to write! And soon after I went up to Saint Edmund Hall in 1959, one of my contemporaries, Jim Harpham, said he'd like to set a sequence of my (sub-Yeatsian) poems, 'One is One and All Alone', for tenor and piano. We actually recorded them.

> When we forsake, as we most surely will,
> Each other for a latest company,
> It is only the restless particles
> Of dust which lift to find the pulsing day...

I assumed it wouldn't be at all long before I had other suitors for my words.

Not so. Not at all. It was more than twenty-five years before I collaborated again.

The composer Nicola LeFanu, daughter of William LeFanu and Elizabeth Maconchy, wrote me a letter to say that she had been commissioned to write a full-length opera for children and adults for the King's Lynn Festival in 1990, with the support of the English National Opera's Baylis Programme. My version of the wonderful Suffolk folk tale of the Green Children had caught her eye, and she wondered whether I would be interested in writing the libretto.

Nicola and I and our families soon spent a joyous day meeting for the first time, exploring Woolpit, and almost immediately plunging in headfirst. We discussed the story's issues of tolerance and friendship, communication and language, we planned project scenes written and composed by children themselves, we recruited almost two hundred children aged between eight and thirteen from five primary schools, we regularly met with the producer Rebecca Meitlis and designer James Merifield.

While writing the libretto, I was teaching at St. Olaf College in Minnesota, and faxes flew between Nicola and me on an almost daily basis as she responded to my drafts. Maybe time makes the heart grow fonder, and the memory of difficulties fewer, but I think of those seasons in 1989 as amongst the most exhilarating in my life, an almost non-stop succession of writing, rewriting, returning to England for workshops and rehearsals and school visits.

> 'The Green Children', the new children's opera, is a piece of ravishing beauty: its text shimmers from start to end with incantations, children's rhymes and its riveting medieval legend. LeFanu's inspired music, with long mourning flute and cello lines for the green children, and with hints of organum on the paired clarinets, encases a rich variety of styles and crisply directed by the composer, proved a sheer joy.' (*The Times Educational Supplement.*)

By this time the Twin Cities Opera Guild in Minnesota had also come aboard and – conducted by the renowned Philip Brunelle, and produced by Lyman T. Smith – mounted a full week of sold-out performances at the World Theatre (now the Fitzgerald Theatre) in Saint Paul. Performances of 'The Green Children' followed in York and Bristol, and in Limerick during two separate seasons, and there are more in prospect. Almost thirty years after the reviews of Bliss' *A Knot of Riddles*, the pendulum had swung!

I was eager to develop my nascent ability to write libretti, and before long a wonderful opportunity to work for a second time with Nicola LeFanu presented itself in response to a commission from the Aldeburgh Foundation as well as a subsequent commission from the Yorke Trust to write 'The Sailor's Tale', with Rupert Bawden as a companion piece to Stravinsky's 'The Soldier's Tale', scored for the same thirteen instruments.

But I couldn't have guessed that my connections and collaborations with composers were about to take an entirely different direction. In 1991, I was appointed to an Endowed Chair in the Humanities in the well-endowed Minnesotan university of Saint Thomas in Saint Paul. One of the trustees, Linda Hoechsler, director of the Minnesota Composers Forum, persuaded St. Thomas to appoint a composer-in-residence, and I was invited to chair the search committee.

I'm aware this piece of writing turns on the nature of collaborations, not on how they came about, but... After being appointed to the board of the newly-formed American Composers Forum, (a position for which I had very scant qualifications) I soon learned about an informal set-up known as the Minnesotan Commissioning Club.

This club consisted of four or five philanthropic families each of which pledged an annual endowment for the commissioning of new music. One of its members was Nick Nash, the recently retired Minnesotan Public Radio's director of music. In this position, he relayed for the first time to American radio the King's College

Festival of Nine Lessons and Carols, now broadcast by virtually two hundred radio stations, and had become a firm friend of Stephen Cleobury, the King's Choral director.

To be in the right place at the right time is sometimes as a matter of luck, but sometimes it seems all but ordained. When Dr. Nash persuaded Stephen Cleobury to commission an American composer for the first time to write a new carol for the 1997 Festival, I was invited to write the words for it.

I procrastinated long after the selection of Stephen Paulus as composer, and very long after the agreed delivery date. Back in England, and by chance living in Cambridge for a year, I asked Stephen Cleobury whether I might come and listen to a choir rehearsal.

The choir was in full fig and throttle; daylight gave way to the blue hour; the candles scarcely flickered. And other than Stephen Cleobury, the student organist and, I think, one verger, I was the only tenant of the chapel. What did I do? Sit in a pew, and sketch. Listen and sketch one little ink drawing after another – something I'd seldom done at any time in my life, and almost never since.

Next morning, my partner Linda, partner in a Fulbright Teacher Exchange, went off to teach at a hard-boiled Middle School in Mildenhall, and I began to write. During the previous weeks, I'd read about and listened to carols galore, ancient and modern, reacquainted myself with my father's *Six Carols* (Elkin) and received a precautionary visit from Nick Nash himself. It was high time to get cracking!

In the event, with some ease and great delight, I wrote four carols within seven days. After putting them through several drafts I relayed them to Stephen Paulus in Minnesota. He selected 'Pilgrim Jesus', as I imagined he well might, because of its echo of the Pilgrim Fathers. When we next met, he played through his fine setting, and I remember urging him to exercise the King's mighty organ to its utmost. I think now that this was ill-advised, although perhaps inevitable, given the triumphant nature of the text. But I'm more aware than ever I was of how there's nothing to match let along surpass the lyrical and tender: Patrick Hadley's and Bob Chilcott's versions of 'I Sing of a Maiden', Elizabeth Poston's 'Jesus Christ the Apple Tree', Judith Weir's 'Illuminare, Jerusalem'.

It was a short step from here to my collaborations with Bob Chilcott, and he set all four carols, 'Pilgrim Jesus', 'The Heart-in-Waiting', 'Nine Gifts' and 'Jesus, Springing', as well as a short poem, 'The Wellspring' (Jesus of Norton):

> Infant of the bubbling spring
> well in my heart.
>
> Child of the sighing marsh
> breathe in my head.
>
> Son of the keen light
> quicken my eyes.
>
> Rebel of the restless creeks
> tumble in my ears.
>
> Disciple of the rising tide
> dance in my heart.
>
> Teacher of the gruff salt-wind
> educate my tongue.

Certainly Britain's most performed choral composer after John Rutter, Bob wastes neither words nor time... Always generous in his praise, he has never asked me to change a word, and the only occasion when we truly exchanged ideas was after I had sent his young daughter *How Many Miles to Bethlehem*, my account of Jesus' nativity, in which each of the characters speak for themselves.

Bob said he would like me to write a prologue and epilogue

for this through-composed mini-drama, commissioned by BBC Radio 3, and we sent each other a few emails about their substance and wording. We called the piece 'My Perfect Stranger', and it was first performed by the BBC Singers, Finchley Children's Music Group and the harpist Tanya Houghton at the Barbican before Christmas 2016.

Encouraged by the sometime Dean of Saint Edmundsbury Cathedral, Frances Ward, I've harboured for years an ambition to write an 'Edmund Oratorio', a full-blooded work that would ultimately lead to Edmund's replacement of the non-existent George (whom we share with Portugal and Albania) as our national saint. If ever there were a project destined to fail! To begin with, Bob showed plenty of interest in what would have grown into a mighty and notorious work, but before we could elicit substantial artistic or financial interest, his publisher stepped in and reminded him of his long list of existing commitments.

With Bernard Hughes, now composer-in-residence at St. Paul's School for Girls in the footsteps of both Gustav Holst and Ralph Vaughan Williams, I collaborated on 'The Death of Balder', a substantial choral and orchestral work, which was runner-up in the British Composer Awards (2009). He was so decided about how to tailor my retelling in *The Penguin Book of Norse Myths* that we both soon agreed that he should do just that, and simply check back with me when he had done so. When he wrote another piece for large forces, 'A Medieval Bestiary' (2010), Bernard invited me to come aboard, and the medievalist Richard Barber and I invented a host of non-lexical noises, while Bernard also incorporated my translations from the Anglo-Saxon *Physiologus* into the piece.

By the end of the century, I'd also collaborated with Giles Swayne ('Hubbub'), Lynne Plowman ('The Return of King Rædwald') and

Janet Wheeler ('Sea Tongue'), and discussed collaborating with Joseph Phibbs and several others. Arid in my twenties, thirties, and early forties, the field of collaboration had become challenging, fertile, and a significant part of my writing life.

Although I relish the way in which composers have responded to my carols, I don't think that they have very much influenced my work as a poet, with the exception of my scene-setting for Chilcott's 'My Perfect Stranger'. But of course they have pushed me towards greater clarity, relatively simple images, and towards the music of language, including silence.

But the last collaboration I want to describe changed all that!

I first met Cecilia McDowall in Chelmsford Cathedral in April 2016 at the première of 'A Time for All Seasons', a piece commissioned from us by Harlow Chorus to celebrate their fortieth anniversary. For this work, I took the famous words from Ecclesiastes 3: 1–8 ("To everything there is a season") and enclosed them within verses of my own, offering a darker perspective. At the beginning, it's no worse than the prospect of birdsong being alarming and sweet daughters singing out of time, but before the end, turbines will fall silent, plates will grind and the sea will curdle. And so –

> Before dust falls to dust,
> with a handful of quietness
> draw near to your creator.

We both approached our first collaboration with caution and courtesy, and both enjoyed it, not least because each of us kept the other abreast of our thinking, writing and composition, and felt free to make critical comments.

I was of course aware that Cecilia was a leading choral composer with a special feeling for the sacred, but that she had also tackled secular material (including 'The Shipping Forecast' with a text by the estimable Sean Street). I also recognised that she had a "communicative gift that is very rare in modern music" (*International Record Review*), and when I was invited by Barnardo's not only to write an anthem for its 150th anniversary (the first performance was in St. Paul's Cathedral in October 2019) but to suggest my composer, I named Cecilia.

I don't really have a feel for writing commissioned poems, and have recently struggled with an anniversary poem for the Almshouse Association, for which I'm an ambassador. The same was true of the Barnardo's poem. It was too full frontal, and St. Paul's Cathedral is far from the best acoustic.

"I have listened to the recording, captured from the dark and infernal recesses of my handbag," Cecilia wrote to me on the following day, "and it is better than I thought it might be. Though *lontano* might best describe the performance or even *indistinto*! But it is all there, wrapped in the St. Paul's miasma – the equivalent of musical mist."

Our next commission came from the Peninsula Women's Chorus in Santa Clara, California on the occasion of its fiftieth anniversary. I offered Cecilia 'Come Home, Little Sister', a poem I'd written years ago after the birth of my second daughter, Eleanor. At its heart is the idea that it is inappropriate to impose a name on an unborn or newborn baby ("you are your own word and cannot grow out of a careless visitation"), and Cecilia wrote a charming draft programme note to explain this, only to receive a response from Santa Clara we both considered 'pompous and inappropriate'! "If you felt there might be anything which could be said to support my shallow interpretation," Cecilia wrote to me, "that would be quite wonderful!" And again: "The bottom line for anything of this nature is it is so terribly time wasting, isn't it, time which neither you nor I have at our disposal. Argh!" So well put, and so entirely true. The sheer amount of time setting up, sorting out and surrounding collaboration as opposed to the heart of the matter, creation, doesn't really bear thinking about.

In 2017 Cecilia wrote to say she had been invited by the National Children's Choir of Great Britain to write a substantial piece with the theme of 'children in conflict' for their twentieth anniversary, and was just wondering whether I had any ideas...

Shortly after, my wife Linda and I flew to benighted Dubai for its enlightened literary festival, and there I met Nujeen, the Kurdish girl with cerebral palsy who – when she was sixteen – was pushed in a wheelchair by her sister Nasrine through seven countries to asylum in Germany. Her incredible story had already been followed on television by Fergal Keane, and described and co-authored by Christina Lamb in *Nujeen* (later retitled *The Girl from Aleppo*). "Nujeen inspires me to dream without limits," wrote Malala Yousafzai. "She is our hero. Everyone must read her story."

I saw at once that Nujeen's story might make a tremendous secular cantata, the story of a refugee, a story of great bravery, great resilience and sheer spirit. There and then, I discussed the idea with Nujeen and Christina (who later and most generously allowed me to base my libretto on her fine account).

Cecilia needed no persuasion. Then she and I travelled to meet the founder, director, and tutors of the National Children's Choir at their bi-annual residential course in Shrewsbury. Step by step by step...

Reviewing now the swollen files of correspondence about the form of the piece, including the vexed question of length, and all the admin surrounding the piece, characterised by the composer as "struggling all the time to do anything at the right time", and then revisiting cornucopia of drafts and Cecilia's many comments, I can scarcely believe that we reduced the whole story to five short sections and a mere eighty, often terse lines.

Accompanying the choir, Cecilia introduced a solo narrative for violin threading its way through the cantata and evoking, at times, an Arabic sound world! "I have come to understand so much more of the terror," she wrote, "the distress and helplessness experienced by those driven from their homes by the horror of war. As composer, I felt it important for the music not to obscure the text in any way, but to allow the words to tell the story, from despair, though hope and ultimately (and surprisingly) joy."

And that, in a nutshell, is why it has been a joy to work with Cecilia: so articulate, so good-humoured, and so completely aware of the delicate and crucial balance between words and music.

'The Girl from Aleppo' has enjoyed a successful life since its first performance in August 2018. My own contribution, and delight, was to persuade the Dubai Festival to welcome Nujeen and Nasrine back in 2019 and to mount a superb fully-fledged performance, on the final evening. Before the performance, Cecilia and I talked to Bettany Hughes on stage:

>This wreath of words is our choice.
>These flowers of song, they are our voice.
>Singing sorrow, singing tomorrow, singing tomorrow.
>Singing the song of life itself.

The Girl from Aleppo (Everyday Wonders)

1. Orphans of the World
Chorale   This wreath of words is what we have,
And flowers of song all we can give.
Singing sorrow but singing tomorrow.
Singing the song of life itself.

Nujeen. Nujeen.
New life. That's me!
But I can't walk, can't balance.
My two legs have lives of their own.
Plaster, braces, operations.
I'm stuck forever on tiptoes.
I often dream about being an astronaut.
Floating in space, your legs don't matter.

The scent of rosewater, hookah pipes,
Pistachios. That's how Aleppo used to be.
Dust, rubble. Every window broken.
Aleppo, Aleppo… like a ghost town.

We Kurds: orphans of the world.
My mother, father, my siblings.
All ten of us in three rooms.
TV was my school, TV was my friend. I learned
Soap-opera English by watching TV.
Shelling, looting, hammering, bombing.
We knew we had to leave.
Just me, my sister Nasrine, and my wheelchair.
Sometimes sisters can be as sweet as birds.

Chorale   Remember me? Remember.
I'm not a baby, not a girl, not a boy.

I'm just a number, an obstacle.
I'm on the wrong side.
Remember. Remember me?

2. Thousands milling at the border (The Journey)
Thousands milling at the border. Suitcases.
Bundles. Refugees – nothing!
We sold heirlooms. Family homes.
One man said he sold his kidney.
We raised money to buy life jackets,
A place on a dinghy, freedom.

3. I'd never seen the sea before
I'd never seen the sea before,
The mist, the spray. How beautiful it is!
Our phones we tied inside party balloons
To keep them dry on the crossing.
Of course I can't swim. I've never been in water.
None of us could swim. I became Poseidon.
That dove pebble a little Afghan boy
Gave me: I held it for luck between my awkward fingers.

4. A lost tribe pushed from border to border
A lost tribe pushed from border to border.
Stampeding for a bus, swarming across fields.
In the camps children drew pictures
With coloured pencils: a flower bright as blood.
The guards lobbed food at us – lawyers, doctors,
Professors, businessmen. We aren't animals.
The jerking, the jolting, the pain, the pain.
And Nasrine always pushing, pushing.
Greece, Macedonia, Serbia, Hungary,
Croatia, Slovenia, Austria…

"Please, Germany? Where is Germany?"
  The policeman smiled.
"*Wilkommen!* Welcome to Germany!"

5. Everyday Wonders
My head, my heart. Skipping and singing.

What delights me are everyday wonders:
People talking to me because I'm smiling.

My head, my heart. Skipping and singing.
Happy frogs croaking, summer rain falling,
Even the ducks seemed to welcome me.
A chance to brush my teeth in the morning.
Everything on time, all the strict rules,
Waking early, my first ever morning at school,
My pink-and-blue rucksack, red subject folders.

Sometimes in my dreams I make friends…
The animals at the zoo, some are as weird
As I am. A smiling refugee. Am I an alien?
Laugh as long as you breathe. Love as long as you live.
These are my favourite sayings.

My head, my heart. Skipping and singing.
Nujeen. Nujeen. New life. That's me.
Chorale   This wreath of words is our choice.
These flowers of song, they are our voice.
Singing sorrow, singing tomorrow, singing tomorrow.
Singing the song of life itself.

From Cecilia McDowall's and my cantata, 'The Girl from Aleppo (Everyday Wonders)' (2018)

On Writing a Libretto

A few stories speak so piercingly to the outsider in each of us that, when we hear them for the first time, we feel as if somehow we've always known them.

Two stories of this kind were written down about seven hundred years ago by the same man. Ralph of Coggeshall was his name, the abbot of a Cistercian monastery near Colchester in Essex, and he was describing "wondrous things" that had happened in Suffolk during his own lifetime. One story related the discovery near the village of Woolpit of two green children – the subject of Nicola LeFanu's and my opera for children 'The Green Children'; and the other described how fishermen at Orford caught in their nets a shaggy, naked, silent Wildman.

In his account, Ralph of Coggeshall says that the constable of the castle, newly-appointed during a time of great civil disorder, has no intention of letting the Wildman go without finding out precisely who his is, and may or may not be complicit in the Wildman's torture; and everywhere there are eyes, eyes watching and assessing how the Wildman looks, how he eats, how he will not or cannot speak, how he sleeps, how he dives and swims (this is more of a wonder than it may seem, for in the twelfth century the sea was regarded as a shuddering wilderness).

Nicola LeFanu and I were eager to work together again, and when we were commissioned by the Aldeburgh Foundation to write a new opera for the 1995 Festival, we looked closely at the story of the Wildman. We saw in it many pressing matters – language and identity, fear and self-preservation, law and order, religious intolerance, and believed such issues could provide sources of great dramatic tension.

Ralph of Coggeshall first calls the Wildman a "man of the

woods caught in the sea". But then he goes on to speculate whether the Wildman was human at all, or some kind of fish, or a vengeful spirit inside the body of a drowned man. It may seem odd to find an educated churchman thinking in such terms, but ghosts, fabulous beast and shape-changers ("I am a man upon the land, / I am a selchie in the sea") were all present in the medieval imagination.

What Nicola and I found compelling was that, throughout his captivity, the Wildman remained silent. Suppose, we thought, he were indeed human and not unwilling but unable to speak: what then would his silence imply? To what extent does sense of self and memory depend upon language? How, we wondered, did the Wildman experience the world around him? And what had happened to him? Why was a human being living on the marshes and in the salt water? When and why did he lose his power of speech? And how could he regain it? In this kind of way, with long discussions in sunlit and dark gardens in north London and Essex and Suffolk, and with a torrent of letters and faxes and telephone calls, we examined the facts provided by Ralph, and began to extrapolate from them.

Nicola and I naturally wanted our cast of characters to reflect but extend the brief responses described by Ralph of Coggeshall. Thus our fishing people live near the breadline as well as the shoreline. Superstitious, salty, and fiercely self-protective, they regard the Wildman as a threat to their livelihood and while others wrestle over what to do with him, they have no doubt. They want the constable to put him to death and, when he refuses to oblige, they decide to take the law into their own hands.

As one might expect, the canon of British traditional tales includes literally hundreds of memories and fantasies associated with the sea. In East Anglia, one thinks immediately of the bells of the medieval church at Dunwich, long since fallen from cliff top into the water, but still tolling under the waves; and of Shuck, the terrifying black dog who haunts the lonely marsh paths in his unending search for his Viking master.

It must have been fisherfolk who first gave tongue to stories such as these. They developed them and relayed their messages from generation to illiterate generation. In a sense, our fearsome fisherwoman Mardle Jane (*mardle* means gossip or yarn) is the embodiment of this oral tradition from which the account of the Wildman himself must ultimately spring. We never meet Jane without hearing her embroider fact and surmise and fantasy in the way storytellers do.

Like the fishing people, the townspeople precipitate or respond to dramatic event according to their own natures. The trader Ralph le Breton is slimy. He is also ineffectual. Wimar the priest, meanwhile, is not simply petty and narrow-minded but also reflects the frustration of life in a small self-referring community way out from the centre. Each man resents being at the constable's beck and call. Ralph wants money, Wimar wants preferment, and both try to turn the presence of the Wildman to their own advantage.

In common with Ralph le Breton and Wimar, the character of Sir Bartholomew de Glanville is based on an historical figure: the first constable of Henry II's newly-built and expensive castle at Orford. For him and his family, the Wildman is a headache, a challenge and a fascination. Theirs is the reasonable, questioning and self-questioning response. Theirs is the imagination and generosity. And theirs, of course, is the agony. Not only does the Wildman cause Sir Bartholomew and his intuitive, passionate Cornish wife Lady Eleanor to examine their marriage, but in their twin children, aged sixteen, we discovered not one but two characters just ready for a sea-change...

Mark and Ankarette are so impatient and innocent and vulnerable as they stand on the very threshold of their adult lives. Mark is fed up at having to stay in service as a squire; he wants to see action, all the more so as his hard-pressed father plainly needs help in defending the castle against Hugh Bigod, Earl of Norfolk. And Mark's spirited but sheltered sister Ankarette, betrothed to a much older man whom she hasn't even met, can't reconcile her own impending 'business deal' marriage with the images of love she knows from lyric and romance. So brother and sister may both see in the Wildman a life enviably free from the constraints and conventions of the society they live in.

I've described the way we've used Ralph of Coggeshall's text as a kind of springboard in addressing issues important to us, assembling a cast and devising a narrative. But linear narrative is not the only means by which the opera develops.

Except for the Wildman himself, the entire cast remains on stage until the final scene. And from time to time all their voices combine to become the many-tongued sea from which the Wildman rises and to which at last he has to return. These sea-voices, expressing the colours and contrary moods of ocean, are also intended to foreshadow and underscore the emotional tides of the opera:

> Dawn-dreep, shell-shine, heart's tide rising –
> Rumouring, memory, sheenskin ripple –
> Fingers, obsidian, asking all knowing –
> Spark and spearflash, sea-serpent, hiss –
> Gossip and knock, knock, wave-whack, plunge –
> Rib to furrow, salt-surge, ocean-rut –
> Overlap, overrun, overcome, undermine –

Since the Wildman is unable to speak, he has to discover his palate and, in a series of soliloquies, to learn or relearn words. The remainder of the cast, meanwhile, speak with many tongues, The Suffolk fishermen have their own dialect, Wimar knows his liturgical Latin, Lady Eleanor is conscious of the power of certain Cornish words, and Ralph thinks first in Breton, second in French, and only third in English! So another strand in the development of the opera is an exploration of divisive, unifying language – the word that alone will unlock the Wildman's identity and memory.

While writing this opera (and I think I contracted an 'opera-fever' from which I hope devoutly never to recover), Nicola and I engaged in endless, cordial, bracing argument. Together we developed the synopsis, and then the all-important series of 'progressions' in which we established the pulse of the opera – the crucial alternation of recitative, soliloquy, aria, ensemble, chorus, and orchestral moment. The composer felt free to comment word by word on the drafts of my prose and poetry, and I in turn felt free to comment on her composition. This is how Nicola described the quite remarkable way in which the Wildman's soliloquies evolved:

> One member of the cast, though, was in my mind even before the opera was contracted: Gwion Thomas. I knew from the outset that his was the voice I wanted for the Wildman. From those earliest glimpses of the music of the opera, I knew not only the sound-world of the ensemble, but something of the extraordinary quality I wanted for the voice of this sea-stranger, who comes to land seeking kin and kinship. Gwion was generous with his time and we improvised, together with Kevin, exploring the Wildman. If the Wildman is a selchie (sealman) then he is fluid, lithe, sensuous, by repute magnetically attractive to women, and also with something of androgyny about him. How does this mesh with the lonely young hermit from the marsh, a strange, silent creature of mud and damp, salt and sand? What is the voice of a man tough enough to withstand the North Sea winter, yet still carrying within him of one who has lived apart from people for so long? What, above all, is the inner voice of one who is mute?
>
> Finding answers to these questions meant much more than endless discussion, reading, experiment, marvellous though that was. It meant a journey into the hinterlands of the imagination. As I

began to discover the Wildman's first soliloquies, I found that word and music were inseparable. Words of my own began to mingle with Kevin's in a kind of quarry from which the music emerged; whether a sound was a syllable or note was often irrelevant; in the ambiguity of the Wildman's language, word and music had become one. Thus a continuous flow was established, back and forth between Kevin and myself, as the soliloquies were discovered, refined, revised, and discovered again. As late as summer 1994, when the opera was largely composed, Kevin was finding new syllables for the Wildman's first soliloquy, to fit with the sounds that had finally crystallised musically; and in January 1995, as I completed the fair copy of the full score, we both heard the need for different vowel sounds in the Wildman's last phrases, and altered music and text accordingly.

In their operatic "treatise on dramaturgy", Richard Strauss and Clemens Krauss examine the relationship of words and music. "*Prima le parole – dopo la musica!*" says the poet. "*Prima la musica – dopo le parole!*" says the composer. "Loving enemies... friendly rivals... brother and sister..." Since the opera repertoire contains plenty of opera with fine music and dire libretti but no opera with dire music and fine libretti, it seems clear that music is the senior partner. But in the making of 'The Wildman' such an issue was scarcely an issue at all. Ours was the story of an unusually close and fruitful collaboration.

From *The Wildman*

Mardle Jane is an old fisherwoman. Mark is the sixteen-year-old son of the constable of Orford castle, Sir Bartholomew de Glanville. Ankarette is Mark's twin sister. Ralph le Breton is a trader. Meg is a castle servant. The whole cast except for the Wildman also form a chorus of sea-voices who sing outside the action.

Mardle Jane	I'll tell you what. That sea-creature of yours, that's stolen away our herring.
Mark	He hasn't been near them.
Mardle Jane	You don't know nothing. Ate them all in the net he were caught in. Not a smig left. (*Meg gestures 'small fry' with her thumb and forefinger*)
Mark	He can't have done.
Mardle Jane	And this morning – the whole catch, that's wholly nasty and green. The whole cran. That old creature put a curse on us. A curse on us all.
Wildman	(*in the dungeon*) Karak Karak sed-gy-wik sed-gy-kik kit-ta-git-ta kek-tek ki-kuk – a a a tom gone to' to' to' torn all – glint gleam m-y o(pen) – pen my? who? you gone? you o-pen?
Mardle Jane	What you going to do with him? That's what I want to know.
Bartholomew	Jane, I'm not making a hasty decision.
Mardle Jane	The whole catch. The whole cran. The devil! Cut out that's tongue! Burn that on the beach.
Bartholomew	I need to know more. Is she right or wrong?

	I need to know more.
Ankarette	He's not a creature.
	I know he's a man.
	He would never harm
	The poor fishermen.
Mark	Blast Mardle Jane!
	I've watched the creature.
	Kept a proper record.
	What will my father think?
Meg	Did that hairy creature
	Really ate our herring?
Ralph	And what will you do now, Constable?
	You're in the pickle.
Bartholomew	Jane, I'll decide what to do with him.
Ralph	Will you now? We'll see.
Bartholomew	Get along with you now!
Mardle Jane	Mardle Jane knows what's ripe, what's rotten. (taps her forehead) They're all about: boggarts and bogles and them nine daughters of the sea. And now this old creature. All this haffling and jaffling.
Ralph	*Ann hini goz! Quelle pagaille!*
Mardle Jane	You mark my words. (*exit Mardle Jane, Meg and Ralph*)
Bartholomew	(*to Mark*) That's Orford for you. They'd believe anything.
Wildman	I you I you I you I you I you I you I you I you I you I you I you I you I me me m'rember m'rem remember names names rember names Jenny Wren, Cocky Robin, Cuth Culver, Sammy Spink! Madge, Mavis, Martinet, Devilin, Tarsel, Titty-wren, Pudden-e-poke. Unna, tinna, wether, tether, pinkie, hater, skater, sara, dara,

dick! Dick Divendop, Henry Hodipeke, Ollie Otter, Simon Seal, Bat Brack, Betty Brock, Bonny Boots, Bitter Better, Betty, Batter, Bitty, Bittering, Bittern! (*he booms*) – naming amming being them they I not knot throat lock halter them they them they naming them naming they talk I not talk I not speak I I I speak

Ankarette How he moves! He moves – he swims through air. He's like a seal. That piper! He caught it on the wing. (*pauses*) Not a word. Not one. Why can't he talk to me? I know he's a man. (*light on Ankarette dims*)

From *The Wildman* (1995)

NORSE
....

When Eric Ravilious travelled to Iceland as a war artist, his feeling was of having come home. And that is what I felt when I read the Icelandic sagas and Norse myths, and first travelled to Iceland almost fifty years ago. I knew I was embarking on a journey challenging and vital: an experience as much physical as intellectual and creative.

So much of who we are and what we do – we scarcely give them a second thought. In our parish, there's one small field known as the Viking Field and, next to it, another in which the farmer always leaves one swathe of golden wheat or barley unharvested. Does he know why? All around us are signs of the long and exhausting conflict between the Anglo-Saxons and invader-settler Vikings that began in 793AD and ended only when Harald Hardrada sailed south in 1066. Our words, our settlements, our days of the week, our attitudes, our heritage: they're all inextricably mixed.

In what will, I suppose, be my last novel, *Kata and Tor*, about the mutual attraction of a Viking boy for an Anglo-Saxon girl, I've tried to identify some of the similarities and differences between the two cultures, as well as dwelling on their beauty and terror.

And of course I've been aware – only too aware – that while the myth-makers of different civilisations tell us how the world began and will end, reflecting particulars of their own environment, it's the Norse mythology that warns us that we'll reap what we sow.

But… that tree. Yggdrasill. The tree of sacrifice. The life-giver. Give me and all those whom I love, if not a sip of morning dew a bottle or two of Akvavit, and let us lie long and deep within it.

Look North

The great poet W. H. Auden stood up. A drift of cigarette ash fell to the floor from his jacket and trousers. Then several sixpences followed one another through the hole in his right trouser pocket and ran rings around him.

"I know your *Beowulf*," he said. "You should translate or tell the great old stories of Northern Europe. Almost everyone looks south. The Mediterranean... the Bible... How well do you know the Norse myths? The Germanic legends? Those are *our* stories – the stories of Northwest Europe."

Now and then, but only now and then, advice or example can set you on fire.

Yes, I'd skimmed through some of the Norse myths when I was a boy, including versions by Annie Keary and Katherine Boult; and I was aware of later versions by Barbara Leonie Picard and Roger Lancelyn Green. I relished Edward Burne-Jones' brooding portrait of Odin – an Odin become the very essence of pre-Raphaelite sensibility – and the superb illustrations by Arthur Rackham for Wagner's '*Der Ring des Nibelungen*', but it was only years later that the stupendous cycle itself worked its way into my head and heart and nervous system.

But now I started to immerse myself in translations of the sources (published by The American-Scandinavian Foundation), and to read widely about myth and religion as well as delving into Scandinavian history and archaeology.

That was that. Quashing the surprise and concern of my family and friends with my sheer certainty, I threw over my rewarding job as editorial director of Victor Gollancz, secured a small grant from the Arts Council, headed north to Iceland for a long camping holiday with my two young sons, and embarked on a version of the Norse myths.

Well! Precipitate decisions sometimes have lasting consequences. This one did, and still does, but that's another saga, perhaps for another time. As W. H. Auden wrote in his *Letters from Iceland*, "Few English people take an interest in Iceland, but in those few the interest is passionate."

When I edited *The Oxford Book of Travel Verse*, I included a superb poem by George Barker, 'The Oak and the Olive'. After living for seven years in Italy, he says he has come to think of it as resembling "a delicious garden inhabited by seven-year-old children, where white and gold sunlight tend to deprive one of the pessimistic faculty" and –

> It is harder to indulge there
> the natural Anglosaxon melancholy
> because I, for instance, found a bough of oranges
> growing through the skylight of my lavatory.

Barker describes the chilling rain in the North as "a moral punitive":

> I write this in
> a Norfolk August and the rains pour down
> daily upon a landscape which derives
> its masculine nobility from the simple
> fact that it has survived. It has survived
> the flood, the winter, the fall and the Black
> nor'easter.

At the heart of this poem is the opposition of innocence and guilt, and I know of no more vivid or convincing contrast of North and South.

Until the end of the nineteenth century, the true North (north, that's to say, of the British Isles) was *extra*. It was outside the cultural mainstream. The best topographical accounts of Iceland were *Letters from High Latitudes* by Lord Dufferin (1858) and William Morris' *Journal* (1871–3).

Boreas, the north wind, froze everything with his icy fingers; it was more dark than light, and for long months entirely dark; it was lonely, dreary, implacable, dangerous, magical.

W. H. Auden himself had a hand in changing cultural conceptions not only with his *Letters from Iceland* and poems such as 'In Praise of Limestone' but with his translations (with Paul B. Taylor) of the poems on mythology, cosmogony and Norse heroes in the *Elder Edda*, made in about 1200 AD. And another crucial stepping-stone was the decision by Penguin Books to publish translations first by Magnus Magnusson and Hermann Palsson, and then by Palsson with Paul Edwards) of many of the witty, thrilling and rapid Icelandic sagas – the cornerstone of West European fiction.

The most comprehensive account of early and changing attitudes to the actual and conceptual North is that by Peter Davidson in *The Idea of North* (2005); while what has happened during the last generation is akin to a tsunami of recognition of the presence and power and significance of North by historians, topographers, poets, novelists for adults and children, artists and composers.

I'm thinking of authoritative studies of the Norse world by Neil Price, (who was also the brains and backbone behind the Netflix series, 'The History of the Vikings') and a host of scholars, as well as novels for adults by Cecilia Holland, Francis Berry and George Mackay Brown, and for children by Joanne Harris and Francesca Simon, among the best to be set in Iceland since the work of Iceland's unique Nobel prizewinner, Halldor Laxness.

While I was giving lectures at the University of Reykjavik some years ago, I was invited to drive out to meet Laxness, and as I sat in his little study entirely surrounded by shelves of the translations of his great books, and listened, I drowsed in the heat of the log fire.

I felt as if I were taking my first steps across the rainbow bridge towards Asgard.

I think I'm right in saying that the Belgian King Leopold was the last king actually to lead his army into battle – this during the First World War – as so many kings and generals had done for centuries before.

In so many ways, Iceland past and present are of one piece, and it seems entirely appropriate that their great president Vigdis Finnbogadottir (who served three five-year terms from 1980 until 1996) should in the same spirit have been not only a forceful political leader, elected on a platform that included throwing out the USA military stationed in Iceland but a cultural leader, translator of Giradoux and Samuel Beckett, and ex-director of the Iceland's National Theatre.

While visiting our late Queen during the Cod Wars, she was entertained by the Lord Mayor of London and spoke at the Mansion House. The burghers must have fully expected to hear their fill of political and economic argument, however charmingly put, but Vigdis began, "I'm an Icelander, and in Iceland our greatest asset is our language." She then proceeded to tell one sharp, witty story after another, and by the end everyone was eating out of her hand.

I described the amount of attention now given to the North, and especially Iceland, as being akin to a tsunami, the great mass of which we could call derivatives: Scandi noir in all its forms, in which silence is as present as language, and landscape, and light and dark play such a crucial part; the vastly popular Marvel Thor films; *Game of Thrones*, based on the novels of G. R. R. Martin, hugely influenced by Norse mythology; and the worldwide success of the film adaptations of J. R. R. Tolkien's novels.

Just three years ago I took part in a rather remarkable conference, at the University of Cork, 'Reimagining the Vikings', at which distinguished academics sat shoulder to shoulder with leading practitioners of popular culture, re-enactors and digital gamesters. The centre held. Just about.

And before that, I had translated the poem 'North' by Rolf Jacobsen to be wrapped around the base of the Trafalgar Square Norwegian Christmas tree – this after taking primary school children to a snowy forest outside Oslo to witness the felling of that tree:

> Look north more often.
> Walk into the wind, your cheeks will blaze.
> Find the rough path. Stick to it.
> It's shorter.
> North is best.
> Winter's sky-flames, summer nights' sun-miracle.
> Walk into the wind. Climb mountains.
> Look north.
> More often.
> It's a long one, this country.
> Most is north.

Within a couple of generations, we have all learned to Look North. The exceptional has become the norm.

My retelling of the Norse myths was first published by André Deutsch in 1980 and then by Penguin Books in 1982, and in her perceptive review of my subsequent 2017 retelling for children, Amanda Craig noted that "It is the humour, moral ambiguity and inescapable impetus towards tragedy that makes Norse myth so unusual." Yes, for all their energy and wit, the Norse myths have the darkest of hearts – and that's partly why they've taken such a strong hold on contemporary imagination.

It's true that many of the gods, giants and dwarfs are perfectly prepared to play deadly tricks, but it is of course Loki – the most vivid and savage of all mythology's tricksters – who is the deadly yeast in the mix, and whose accusations and betrayals must lead to our world's self-annihilation.

In his *Prose Edda*, Snorri Sturluson (1179–1241) tells us that Loki is "handsome of face, but has an evil disposition".

The trickster is greedy, selfish, and treacherous; he takes on animal forms; he appears in comic and often disgusting situations, and yet he is regarded as a kind of culture hero, who provides mankind with benefits such as sunlight and fire. At times he even appears as a creator. He can take on both male and female form, and give birth to children. He is, in fact, a kind of semi-comic shaman, half way between god and hero, with a strong sense of mischievous glee.

But as time goes on, the playful Loki gives way to the cruel predator, hostile to the gods. He not only guides the mistletoe dart that kills Balder but stands in the way of Balder's return from Hel; his accusations against the gods at Ægir's feast are vicious and unbridled; even when fettered, he remains an agent of destruction, causer of earthquakes. And when he breaks loose at Ragnarok, Loki reveals his true colours: no less evil than his three appalling children, the serpent Jormungand, the wolf Fenrir and the half-alive, half-dead Hel, he leads the giants and monsters into battle against the gods and heroes.

While I was writing my children's version of the myths, five years ago, my idealistic young editor was shocked by some of the attitudes and actions of the Norse gods and their makers, so I attempted to redress matters a little in this way:

> …I suspect you think there's very little to be said for the northern gods, but let me translate them into their makers, or even into your own acquaintance. Think of some friend like Bragi with a gift for poetry; or someone like Frigg

who – excuse my Latin – is a *mater familias*;
some old salt accustomed to iron rations.
A corn-silk blonde? A heavy drinker?
A woman driven by her instincts and passions?

Not only this. Look for the lines between lines.
Black scarves swirling, sweeping over tundra,
black grit smoking and scorching boot soles,
black bears, polar bears, packs of wolves,
mountain hares zigzagging across the glaciers
while the midnight sun bounces along the horizon
but then disappears for weeks on end.
Each fire flickers in its own hearth.
Nothing is ever easy on Middle Earth.

Home from the halls and highlights of Asgard,
I think you'd be smitten by the readiness
of the gods to take risks and laugh at themselves,
and admire their unflinching curiosity.
Their rampant sexuality might not be to your liking
but you'd be exhilarated by their energy and wit.
Maybe their childlikeness would disarm you
and you'd mourn at how, gods as they were,
they were fatalists, trapped in time…

My own interest in the Vikings and their gods is unabated. In the steps of Rosemary Sutcliff and Henry Treece, I've written two novels (*Bracelet of Bones* and *Scramasax*) in which a Norwegian girl joins a trading ship and sails east and south, vowing to catch up with her father who has followed the young Harald Hardrada to Miklagard (Byzantium), and then travels with them both to Sicily.

Harald was the greatest warrior of his age, and I've recently published a cycle of short poems in his persona during his formative years in Byzantium as part of the Varangian guard.

Passionate and decided, fierce and terse and I hope sometimes witty, they're not narratives but revelations, turning on Harald's engagement with warfare, leadership, love and the contrast between the appearance and values of the glittering hard-edged northern world, still half in thrall to the old Norse gods, and the softer, more seductive south.

In this cycle Harald muses that –

> We see only shadows of the gods,
> and they've very little interest in us.
> What they're said to have said
> is only what we wish they'd say.

Hardrada understands that we make our own fate, and it's in that spirit that he sets sail as an old man for England and his meeting with Harold Godwinson at Stamford Bridge.

Hilda Ellis Davidson was my lodestar as I wrote my versions of the myths. So let me end with her wise words in *Gods and Myths of Northern Europe*:

> In spite of this awareness of fate, or perhaps because of it, the picture of man's qualities which emerge from the myths is a noble one. The gods are heroic figures, men writ large, who led dangerous, individualistic lives, yet at the same time were part of a closely-knit small group, with a firm sense of values and certain intense loyalties. They would give up their lives rather than surrender these values, but they would fight on as long as they could, since life was well worth while. Men knew that the gods whom they served could not give them freedom from danger and calamity, and they did not demand that they should. We find in the myths no sense of bitterness at the harshness and unfairness of life, but rather a spirit of heroic resignation: humanity is born to trouble, but courage,

adventure, and the wonders of life are matters for thankfulness, to be enjoyed while life is still granted to us. The great gifts of the gods were readiness to face the world as it was, the luck that sustains men in tight places, and the opportunity to win that glory which alone can outlive death.

Axe-Age, Wolf-Age

"Dear men..." the new Archbishop of York dictates in a gravelly voice. I can see him compressing his leathery lips and hear him gritting his teeth.

Taking the pen name of Lupus (wolf), Archbishop Wulfstan unleashed a furious tirade just after the first millennium, aimed at the whole population of England:

> There has been warfare and famine, burning and bloodshed in every district time and again, and theft and murder, plague and pestilence, murrain and disease, malice and hate and the plundering of robbers.

The Archbishop's purpose was quite simple. In proceeding to list horrifying crimes in detail – gang rape, the disintegration of families who turn against and sell one another, treachery, the deadly spells of wizards and witches – he warns the people of England that they must either learn to love God and observe His laws or they'll never bring to an end the swingeing raids of the loathsome, pagan Vikings, and the payment of extortionate *dangeld*. Indeed, writes the Archbishop, you'll precipitate the Second Coming.

> Dear men, understand that this is true: the world is in haste and it approaches the end, and because it is ever worldly, the longer it lasts, the worse it becomes; and so it must necessarily greatly worsen before the coming of the Antichrist because of the sins of the people, and indeed it will become then fearful and terrible throughout the world...

Superstitious, porous, lawless early eleventh century England was plainly a rather uncomfortable place in which to live. Perhaps only monks and nuns living in the monastic foundations, and sometimes not even they, felt relatively safe.

But in predicting the Second Coming – that is to say, the return of Jesus Christ who 'shall come to judge the quick and the dead', and thereby the end of our world – Wulfstan was not only in line with Christian teaching based on early Hebrew beliefs, but (whether he knew it or not) with Norse mythology.

While it would be naïve to believe that, writing in early thirteenth century, the great Snorri Sturluson – poet, sagaman, historian and critic, as well as political leader – was accurate in all respects, he explains that he was retelling the ancient myths because of the likelihood that they would be forgotten in a country that officially adopted Christianity in 1000 AD.

In his fearsome account of Ragnarok (the 'Destruction of the Powers'), Snorri describes the apocalyptic battle between the gods and giants, involving all creation, in which virtually all life is destroyed, and the nine worlds of the Norse cosmology are submerged.

True, a spark – a seed – of life survives in the form of the young man and young woman sheltering within the all-embracing world ash tree, Yggdrasill; they will bear children and their children will bear children. There will be a new cycle of life on our planet. But for you and for me, for all of us: our world is destined to end in much the same manner as it was created, with the meeting of ice and fire in the vast space between them known as Ginnungagap.

Successive winters with no summers between them... tidal surges... toppling trees... places of raging flame, swirling smoke, ashes, only ashes... All this, and "The sun will be dark and there will be no stars in the sky. The earth will sink into the sea."

The Norse myth of Ragnarok makes it quite plain that the end of life on Earth is not some unforeseeable disaster but self-induced. It is precipitated by the self-interest of the gods, giants and dwarfs – all of them: their want of vision, lack of wise leadership... these and a growing sense of helplessness that things are irredeemable and can only get worse – a failure of imagination.

So what description of how life on our planet will end could possibly be more savage? And what could be more prescient? What could be more of a warning?

On Ian Crockatt's *Crimsoning the Eagle's Claw*

Not a storm-surge, not yet, but the tide of scholarly and popular interest in Viking culture has never flowed more strongly. One has only to glance at a recent bibliography to see the welter of papers, conferences, translations, and histories written since the turn of the century, while the market-place has been flooded by adult and children's graphic novels, films, cartoons, and computer games. Intellectual enquiry and general appeal came together in the major exhibition, *Vikings: life and legend*, at the British Museum in 2014.

But although more than five thousand skaldic poems composed between the ninth and thirteenth centuries survive, they have been swept aside not only because they are so very dense and allusive, and packed with kennings, but because translators have baulked at the poem's extremely demanding verse form.

In his exemplary introduction, Ian Crockatt describes the classic skaldic stanza, the *dróttkvæt*, as exoskeletal, in which the form necessarily if only scarcely contains the contents, and makes a memorable comparison – but I won't steal his thunder! Crockatt then convincingly argues that a translation can only be successful if it "seeks equivalents for the original's sound-patterns and imaginative reach as well as its narrative sense." William Morris was the last translator to attempt this, one hundred and fifty years ago.

So it's wonderful to report that the forty-one skaldic verses in *Crimsoning the Eagle's Claw*, most of them preserved in the 'Orkneyinga Saga', are really fine translations of fine poems. When I first read a few of them several years ago, I noted how passionate they were, how they had got under my skin, and were waking me in the middle of the night. In this short foreword, I would just add that the best of them are akin to fierce sparklers, momentarily lighting the dark; they're like random jottings and observations; spirited, almost gamey, and marvellously skilful.

What I (and I certainly won't be alone) find immensely exciting is that in these aristocratic, vivid, sensuous poems, I'm meeting a Viking face to face, and of course this gives the book both coherence and thrilling immediacy. Here's the Norwegian who was an Earl of Orkney; the man who founded the beautiful pink cathedral in Kirkwall to house the remains of his martyred uncle, Magnus. Here's a member of the Varangian Guard in Byzantium with stories of the old gods seething in his blood, who became a Christian. A sensitive extrovert... daring yet tender... a lover, a pilgrim, a warrior, a wit: Rǫgnvaldr was all these, and 'bragging' of his own skills, he concludes: "Best of all, I've mastered / harp-play and poetry."

A number of Viking poets came from Norway to Orkney, among them Turf-Einar Rognvaldsson ("I can promise you the greatest favour you could wish for", he told his father, "and that's never to see me again!") and the anonymous skald who composed the 'Darraðarljoð', the spear-song sung by the Valkyries after the Battle of Clontarf in 1014, and the author of the 'Orkneyinga Saga'. And as one might expect, their work and Rǫgnvaldr's poems bear the stamp of the Northern Isles (just look at Crockatt's glossary!) that lists no less than five but little known Orkney writers such as Samuel Laing and Robert Rendall, and the islands' three important twentieth century writers, Edwin Muir, Eric Linklater, and George Mackay Brown. Indeed, they're all part of one thriving cultural story.

Rǫgnvaldr's poems give us precious glimpses of a life lived to the full. They are spirited and generous. They're celebrations. And they are manly.

In a charming *dróttkvæt* of his own by way of envoi, Ian Crockatt makes a promise to Rǫgnvaldr. His superb translations ensure that it is very likely to come true.

From *The Death of Balder*

The gods and goddesses did not sleep; they kept a silent vigil in Gladsheim. Ranged around Balder's body, so white that it was gleaming, each of them was prey to his own thoughts and hopes and fears – what chance Hermod had of bringing Balder back from the dead, how to avenge Balder's death on his own unhappy brother Hod, what kind of punishment would begin to suffice for Loki, and what meaning the death of one must have for them all.

Day began to dawn: a lightening in the east at first mysterious, then quickly gathering speed and spreading in every direction.

Then with aching hearts, four of the gods lifted Balder's body on to their shoulders, and all the others formed a long cortège. They carried him down to the sea and laid his corpse near Ringhorn, his own great boat with its curved prow.

The gods wanted to build Balder's pyre in the waist of the boat, up against the mast. They took hold of the stern and tried to launch the boat, but their grief had so exhausted them that they could not summon up the strength to shift it on its rollers.

Then the gods sent a messenger speeding to Jotunheim to ask for the help of the giantess Hyrrokin. A great crowd out of Asgard sat near the water, watching the pulse of the waves. They were pensive and subdued, none of them so strong that he could escape the flux of his own feelings and comfort the others.

In a while Hyrrokin came. She was huge and grim, riding a wolf with vipers for veins. As soon as she leaped off her steed, Odin summoned four berserks and told them to watch over the wolf (and the vipers) and ensure they caused no harm.

The very sight of the four men in their animal skins angered the wolf; its eyes flickered and it snarled.

The Berserks seized the viper-reins but they were unable to hold the wolf fast. First it dragged them one way, then another, slithering helplessly through the sand, as it tried to break free. Then the Berserks became as mad as wolves themselves and in fury they rained blows on the wolf with their club-like fists. They struck it down and left it for dead in the sand.

Hyrrokin, meanwhile, stalked up to Ringhorn. She looked at the boat, so large and yet so sweeping and graceful, and gripped the prow. Then she dug in her heels and with a horrible grunt she pulled – pulled so hard that Ringhorn raced screaming down the rollers and crashed into the water. The pine rollers burst into flames and the nine worlds trembled.

"Enough!" shouted Thor. His fingers closed round his hammer and he felt his old strength surging back into him.

Now Odin strode through the shallows and gripped the gunwale. He climbed into the boat and stood over the body of his dead son. For some time he gazed at him. Slowly he took off his arm-ring Draupnir, the gold ring that dropped eight rings of equal value on every ninth night, and slipped it on to Balder's arm. Then Odin bent down and put his mouth to Balder's ear. Again he gazed at his son; then he left Ringhorn.

At a sign from Odin a servant stepped forward with a lighted brand. He set fire to the pyre and at once a steady plume of smoke, twisting and spiralling, rose into the calm air.

Thor raised his hammer. Slowly and solemnly he intoned the magic words to hallow the cremation.

Then a dwarf called Lit, who had lost all interest in the proceedings, came running along the water's edge. He passed right in front of Thor and Thor was so enraged that he put out a foot and tripped him. Before Lit had time to pick himself up, Thor gave him a terrible kick. The dwarf flew through the air and landed right on the licking and curdling pyre. In this way, he was burned to death beside Balder.

The painter was released and with it the pent emotions of the mourners. They wept as the boat began to drift out, rocking, across the water. They wept and they talked about Balder – the most beautiful, the most gentle, the most wise of them all.

Ringhorn rode across the water. Sea winds caught at her and tugged her away. First she was more boat than flame, but soon more flame than boat. She was a quivering shape, a farewell on the horizon, moving on under a great cloud of her own making.

From 'The Death of Balder' (first published in *The Norse Myths*, 1980)

PLACES

....

Now and then (and sometimes by happy accident), a writer alights on a perception and words that perfectly distil – and I do mean distil, not simplify – a time or a place. They become common coin, and we all know a few of them. "Oh, to be in England now that April's there"…"the great hills of the South Country come back into my mind"… "Should auld acquaintance be forgot"… words that bring with them, like as not, a sense of longing, an ache in the heart.

But of greater moment is the work of those poets, novelists and writers who, by circumstance or intention, have concentrated on some territory with such force as to make it, in effect, their own. Dr. Johnson in London, the Wordsworths in the Lake District and Brontës on the moors with their "arid wilderness of furze and whinstone", Daphne du Maurier and Charles Causley in Cornwall, George Mackay Brown in Orkney, Thomas Hardy in Wessex. I'm in awe of them. And this is without beginning to think about places beyond the British Isles.

And there's one further step, of course: impelling, human and divine. In the words of Traherne: "The corn was orient and immortal wheat, which never should be reap'd nor was ever sown. I thought it had stood from everlasting to everlasting… Everything was at rest, free and immortal."

On *The Oxford Book of Travel Verse*

The British have long prided themselves on being a nation of enthusiastic and resourceful travellers. As pilgrims and missionaries and in the armed services and as mercenaries, as diplomats and teachers and merchants, as Grand Tourists and package tourists, they have quartered this shining planet.

It is perfectly possible to describe this penchant for travel in terms of geographical situation, and historical challenge and necessity. But deeper than specific reason and local condition lies common impulse, so it may not be out of place to begin by saying something about how writers have described or reflected those basic states of heart and mind that have always prompted, or even driven, humankind to travel – restlessness, boredom, escapism, a sense of adventure, a predilection for risk, and a longing for the experience travel can offer of simplicity and wholeness and the old-made-new.

More than one thousand years ago, an Englishman cried –

> the solitary bird screams,
> irresistible, urges the heart to the whale's way
> over the stretch of the seas...

And in our own century, with his haunting words "I must down to the seas again, to the lonely sea and the sky", John Masefield echoed the Anglo-Saxon poet. Both of them are identifying the travel impulse or wanderlust as a kind of generic restlessness. Theirs is a pure longing entirely divorced from reason.

Not dissimilar (but not quite the same!) is the mainspring romantically ascribed by Kipling to his tramp, who sees himself as one of a breed who –

> cannot use one bed too long,
> But must get 'ence, the same as I 'ave done,
> An' go obsevin' matters till they die.

Here already motive has crept in. The tramp's restlessness is coupled with burning curiosity. Likewise, Robert Browning seems to attribute to 'Waring' (his friend Alfred Domett, who absented himself from London for twenty-nine years) not only travel-fever but also boredom:

> What's become of Waring
> Since he gave us all the slip,
> Chose land-travel or seafaring,
> Boots and chest or staff and scrip,
> Rather than pace up and down
> Any longer London-town?

It is not very far from here to the argument advanced by Robert Burton in *The Anatomy of Melancholy*. Why should people travel? On the one hand, says Burton, "peregrination charms our senses with such unspeakable and sweet variety"; on the other, the person who never travels is "a kind of prisoner... that from his cradle to his old age beholds the same scene; still, still the same, die same!"

A longing to escape Burton's treadmill of the same has, in our own time, with its huge growth of tourism, certainly become the most widespread travel-impulse of all. Escapism *per se* has not occasioned much good writing about the experience of travel, but of course it also lies behind much armchair travel writing, or what is sometimes rather grandly called travel in the mind. Samuel Taylor Coleridge in Xanadu and Edward Lear at sea with the Jumblies and W. B. Yeats on Innisfree have much in common with Louis Stevenson when he says:

I should like to rise and go
Where golden apples grow:
Where below another sky
Parrot islands anchored lie.

They are all writing of imaginary otherworlds; they find consolation in the marvellous.

To experience the kind of "sweet variety" Burton speaks of means to lay oneself to the vicissitudes of travel. One cannot stay packaged in a cocoon and hope to experience the germ of Italy or Greece or, indeed, anything distinctive and singular at all. The traveller must learn to expect discomforts, delays, disappointments such as those weathered by Miss Emily Brittle on her way to India, James Boswell in Mannheim, and David Constantine watching for dolphins; and then, won incidentally or waiting at the end of the road, there may occur some sight or meeting or experience that is worth all the effort and, one knows, achieved only because of it. This is why a relish for the unexpected, adaptability, and a sense of humour have regularly been seen as desirable qualifications for the good traveller.

Albert Camus took this line of thought one step further. "What gives value to travel", he wrote, "is fear." He continues:

> It is the fact that, at a certain moment, when we are so far from our own country (a French newspaper acquires incalculable value. And those evenings when in cafés you try to get close to other men just to touch them with your elbow), we are seized by a vague fear, and an instinctive desire to go back to the protection of old habits. This is the most obvious benefit of travel. At that moment we are febrile but also porous.

But that fear is not only a traveller's companion; it can also be his incentive. I am not thinking of the tens of thousands who follow relatively tame and trodden paths, but of the hundreds who are trail-blazers. These are the travellers who actually court hardship, in whom a sense of adventure has hardened into a readiness regularly to face danger as an explorer or mountaineer or round-the-world sailor. It is not difficult to sense the relief of Thomas Perry, one of Captain Cook's seamen, as he at last turns his back on the Antipodes and heads for home, while the mountaineer Wilfred Noyce's 'Breathless', written at Camp IV on Mount Everest, is a poem torn from the teeth:

> Grind breath
> once more then on;
> don't look up
> till journey's done.
> Must look up,
> glasses dim.
> Wrench of hand,
> faltering limb.
> Pause one step,
> breath swings back;
> swallow once,
> throat gone slack.

There is one more theory (at least) about the travel-impulse, and it is attractively argued by Samuel Rogers. In adulthood, he says, ambition and worry and fatigue and sickness of spirit replace the taste for natural and simple pleasures and golden hours of childhood.

Now travel, and foreign travel more particularly, restores to us in a great degree what we have lost... at every step, as we proceed, the slightest circumstance amuses and interests. All is new and strange. We surrender ourselves, and feel once again as children.

This sense of wonder, like fear, both arises from the experience of travel and leads to it. The prospect of rejuvenation! Rogers' words are corroborated time and again in poems in which the everyday is seen as unfamiliar. The drawing of water from a well or the sight of a man ploughing or a restaurant scene in Cairo or Shanghai seem wildly exotic. David Holbrook, indeed, comments on just this while taking a day trip to France and noting the marvellous otherness of lives and sights and sounds 'hardly a stone's throw away'.

> Nothing I want nothing but to look at the bread,
> The big sticks, *les baguettes, les ficelles*,
> *Les croissants*. I just want to stand here
> And smell the smell of France, and study
> The culture of *le boulanger*.

This is where the traveller's viewpoint and poet's purpose draw close. One sees the slightest circumstance as new and strange; the other wishes to make it seem so. First, however, the poet has to make that circumstance new to himself. And to travel, with perceptions heightened, is one helpful and attractive means of doing so.

The idea of making a journey to a sacred place as an act of devotion was certainly not unknown to the Anglo-Saxons, but it was, of course, in medieval Europe that pilgrimages became really popular. A new interest in the idea of travel as adventure, partly generated and partly reflected by a wave of guidebooks and pilgrims' diaries, and further fuelled by the highly successful *Mandeville's Travels* (1357), attracted a steady stream of visitors to Compostela and Rome and Jerusalem and many other venerated places. In his itinerary *Jerusalem History*, Jacques de Vitry tartly commented that:

> Some light-minded and inquisitive persons go on pilgrimages not out of devotion, but out of mere curiosity and love of novelty. All they want to do is travel through unknown lands to investigate the absurd, exaggerated stories they have heard about the east.

Maybe Chaucer's Wife of Bath was one such:

> And thryse had she been at Jerusalem.
> She hadde passed many a straunge streem.
> At Rome she hadde been and at Boloigne,
> in Galice, at seint Jame and at Cologne.
> She coude much of wandring by the weye,
> Gat-tothed was she, soothly for to seye.

The medieval itineraries that were written in verse, such as 'The Stacions of Rome', on the whole make flat-footed and wearisome reading. But the medieval enthusiasm for these long journeys and the physical hardship they entailed is evident in 'The Way to Jerusalem' and 'The Pilgrims' Sea Voyage and Seasickness':

> For when that we shall go to bedde,
> The pumpe was nygh oure beddes hede,
> A man were as good to be dede
> As smell thereof the stynk!

My anthology's interest in Christian experience and churchmen does not cease with the end of the Middle Ages. On the contrary, administrators such as William Strachey, first Secretary of the Colony of Virginia, speak in the name of Church as well as State; to the voices of pilgrims like Henry Newman and G. K. Chesterton, author of one of the inexplicably few good travellers' poems about Jerusalem, are added those of churchmen resident abroad, such as Reginald Heber, Bishop of Calcutta; while Thomas Pringle, a Scot who took his family to South Africa in 1820, comes upon evidence of thwarted missionary endeavour in the mountain-wilderness:

> A roofless ruin, scathed by flame and smoke,
> Tells where the decent Mission-chapel stood;

> While the baboon with jabbering cry doth mock
> The pilgrim, pausing in his pensive mood
> To ask – 'Why is it thus? Shall Evil baffle Good?'

Finally, the medieval passion for relics and modern curiosity – the proper curiosity that keeps its eyes and mind open – come nicely together in Geoffrey Grigson's 'Discoveries of Bones and Stones', a poem that also touches on something the traveller is constantly aware of, 'the casualness of discovery'.

There was nothing casual, however, about the daring and determined gentlemen who discovered and colonised the New World. Edmund Spenser lauded their enterprise in laying open new regions, "Indian Peru" and the "Amazon huge river" and "fruitfullest Virginia"; in Tamburlaine, Christopher Marlowe thrillingly celebrated the growing awareness of geography and new colonial ambition; while George Chapman emphasised the travellers' sense of patriotism and the recurring quest for gold:

> Guiana, whose rich feet are mines of gold,
> Whose forehead knocks against the roof of stars,
> Stands on her tip-toes at fair England looking,
> Kissing her hand, bowing her mighty breast,
> And every sign of all submission making
> To be her sister, and the daughter both
> Of our most sacred maid.

These explorations find their greatest direct expression in the pages of Richard Hakluyt's *Voyages*, a work just as germane to the understanding of the Age of Elizabeth as the plays of Shakespeare. And here, the same spirit is at work in Sir Richard Grenville's superbly confident 'In Praise of Seafaring Men'; an epigram about Sir Francis Drake, and in poems from the New World. What a pity it is it that Sir Walter Raleigh, the greatest of all poet-travellers, never chose to write directly about his voyages.

The more sober successors to these Elizabethan and early seventeenth-century travellers are the eighteenth- and nineteenth-century diplomats, local government officials, soldiery, landowners, and teachers who (sometimes philanthropic and sympathetic, often ruthless) consolidated England's dominion over her newly established colonies – India and Canada and Australia and all places pink! One catches something of the optimism with which they habitually travelled in George Berkeley's 'Verses on the Prospect of Planting Arts and Learning in America':

> There shall be sung another golden age,
> The rise of empire and of arts,
> The good and great inspiring epic rage,
> The wisest heads and noblest hearts.
>
> Not such as Europe breeds in her decay;
> Such as she bred when fresh and young,
> When heav'nly flame did animate her clay,
> By future poets shall be sung.
>
> Westward the course of empire takes its way;
> The four first acts already past,
> A fifth shall close the drama with the day;
> Time's noblest offspring is the last.

Some of these travellers wrote observantly about the relationship between occupier and occupied, and not always in terms flattering to the British. Sir Alfred Lyall, for example, paints a far from unsympathetic portrait of a Rajpoot rebel, hounded by the English in his own homeland; and in 'Studies at Delhi' he turns from the English playing badminton next to the site of a recent Indian Mutiny battle to scrutinise one spectator:

> Near me a Musulmán, civil and mild,
> Watched as the shuttlecocks rose and fell;
> And he said, as he counted his beads and smiled,
> "God smite their souls to the depths of hell."

The lines of a man accustomed to watching and listening, to noting discrepancy between word and thought and seeing both sides of a question.

The diplomat-poet and politician-poet are, of course, familiar figures in the history of English verse and Lyall, Foreign Secretary to the Government in India, was working in a long and distinguished tradition: Chaucer left no direct impressions of his sojourn in Italy, but Sir Thomas Wyatt in Spain and Sir George Etheredge in Regensburg, Matthew Prior at the Hague, Ambrose Philips in Copenhagen, and Lady Mary Wortley Montagu, accompanying her husband to Constantinople, all wrote delectable poems arising from their travels, while George Turberville, secretary to Queen Elizabeth I's Ambassador to Moscow, penned marvellously detailed and scathing verse letters about Russian character and landscape to his friends in England:

> The cold is rare, the people rude, the prince so full of pride,
> The realm so stored with monks and nuns, and priests on every side:
> The manners are so Turkie like, the men so full of guile,
> The women wanton, temples stuffed with idols that defile
> The seats that sacred ought to be, the customs are so quaint,
> As if I would describe the whole, I fear my pen would faint.
> In sum, I say I never saw a prince that so did reign,
> Nor people to beset with saints, yet all but vile and vain.
> Wild Irish are as civil as the Russies in their kind,
> Hard choice which is the best of both, each bloody, rude and blind.

During the second part of the eighteenth century, educated English travellers began to visit southern Europe in greater numbers than ever before. In the name of education, parents sent their sons abroad, usually accompanied by a guardian-cum-tutor, to learn French and Italian, marvel at the awesome landscape of the Alps, and see the glories of classical Rome and Renaissance Florence and Venice for themselves. In short, they conceived the idea of a Grand Tour, a journey by carriage or on foot through France, the Rhineland, Switzerland, and Italy lasting for anything up to two years.

In 'The Progress of Error', William Cowper derides the whole process of the Grand Tour as superficial, and Samuel Taylor Coleridge in 'The Delinquent Travellers' pokes fun at the new passion for travel:

> Keep moving! Steam, or Gas, or Stage,
> Hold, cabin, steerage. hencoop's cage –
> Tour, Journey, Voyage, Lounge, Ride, Walk,
> Skim, Sketch, Excursion, Travel-talk –
> For move you must! 'Tis now the rage,
> The law and fashion of the Age.

Travel may broaden the mind but it does not necessarily deepen it. Many Grand Tourists did, of course, respond superficially to what was, literally, a chance in a lifetime. But many others would have agreed with Lord Byron in Italy that, although "States fall, arts fade", and they were confronted by little more than a series of ruined shells and deserted landscapes, the power of Imagination could so play over them that "For us repeopled were the solitary shore".

These travellers tended to look down their noses at contemporary Italy. Joseph Addison, for example, deplored the lack of individual liberty ("Thee, Goddess, thee, Britannia's Isle adores", he wrote) and he found the Italians paltry and altogether unworthy inheritors of their great Classical and Renaissance legacy. While in France, in the name of the same liberty, William Wordsworth passionately subscribed to the ideals of the Revolution, with its famous cry of "*Liberté! Égalité! Fraternité!*"; and in Greece, Lord Byron gave money and formed the 'Byron Brigade' and fought for Greek independence:

> The mountains look on Marathon –
> And Marathon looks on the sea;
> And musing there an hour alone,
> I dreamed that Greece might still be free.

For the Romantics, a journey was scarcely worth the candle if, at its end, they had not endorsed some cause or witnessed – as Wordsworth had it – "types and symbols of eternity". But they were not the only poets writing at the end of the eighteenth and beginning of nineteenth centuries to be inspired by travel. Other writers, more old-fashioned maybe, inheritors of the light tread and wit of Pope and Dryden, and little concerned with the eternal verities, took as their theme the hazards of travel. Thomas Hood warns "how a little English girl will perhaps be served in France", while for Thomas Moore, moving from the high to low style in just four lines, it is the ubiquity of the English themselves that is travel's worst hazard:

> And is there then no earthly place
> Where we can rest, in dream Elysian,
> Without some cursed, round English face,
> Popping up near, to break the vision?

William Parsons, a regularly entertaining epigrammatic poet, cleverly exposes in just six lines both the duplicity of the Italians and the naiveté (at least when away from home) of the English. And Sir George Dallas, in his 'The India Guide', most amusingly illustrates the alarm, or at least the sense of exposure, that so many travellers experienced after leaving the shelter of their own homes and, for the first time in their lives, rubbing shoulders with all sorts and conditions of men.

From the middle of the nineteenth century, travel verse becomes more voluminous and more various. The Victorian poet-travellers did not have the preconceived notions of classical grandeur of their eighteenth-century forebears or the lofty ideals of the Romantics. In Europe, we find them off the beaten track, able to take advantage of improved (though not necessarily more enjoyable) travelling conditions, and the advent of the railway system:

Breakfast at 6, and train 6.30,
Tickets to Königswinter (mem.
The seats unutterably dirty).

And we find them often ruminative, prompted by the experience of travel to compare past and present: Matthew Arnold brooding on the "giant stones" at Carnac and thinking of his dead brother; William Makepeace Thackeray, tucking into a bowl of bouillabaisse and gently reminiscing; George Eliot brooding on Spain's Moorish inheritance...

Outside Europe, the Victorians not only continued to people the colonies but extended the Grand Tour itinerary to include Egypt and the Holy Land – the first English to travel in appreciable numbers to the far end of the Mediterranean since the crusaders and pilgrims of the Middle Ages. The poems by William Lisle Bowles and J. W. Burgon stand at the head of a tradition of verses about trips up the Nile and visits to Pharaonic archaeological sites that has continued from that day to this, while the abuse of monuments described by Richard Hengist Horne surfaces again in the form of an anonymous graffito-poem scrawled on the Taj Mahal. Alas, there seems to be few Arabist poets to stand alongside such prose-writers as Doughty and T. E. Lawrence and Wilfred Thesiger; but the long-standing English attraction to a hot dry climate and desert is, however, wonderfully well celebrated in Wilfred Scawen Blunt's 'The Oasis of Sidi Khaled':

> How the earth burns! Each pebble underfoot
> Is as a living thing with power to wound.
> The white sand quivers, and the footfall mute
> Of the slow camels strikes but gives no sound,
> As though they walked on flame, not solid ground.
> 'Tis noon, and the beasts' shadows even have fled
> Back to their feet, and there is fire around
> And fire beneath, and overhead the sun.
> Pitiful heaven! What is this we view?
> Tall trees, a river, pools, where swallows fly,
> Thickets of oleander where doves coo,
> Shades, deep as midnight, greenness for tired eyes.
> Hark, how the light winds in the palm-tops sigh.
> Oh this is rest. Oh this is paradise.

At first pegged back by the turmoil of the First World War and the ensuing economic doldrums, foreign travel for professional (and peaceable) purposes has during the last few generations increased from year to year, while travel for pleasure, above all as escapism, has become overwhelmingly popular. When we meet an aborigine in the company of Hugo Williams and with Lawrence Durrell watch half-castes (as once we called them) drinking coconut milk in Rio de Janeiro, when we pad across an archaeological site in Greenland with Francis Berry, sit with D. J. Enright dreaming in the Shanghai Restaurant. and then go on with James Kirkup to watch a steamy bout of Sumo wrestling, we very soon get an idea of the immense range of thematic and geographical possibilities available to the enterprising modern poet-traveller.

For a few poets writing during the second half of the century, travel and the experiences occasioned by travel have become a central preoccupation – and they take their place alongside prose-writers such as Eric Newby and Patrick Leigh-Fermor and Jan Morris in what is generally regarded as a golden age of travel writing. To read the work of such writers as Alan Ross and D. J. Enright and, above all, Lawrence Durrell is to enter a world that is at its best governed, in Durrell's own phrase, by "a science of intuitions": the poet so identifies with some landscape and its people and their interrelationship that, without necessarily being particularly knowledgeable about them, he can interpret them convincingly, even profoundly.

Many good travel poems work in the same kind of way, their first attraction is exotic surface colour and vigour; their second is a demonstration of difference, genuine difference of custom or behaviour or between the world of appearance, between the world of the poem and the poet's own experience; the third is their revelation of the correspondences, the shared humanity that enables us to empathise with the apparently disparate. In 'Anthropology: Cricket at Kano', in which a Tuareg tribesman sees meaning in the game's rituals, Stewart Brown takes things one stage further, acknowledging the correspondence but concluding:

> So, at stumps, nomad and exile
> pursue their disparate paths,
> amicably separate, rooted in certainties
>
> centuries old, our rootlessness
> a fragile bond that will not bear embrace.

With this allusion to identity and rootlessness, travel poetry engages with one of the main concerns of twentieth-century literature. Such talk of belonging is not confined to Brown's poem. On the contrary, the idea that through travel people learn not only about other people and places but about themselves is a leitmotif of modern travel verse. And George Barker gave this theme of self-discovery a wider meaning in 'The Oak and the Olive', writing not only as an individual but as Englishman and north-west European.

As often as not, it is the very moment when the traveller pauses and looks over his shoulder that he finds himself looking into a mirror. Sudden longing for home, or the act of returning home, also leads him, as it did W. H. Auden, on an inward journey:

> Red after years of failure or bright with fame,
> The eyes of homecomers thank these historical cliffs:
> 'The mirror can no longer lie nor the clock reproach;
> In the shadow under the yew, at the children's party,
> Everything must be explained.'

The Kings of the Irish

Back to the Aran Islands, swimming under the paws of Ireland in the brash Atlantic. Back along the spine of Inishmore, marvelling at acres of limestone pavement shining after an evening shower. Back to Kilmurvey House.

The door was open. I stepped down the gloomy passage and into the bright kitchen, and at once knew why I had come back

Bridget and Treasa Johnston Hernon's kitchen exhales a kind warmth, generated by the splendid old cooker. The upright chairs ranged around it are shiny with use, promising racy conversation and laughter. There are several aromas in the air – the soda bread baking in the oven, the greasy black pudding fried at breakfast and the floury smell of boiled potatoes, the best I have ever tasted.

"It's Kevin, so it is!" says Treasa.

"Arra!" says Bridget, "it's Kevin at last."

Bridget is in her sixties now, and her daughter Treasa almost thirty. They speak simultaneously, and both smile generous smiles. Together they preside over the island's most highly reputed guest house, twin hostesses at a kind of continuous house party attended by a succession of relatives and visitors.

"The Hernons," said Bridget, "the Hernons are the greatest conglomeration of people you ever saw in your life."

I have come back to the Aran Islands after eighteen years, and settle into a chair as easily as if I had been sitting in it the day before yesterday. This kitchen will be my home base.

What will the weather be like tomorrow? Bridget will know. What should I pay for an Aran Islands' sweater? Treasa will tell me. More than that, the kitchen is a microcosm: the policeman arrives, or the priest comes for a squabble, or the driver of a mini-van… all to pause, drink tea, exchange local news.

When I first visited Aran, there was no electricity, only generators, gas cylinders, and candles. Even now, high on the wall, a battery clock hums to itself. It is set wrong and hung crooked, as if to cock a snook at the importance of time.

"Days, months, years, Kevin!" says Bridget. "God, yes!" And then, brightening: "I'll tell you what. It's when you're working and you're happy, you don't notice time."

*

Ireland's eastern seaboard is relatively clear-cut. Land ends, sea begins. But the western seaboard is ragged and strewn with rocky outcrops, islets, populated islands. Inishbofin and Inishturk, Achill and Mweenish, Garinish and Gola – a musical litany. People live on no fewer than seventy-five islands off the coast of Ireland.

The Aran Islanders – the 1,350 people living on Inishmore ("the big island"), Inishmaan ("the middle island") and Inisheer ('the west island') – are the most celebrated of Ireland's wind-swept communities. This is partly because they live in so desolate a place, on islands without trees, in little hamlets of low-slung cottages; partly because of Inishmore's stunning horizontal limestone expanse and its huge cliffs dropping sheer to the gnashing ocean; and because the scatter of ancient megalithic and early Christian monuments seem not to have been imposed upon the landscape but to grow out of it.

"No girl at all on Inishmore would marry to Inishmaan or Inisheer," an Inishmore woman told me.

"Why not?" I asked. "Wouldn't a girl prefer an Aran islander to a man from the mainland?"

"It would be too lonely there," said the woman.

And conversely, I've heard people say that the mainland is altogether too large and intimidating. This was perfectly described almost a century ago by Maurice O'Sullivan in his classic *Twenty Years A-Growing* (1933):

Half-way up the Clasach I looked back and saw the crowds ascending the road from the chapel.

"Oh Lord, look at all the people coming to the races!"

"Oh, mo léir, aren't there many people in the world!"

When we came in sight of the parish of Ventry, Tomás was lost in astonishment.

"Oh, Maurice, isn't Ireland wide and spacious?"

"Upon my word, Tomás, she is bigger than that. What about Dingle where I was long ago?'

"And where is Dingle?"

"To the south of that hill."

"Oh Lord, I always thought there was nothing in Ireland, only the Blasket, Dunquin and Iveragh. Look at that big high hill beyond."

*

Inishmore is not for those who need spoon-feeding or who insist on having a shower in their rooms. It's for those who want simple clean lodgings, an unhurried pace and dramatic weather, who respond to time-honoured stone acres, rugged shores and wind-tormented seas, and who welcome hearty food and unexpected companionship, the flickering of the fire and lively talk.

I sit in the kitchen of Kilmurvey House, listening to the young curate, Father O'Donohue, who has just come from the morning's six-monthly court proceedings in Kilronan. One man drunk and disorderly. Two men in a fistfight. Two women who went to the pub for lunch on the day of the annual First Communion and were still celebrating after the pub's closing hours, more than twelve hours later.

"The judge asked when the Communion began," Father O'Donohue reported. "'Eleven o'clock, your honour,' said one of the women."

"Arra!" cries Bridget, throwing up her hands, always so quick to seize the bright thread of humour in the fabric of island days. "The Aran Isles forevermore!"

Come to Inishmore by boat and you will land, as I did, at the little jetty in Kilronan, the island's only real village, though it amounts to no more than a spatter of grey houses with a couple of shops, several cafes and bars, two bicycle-hire sheds and a post office.

But no matter how long you intend to stay, the island's most dramatic and magnetic centre remains the same today as it has for the last 2,000 years – the spectacular prehistoric fort of Dún Aonghasa.

At first you don't realise quite how vast Dún Aonghasa is, because it was built with great hunks of limestone, much like the maze of stone hedges that give so much of the treeless island its unique hive-like appearance.

Erected by the Belgic Celts sometime between 500 BC and 100 BC, Dún Aonghasa consists of three massive semicircular ramparts, the inner wall thirteen and eighteen feet high, perched right on the edge of a cliff dropping almost three-hundred feet to the Atlantic.

I sat as near to the edge of the cliff as I dared and listened to the ocean roar into the caverns underneath. Waves, unhindered by even so much as a rocky outcrop for 3,000 miles, smashed into limestone, rose in slow motion like dancers and collapsed again.

The sea spray was lifted on the fierce updraft, and I tasted the salt on my tongue.

We know that for centuries – up to and just after the birth of Christ – waves of Indo-European migrants moved west across the empty green face of Europe, overlapping, fighting, intermarrying, settling: the Slavs, the Germanic peoples, the Celts.

And here, on the edge of a stupendous cliff, with their backs to the Atlantic, the driven Celts made this one last stone stand.

Was Dún Aonghasa once circular? Did the cliff collapse and part of the fort drop into the seething water? Or was it, like one fort in County Clare on the Irish mainland, actually built in the shape of a horseshoe?

Was the *chevaux de frise*, an army of pointed stones raised and tilted against oncomers, erected around the ramparts to repel not only armies of wild men but also herds of wild pigs? Was the place used for trading, for sacred ceremony, for observation of sun and moon and stars, as well as for defence?

These are the questions archaeologists and historians have asked about this fort. And because there's so little agreement, there is still room for the nonspecialist to speculate.

I see Dún Aonghasa as a kind of symbol. I see it as standing for heroic last-ditch resistance, then and now, here and everywhere. I see it as the statement of a people with nowhere further to go.

*

I've been searching for the riddle master, and I cannot find him. He is a man permanently employed by the Office of Public Works to maintain the ruins of the Iron Age forts and medieval churches on the island – the Black Fort, the Church of the Four Comely Saints, Turmartin Tower and the Seven Churches, of which only two remain.

From time to time this man falls into conversation with passersby and asks them riddles. Sometimes he plays for a wager, say a pint of Guinness. Today it was the turn of two Americans staying at Kilmurvey House.

"How can you tell Adam from the other people you'll meet in paradise?" he asked them. They cleverly guessed that Adam would be missing a rib, but the riddle master rejected that idea. He was, however, in no hurry to provide the answer himself.

Sitting after supper in the warmth of Bridget's kitchen, it occurred to me that the Aran Islands abound with unanswerable questions. It's a place of mysteries, stories of fairies trooping up at Black Fort and Dún Aonghasa, and of a recently deceased priest who still makes his rounds as a ghost, accompanied by a greyhound without legs.

All that seemed rather improbable as the everyday talk ebbed and flowed around me. "Agas, they're mighty cookers, but the price is fierce" … "Tomorrow will be a bit whiskery" … "Off you go now, and mind you behave yourselves."

This last directive was intended for me and my fellow guests – a German woman returned here, like me, after a long absence, and a couple from Dublin. We were about to visit the local pub. Donning our hats and coats, we stepped out into the starless night. It was so dark that, in the name of a drink, we kept walking into stone walls. So we linked arms and, four-abreast, advanced into the night.

Then out of the dark night welled a darker shape. The German woman gave a start and yelped. The shape – a man, if that is what he was – walked right through us, and we through him, or else he glided between our linked arms. We turned around, but there was no sign of him.

Thomas Dirrane's pub consisted of a single room, perhaps seven-and-a-half feet high. the floor was bare concrete. There were benches along the walls, and on the benches 18 islanders, all men, who courteously greeted and studiously ignored us. So we bought our draught Guinness and sat waiting, as the saying is, for a chance.

The talk of the men of Inishmore is not at all like that in the rest of Ireland. It is not a gabble and it is not strident; it is a sustained susurrus, not altogether unlike the humming of a swarm of bees or the sound of the distant summer sea. I think no one significantly raised his voice during the two hours we were at Thomas Dirrane's.

The atmosphere thickened with smoke from pipes. Suddenly a man was on his feet and into a song – a protest song of the 1916 Rebellion with its refrain indicting the 'English monsters'. The audience were totally attentive, from time to time joining in the refrain in a haphazard sort of way, and clapping politely at the end of the song. Then the singer removed a pint and sank it without drawing breath.

*

When I first came to the Aran Islands, I saw decline everywhere: few tourists, little fishing, the population dropping more than twice as fast as in the west of Ireland. The European Economic Community helped slow down this decline. New markets have opened, and Aran Islanders have found new income from increased fishing for lobster, whitefish (cod, whiting and flatfish) and prawn, and from smoking their own salmon.

Standing on a cliff top in the drizzle that slanted in off the sea, I talked to a young fisherman. Under his woollen cap he had dark curly hair and, like so many of the islanders, a long narrow face and clear blue eyes. With a single rod he had caught seventy mackerel in an hour and a half.

"And I caught one hundred last night," he said, "so I did. And three times, I caught seven on the one line."

"Where will you sell them?" I asked.

The man was throwing the shining fish, all of them looking rather surprised, into an old sack lined with a plastic bag. "Up and down the island," he said. "I'm only fishing to help pass the time." He told me he fished from a curragh (a canvas-and-frame boat) for lobster, some of which goes to Paris and fetches a "good price" – about £5 a pound, he estimated.

The Aran Islanders' association with the Continent is relatively recent, but like people throughout western Ireland, their links with North America are more than one hundred and fifty years old.

Since 1820 more than four million people have emigrated from Ireland to America, and it is probably no exaggeration to say that every Aran Islander has a family association with America.

"There are ten men off the islands in America working," one islander told me. "They're working illicitly. And I know of five more going out this month."

Most of these emigrants stay abroad. Builders and plumbers, carpenters and nannies. Their photographs adorn the front rooms of little cottages, keeping company, as often as not, with time-worn pictures of John F. Kennedy and the pope.

I went to see Mary Hernon, who, according to Bridget, is the best knitter on the island. She and her husband, Pat, both in their seventies, received me with the simple courtesy that is at once deeply refreshing and humbling to those of us who rush around and regard time as an enemy.

For a while we talked about the different stitches that go into the elaborately decorated Aran sweater. The trellis symbolises the island's stone-walled fields; the basket stitch represents the fisherman's basket; the tree of life conveys family unity and strong sons; and the link is emblematic of the eternal tie between those who stay and those who leave home and travel to distant countries.

"Have any of your family gone to America?" I asked.

"Sure enough!" replied Mary. "I've five cousins there. My aunt is there too, and last week she asked me to knit sweaters for them. Six sweaters in all."

"That's plenty of work," I said.

"She's my godmother," said Mary. "I wouldn't want to let her down. After my mother died, each year she remembered and sent me something."

For a while we sat in companionable silence. A donkey ambled up and looked in the window.

"More fishing," I said. "More tourists. When I was here before, things were dying away."

"Yes," said Pat, "things is changing."

"And we're dying away ourselves," said Mary. Both gently rocked and laughed.

For the moment, looking east and looking west, the Aran Islands enjoy a precarious prosperity. The fishing is good, though the lobster is in danger of being fished out. There is a little outpost of AT&T here, employing up to thirty people making cables. And from July to September, tourists arrive.

But for all this, there are simply not enough jobs to stabilise the population. Inevitably it is the young who leave, looking for work, unwilling to accept the inertia and claustrophobia of the long winters. While it is true that the Aran population is declining at about half the rate of the other Irish islands, the long-term outlook is probably no more secure than it was twenty years ago.

Mairtin Mullin, driver of one of Inishmore's ubiquitous minivans, has just invested his life's savings in a half-share of a new boat.

"Not new, Kevin," he says in that soft island voice.

"How old?"

"Twenty-five years," he says. "That doesn't matter. It's how it's made, that's what matters. A boat can be five years old and finished, and another boat can live for years and years."

"Will you go out in it yourself?"

Mairtin shook his head.

"But it's profitable," I said.

Mairtin smiled a melancholy smile. "When winter comes with no visitors, and you have a wife and children, and there's more time to eat..." His voice trails off. "Life's not easy on the islands."

The Aran Islands are changing, but they change slowly. They have not lost touch with their old values and identity. Gælic, for instance, is still the islands' first language and is said to be spoken with greater authority and purity than anywhere else.

Some of the old folk tales and folk songs are still in currency too; it's not unusual to hear an old man break into song in one of the islands' pubs.

Curraghs are still used by the inshore fishermen. Made of tarred canvas stretched over wooden frames and drawing not more than six inches of water, the slender boats are rowed by two or three men with oars shaped like matchsticks. They bob and twist through the water and, when beached and overturned, they look like basking seals.

*

The islanders' arduous way of life, fishing in the moody seas and wrestling a living from the intractable land, was celebrated in filmmaker Robert Flaherty's epic documentary of 1934, *Man of Aran*, starring the islander Maggie Dirrane.

"That film put Aran on the map for America," Bridget told me.

I had just come back from a screening of the film in Kilronan and was rhapsodising about the way in which one astounding scene succeeded another: a boy casually sitting on the edge of a cliff, hooking fish almost 300 feet beneath; a woman lugging panniers of seaweed from the beach to the flagstone field where, with sand and grit and precious earth, it is used to build up beds for growing potatoes; savage storms and huge exploding waves; a man standing in the prow of a curragh, poised to hurl his harpoon...

"Flaherty once stayed here," Bridget said. She got up and staggered back into the kitchen carrying a solid brass harpoon gun. "One and the same," she said.

I knocked on the door of a white cottage in Onaght that looks out over the Seven churches, across the water to the Twelve Bens of Connemara, in the far distance.

A woman in her seventies now, time-worn but still with the same grace and pride of manner and that same, arresting, wild beauty, opened the door. Maggie Dirrane.

"I have come to see you," I said.

Inside the threshold she took one hand of mine in her two hands and said *"Mile Cead Failte"* – a thousand blessings. Then we sat each side of the turf fire she blew into life, and talked the length of the drifting afternoon. And as we talked, the hens clucked and tutted outside the door, and the large clock tocked as dependably as a heart's beat; those were the only sounds.

There can be no star of any great film whose life was so little changed by that film. It is true that Maggie Dirrane travelled to London for the première, where she was highly amused that a policeman should have taken her arm to cross the road; and when we were talking about developments on the island, her comment, "Sure, it's as capable as the Hotel Russell we'll be getting," indicated where her stopping place en route had been. But she lives now where she has lived always, how she has lived always, in great simplicity, ready to reminisce, philosophical about the future, mildly reproachful about journalists. I told her that I hoped to write something about Inishmore and more than once she said "I know that you won't write anything bad about me". More than once I reassured her that I had not come from any newspaper; then she noticeably relaxed.

Maggie Dirrane has not been to see *Man of Aran* since the première, although it is shown on the island each summer. "Sure, now you're as bad as the rest of them," she said, "wanting me to go to the film. They sent up a car for me but I wouldn't go." Perhaps it is not lack of curiosity that keeps her away, but simply a reluctance to claim the exceptional attention she would get from tourists, undue notice in this place where all the islanders are, truly, equal. At any event, she showed me the stills with justifiable pride and is evidently not averse to thinking and talking about the film at the appropriate moment.

A car passed outside. Maggie shook her head. "Gosh, talk about cars," she said, though we had been doing nothing of the kind, "you have to watch out on your way to Mass." There are forty cars on Inishmore now. ("And there's another every day," said Christy Bourke, the policeman.)

I asked Maggie Dirrane about the island's stories, traditions, songs. Often she said, "The best people are dead," and of my half-belief in the leprechauns, "The young people would laugh at you." But she did not and, after a while, suddenly took my right hand and began to sing. She sang the old songs of Aran in a quiet, cracked voice – many of the songs she recorded for Sidney Robertson Cowell's disc, 'Songs of Aran': 'The Ale Woman', and a spinning song, and 'Do-een Do A-diddle Am', a quiet song for sleep; and also 'Suabrel', a song which I have been unable to identify and which begins in translation, "I dyed my tunic, I dyed it green." As she sang, Maggie Dirrane moved my hand in hers vertically and horizontally to the beat of the music, a gesture commented on by Cowell:

Sometimes he would face me and with my right hand in his would swing hands to the rhythm of the song, in the manner of an old and formal tradition that I found among Scottish Gælic singers on Cape Breton Island in Canada as well. It is a hint of a not-too-distant past where (as still on the Faroe Islands) song and dance were one thing.

As I left, Maggie Dirrane put her hand on my head; a bird flipped out of the eaves. I am haunted by that picture of her, seaweed on her shoulders, and her proud bearing; and by another picture of her, unchanged except by years, so courteous, instrument both of a gay laugh and a sudden look of utter desolation.

Bridget was agog. And so too were her daughter Treasa and her friends, and Ellie, the serving-girl. As if I had been on some great pilgrimage.

"She did not," said Bridget. "She never sings now. Not at all."

"She did," I said.

There was a great deal of amusement. "Janey," said Bridget, "isn't it good to laugh now?"

Then I told them that Maggie had taken my hand. There was uproar. "She did not," cried Bridget. "Janey, why, she wouldn't take the hand of the Archbishop of Tuam!"

*

"Will you go to the ceilidh?" asked Bridget, bright-eyed at my chance.

She could not have hoped for greater enthusiasm. "When will it be?" I asked. "And where?"

"Tonight," said Bridget, and explained that it was to be an American Wake Ceilidh, and that it was on account of Brid Mullen – the sister of Ellie, the serving-girl at Kilmurvey House – who was "going away to America in the morning".

Once more my *wyrd* danced for me; this was the first time in more than two years that there had been a ceilidh in a family cottage on Inishmore, as opposed to a public ceilidh in Kilronan Hall. Mr and Mrs Mullen had sent word, said Bridget, that they would be happy if I would go. "Only take a present," she said. "Take a bottle of beer for the man of the house."

Early in the evening I walked to Thomas Dirrane's pub and collected some bottles of stout and, at perhaps eleven o'clock, set off for the Mullen's cottage in remote Bungowla. It was a cloudless, starlit night.

This time the journey to Bungowla was far from solitary. Small groups from Kilmurvey and Onaght were making for the ceilidh, and others from the south-eastern end of the island. there was the continuous sound of talk and laughter on the still night air. Then, as I rounded the last corner into Bungowla, I heard the music of the accordion ad, drawing nearer, saw the Mullens' cottage packed out with young men and girls.

I hurried forward into the cottage where we paid our respects to Mr and Mrs Mullen and to Brid.

"I'm only going for a year, or two years," said Brid, gaily. Yet if precedent is any guide, it is most unlikely that this girl, who had arranged to live and work in an American family, will return to the Islands. It was more than likely that this night was the last on which she and her family, never before parted, would remain one unit. No one admitted it; no one was unconscious of it.

In the small kitchen every chair and every lap had been pressed into service. People were jammed two or three deep against the walls, leaving a small square in the middle of the room. Segregation of the sexes was, however, entire, and it was only in the dance that male and female met. And dance they did, an endless succession of jigs in which the footwork of both girls and men was prodigious, the Viennese waltzes, occasionally broken by the recital of an unaccompanied song. There may have been high heels, a little nail varnish, and the singing of that extremely popular (and in the circumstances particularly haunting) song, 'Nobody's Child'; but through half-closed eyes, or the haze of smoke, there was little in this scene to date it.

The gaslight wavered and invested everybody and everything in the room with a greenish tinge. In the corner of the room stood the dresser with its Delft; the floor was concrete, parts of it covered with lino; a couple of religious pictures adorned the walls; and the walls themselves had recently been painted pale brown. And the faces, they too remained the same.

"These strange men with receding foreheads," wrote J. M. Synge, "high cheek-bones, and ungovernable eyes seem to represent some old type found on these few acres at the extreme border of Europe, where it is only in wild jests and laughter that they can express their loneliness and desolation."

As is the tradition, Mr and Mrs Mullen entertained small groups in an inner room, where they partook of tea and buttered bread and biscuits. The contrast between the cool of this room, the courteous gestures and quiet unhurried talk, and the increasing liveliness and noise in the kitchen, was very marked.

The idea that the islanders become more excited, more wild as the night goes on in order to fight off the sense of impending departure was first put into my head by Synge. It would be easy to overemphasise it, but I can only write that it seemed like this at Bungowla also. One or two of the men, having been too long in Thomas Dirrane's pub before coming to the ceilidh, were drunk and had slumped on their stools or in a corner of the kitchen, asleep. But the majority – and to my surprise Peter Gillon, the 'dreamer' was very much to the fore – danced with increasing abandon as the night wore on. The man with the accordion and the man with the spoons played until the feeling began to go out of their fingers. Then I, too, threw myself into the dance. There was nothing I could say with words to tell the Mullens that I, a stranger, in some way perceived their loss; I was swept simply into the prevailing expression of it.

Has it ever been better expressed than by Maurice O'Sullivan in *Twenty Years A-Growing*, 1933?

Time was passing and the appointed day approaching. A mournful look was coming over the very walls of the house. The hill above the village which sheltered the houses seemed to be changing colour like a big, stately man who would bend his head in sorrow. The talk throughout the village was all of Maura and Kate going away.

On the last night young and old were gathered in the house, and though music and songs, dancing and mirth, were flying in the air, there was a mournful look on all within, No wonder, for they were like children of the one mother, the people of the Island, no more than twenty yards between any two houses, the boys and girls every moonlight night dancing on the sandhills or sitting together and listening to the sound of the waves from Shingle Sand...

Liam O'Flaherty wrote a marvellous story, 'Going into Exile', about an American Wake Ceilidh. With passion and without melodrama, he presents the state of mind of the father, withdrawn, unaccustomedly gentle in a gruff way, unable imaginatively to accept that his two children must leave; he presents the mother, at last unashamedly emotional, ferocious in her animal possessiveness of her children; and he presents the children themselves, Mary and Michael, in a limbo, looking back and looking forward, sad and happy. And O'Flaherty records the inexorable passage of time:

At last somebody said: "It's broad daylight." And immediately everybody looked out and said: "So it is, and may God be praised." The change from the starry night to the grey, sharp dawn was hard to notice until it had arrived. People looked out and saw the morning light sneaking over the crags silently, along the ground, pushing the mist banks upwards. The stars were growing dim. A long way off invisible sparrows were chirping in their ivied perch in some distant hill or other. Another day had arrived and even as the people looked at it, yawned and began to search for their hats, caps, and shawls preparing to go home, the day grew and spread its light and made things move and give voice...

So, too, day began to dawn at Bungowla. The gaslight shadows of the men standing at the doorway of the Mullen's cottage faded. The sea growled. People began to leave; and Brid, for all her physical presence, she seemed already all but lost to her family, and to the Islands. It was a night of waves – waves of music, laughter, emotion, water on the shore a hundred yards away. And it had ended.

*

In Bridget's kitchen there's a little sign on the wall bearing the legend: 'Whichever room I show my guests, it seems they like my kitchen best'.

"What would you want your guests to go away with?" I asked her.

"That's a good question," said Bridget. Then, after a while: "I've seen people crying as they left here. It's not the place that makes a place. It's the people."

I never did find Padraig Dirrane, the riddle master. But then, it's appropriate for a riddle master to be elusive. If you should happen to meet him, you can give him an answer, the one I left with Bridget.

"Tell the riddle master," I said, "Adam won't have a navel."

"In the name of Saint Anthony," cried Bridget, her eyes shining, "what are ye talking about?"

Let There Be Light

And God said, Let there be light: and there was light.

But as soon as God saw the astounding quality of the light that He had created in north Norfolk, He must have been tempted, mightily tempted to leave it at that: not only to call it Day but to call it *a* day!

There are hours in this landscape when the light is so quick and keen that it articulates each last leaf and shell; when it burns; when we see, or think we see, what we cannot possibly see…

True, I knew a renowned poet living in Norfolk who never wrote for more than twenty minutes at a time, always had his cat on his lap and always had music on the radio. But he was the exception. The fact is that artists do hanker after the sort of working conditions north Norfolk can offer: its light and the space that light reveals, sustained quietness, involvement with elements and the natural world, the relative lack of light pollution, the sense of possibility.

It is, however, perfectly possible to find a place conducive to work – I think I'll resist that word inspiration – without being deeply interested in that place. Once, I wrote a sustained meditation on British megaliths while living in the middle of a Minnesotan forest, and in the same way writers and artists such as P. G. Wodehouse, Patrick Hamilton, W. H. Auden, and Matthew Smith have visited or lived in north Norfolk, without making more than incidental use of it, or without using it all. It's interesting and fun to know that Wodehouse's *Money for Nothing* is set at Hunstanton Hall, but knowing it doesn't actually help us to any deeper appreciation or understanding of the novel.

What is much more interesting is the way in which the north Norfolk coast has spoken deeply to many artists, some living here, some visitors, some Norfolk born-and-bred, some 'furriners', and even been seminal to their achievement.

So let me be specific, just as our light is specific and a foe to waffle and generalisation. Our landscape is seven-eighths sky: a vast inverted arena, a sky-dome in which there are often several simultaneous theatres of action. It's a landscape of horizontals – skyline, ribbed fields, decaying ribs of boats – in which verticals, including human beings, often look arresting. It's a landscape of the most subtle colours: shining pearl, pewter, iron, obsidian, many-coloured mud, olive, lavender…

Sharp-edged as it is, this landscape is also elusive. Witness to how many artists engage with the coastline as well as how many prospective purchasers there are, the manifold galleries in north Norfolk teem with second-rate images. For all the great work of the nearby Norwich School, north Norfolk has not yet had its Palmer or Constable, its Elgar or Britten, its Dickens or Dylan Thomas.

Another way of seeing our coastline is to think of its components as being in a continual state of flux: a fascinating complex of ocean, sand dune, spit, shingle ridge, creek, saltwater marsh, freshwater marsh, and field that all depend on one another, and are never the same from one day to the next.

At one level, the relationship of these constituents is mysterious, arresting, even thrilling. There is little in Britain more beautiful or subtle than an aerial view of the amoebic or anyhow embryonic shape of Scolt Head island and the saltmarshes penetrated by a Byzantine network of shining creeks, and little more dramatic than late sunlight on the faces of the far dunes, ribs of shadow sweeping in over the saltmarsh. But at another level, this shifting scape, and our own attempts to manage it, raise questions about identity, change and survival.

There is of course a paradox in artists finding anchorage in a place that is, of its nature, in a state of flux. But crossing-places are always potent, and many have responded to it.

Let me tell you what I admire. I admire the way in which E. J. Moeran, in the slow movement of his 'Symphony in G Minor', portrays the simultaneous beauty and danger of sand-dune and saltmarsh, and the way in which P. D. James uses them for her own dark purposes in *Devices and Desires*. I admire the dramatic marine weavings of the fisherman John Craske, who showed so graphically the hardship of living on the edge. I admire the brilliant black-and-silver skyscapes of the photographer John Hansell and the way in which, in his etchings, Norman Ackroyd juxtaposes the specific (each reed in a reed-bed, say) with the immensity of marsh or turbulent sky. Almost as much as anything, I admire William Rivière's first novel, *Watercolour Sky*, in which land, sea, and sky somehow become one indivisible breathing lung. Above all, I admire (for all his vile politics) the Henry Williamson of *The Story of a Norfolk Farm*, an individual in wartime Britain heroically struggling with his intractable acres, taking the view that a country that "neglected its soil, neglected its soul."

Inland, meanwhile, just a breath or two away from the sea and the astonishing, wide beaches where solitaries walk, looking for all the world as if they're the first humans to have been created, are the quiet green lanes that to Sir John Betjeman suggested "lost innocence", and the crusted villages with their continuities and secrets. On the face of it, they're peaceable, sometimes pretty places, hazelnut cluster of brick-and-flint cottages; in actuality, they used to be little less grim than the village of Dulditch so memorably described by Mary Mann in her unflinching, yet often witty, Hardyesque fiction.

Whereas the coastline breathes flux, these hamlets and villages breathe tradition. First built as passports to heaven at a time when churchgoing was a matter of course, our medieval churches remain architectural wonders, repositories of great art, and places of peace. Outside thick walls, winds swirl, skies swirl, leaves swirl: inside, the tiles are honey-polished, saucered by the steps of the faithful, and there our longings and fears, our passions (and maybe our God) await us.

Almost irrespective of our religious persuasions or the lack of them, churches have punctuated most of our lives. We celebrate our christenings, marriages and funerals within them. In a medieval church, we are at once alone and in a throng. George Barker knew all about this (from 'At Thurgarton Church'):

> I enter and find I stand
> in a great barn, bleak and bare;
> like ice the winter ghosts and
> the white walls gleam and flare
> and flame as the sun drops low.
>
> And I see, then, that slowly
> the December day is gone.
> I stand in silence, not wholly
> believing I am alone.
> Somehow I cannot go…

As the Church of England wrestles with itself and church attendance falls, it seems all the more desirable that its buildings should be used as places where not only the religious life but the cultural activity of a community is promoted.

In the summer of 2008, the glorious beached ship of a church at Salthouse entertained the most exciting mixed exhibition that I've seen in north Norfolk in a generation, 'SEAhouse, LIGHThouse, SPIRIThouse', curated by that defender of the faith of East Anglian art, Ian Collins. In this risk-taking show, several artists pointed to where matter and spirit may meet and, so to say, hallow the north Norfolk coast. Floating between the floor and roof of the nave, a swirl of starfish, 'Azimuth' (Liz McGowan) reminded us how to navigate by the stars. A Richard Long-like installation (Margie Britz) elevated clay to the clerestory and revealed the many colours of north Norfolk beach mud. An arrangement of mirrors had us craning our necks and looking over our shoulders, almost entering into the mind of the church's architect; a photograph of the exterior of Salthouse church (Harry Cory Wright), printed on a piece of stretched gauze the size of a large flag, paradoxically enabled us to see the church's interior *through* it; and a small oil painting by Tessa Newcomb, 'Then the Light Came', so utterly defied its frame that a simple unadorned altar and unstained glass window grew as large as the world.

As was apparent from many of the exhibits in this show, the great buildings of north Norfolk – the churches, the halls and houses that have remained in the hands of the same families for generations – continue to attract artists. Not so, however, urban landscapes and communities: fishing ports and resorts like Hunstanton and Wells-next-the-Sea, Sheringham and Cromer, that somehow combine faded grandeur with vulgarity. The joys of Cromer (including sea-bathing) were noted by Jane Austen and Elizabeth Gaskell, and extolled by Swinburne. But this and the other towns of north Norfolk still await their contemporary laureate.

You don't have to live here or even to be a regular visitor to discover that the place's lineaments may satisfy some inner need. Childhood is a bottomless quarry, and a number of writers – among them L. P. Hartley, Compton Mackenzie, and Katherine Pierpoint – have drawn on joyous childhood holidays here. Others have come for a rest-cure, drawn by the coast's sharp, salty air, among them the poet William Cowper ("God made the country, and man made the town") who lived for a few months in Mundesley and often revisited it, and Arthur Conan Doyle.

Parkinson's Law tells us that nature abhors a vacuum, and so it's no surprise that the empty, often bleak coastline abounds with folk tales. The saltmarshes are full of boggarts, bogles, will-o'-the-wykes, and Dead Hands. And it was while Conan Doyle was staying in Sheringham that he heard the story of Shuck, the huge black dog who roams the coastal paths, still searching for his Viking master, and immediately began to plan his novel, *The Hound of the Baskervilles*.

When I face south, I'm immediately aware of the presence of the past in this somehow time-defying landscape: here an archaeological dig (such as those underway at Ringstead and Binham), or an avenue of north Norfolk's 'native' tree, the holm oak; there the prehistoric chalkway that leads to the Icknield Way and the Ridgeway; and still almost everywhere, signs of the last world war, cracked and musty pillboxes in ploughed fields, concrete military roads with green spines and blisters.

When I turn and face north, I'm aware of the never-ending conflict of land and ocean, and of mighty human attempts to stop or at least stay the sea in her chains. Here, the dykes raised by Dutchmen, and the stony beach at Cley, shockingly rearranged (if that's the word) by a savage storm; there the controlled giving of ground at Titchwell. I'm aware, as was an Anglo-Saxon poet more than one thousand years ago, of the power of the sea itself:

> Wherefore my heart leaps within me,
> my mind roams with the waves
> over the whale's domain… returns again to me
> eager and unsatisfied; the solitary bird screams,
> irresistible, urges the heart to the whale's way
> over the stretch of the seas.

All this is grist to the artist's turning mill. Tides rise and fall – and no wonder we have many words to describe them: flowing, ebbing, dropping, making, on the drag. Then, one morning, the air begins to palpitate. Soon it quivers with the noisy, wild threshing of thousands and thousands of wings, the yelping and honking and wink-winking of a whole colony of pink-footed geese, coming home.

This is what many artists feel about Norfolk. We feel we have come home. We know that the end of each journey is also a beginning. The mind's mist begins to lift, all around there's a lightness and a brightness, and we can walk clean into the possible.

Scolt Head

It's Saint Luke's Little Summer: this cluster of days so often benign before autumn in earnest comes trumpeting in, and cloud-waves bank and roll, and salt-waves dash.

Nearby, drops of water are trinketing and percolating back into the swilling creek from the slimy old splash-boards. Little dinghies are giddying around, uncertain where exactly to look, while the larger ones, some clinker, some fibreglass, are still straining at their leashes.

Here on the Staithe, it's almost high water and the tide on the make, as a few older people still say, has left its usual deposit of flotsam and jetsam (such a pleasing pair of words) as well as a flip-flop and a beautiful, sinister jelly fish. But this time round, I'm hoping it will also bring with it some salty words.

A few minutes ago, I fished out a length of splintered sea-wood. It's mauve. No, violet. Lavender. All three. No wonder portrayal of the north Norfolk skies is so indefinable. Not even Crome or Cotman quite caught it.

I lifted the wood just above the level of the saltmarsh and aligned it with the horizon. Away west, I could make out the far nugget of the Royal West Norfolk Golf Club at Brancaster. To the east, I could see the great dyke that divided saltwater and freshwater marshes until the 1953 floods. Raised by Dutchmen, it leads in seven long legs from the Staithe to the far dunes and barefaced Gun Hill, undiminished since my childhood.

But the central three-fifths were taken up by the island of Scolt Head, the tidal island I've inhabited in memory and dream, punctuated by many visits, for as long as I can remember.

Scolt Head, seen from above, is a foetus.

A foetus beginning to uncurl, maybe, bracing its back to face the furious world, but still tied to its mother and embraced by the dark womb of the sea.

Seen from afar, across the forbidding saltmarshes or from out at sea with its tricky currents and shallows, sand banks and unpleasant short seas, the island is a bar of land about four-and-a-half miles long and at the most one mile across, lying low with significant dunes only at the east end and around its one building, the Sheld-Duck Hut.

It's a glorious complex, a mesh, a mix of sand-dunes, marram, sand-flats and shingle ridges, saltmarshes, stiff and grassy and sometimes floral vegetation, little pools that used to be called pulks, and the muddy tidal creeks little and large infiltrating its landward side.

To live in north Norfolk is to live in different kinds of flux, and the weather is often dramatically different here on the coast to a few miles inland. But I have a notion (call it an optical illusion!) that the clouds tend to dawdle over the offing and the island but sweep more rapidly over the wide saltmarshes. To see their shadows very slowly starting to peel away from the island beyond, until it is brilliantly lit, pink and gold, is one of the most electrifying sights in my world.

Sheld-Duck was put up in 1924 by the Norfolk and Norwich Naturalist Trust – 'built' seems rather too permanent a word for a single-storey glorified wooden shed, albeit made of Norfolk oak – and it replaced an older warrener's hut on the same comparatively sheltered site.

The only person ever to live in it was the island's Watcher, Miss Emma Turner, with her two terriers, and inevitably the press identified her as "the loneliest woman in England". But Miss Turner stayed only for a year before she was succeeded by Charles Chestney, and he and the later Keepers or Wardens (not Watchers) have largely lived on the mainland. For a number of years now, the Keeper's Hut, the Chestney Hut as it's most often called, has been used by Cambridge University for field studies.

Between my hands, I'm holding an early and perhaps the first log book of Sheld-Duck, almost as precious to me as an illuminated medieval manuscript.

In addition to the signatures, many by groups of Rangers and Girl Guides, there are photographs (close-ups of species of birds and lounging seals), lists of nests and plants found on the island, sporty young women and older women sensibly dressed except for their hats more suited to Newmarket than gusty Scolt Head, tweedy and flat-capped men, newspaper articles, verses, little watercolours, small records of expenditure and rental receipts... And of course some of the same names, visitors enchanted and often returning, recur throughout the book. The first entry is dated 22nd June 1930 and the last August 30th 1949.

For a few hours before and after high tide, you can sail to Scolt Head from the many moorings at Burnham Overy Staithe – today well over sixty boats are still swinging on their anchors – and many people do, beaching their little boats on the sandy shelf at the east end, for a while inhabiting the scruffy nests in the dunes half-protected by marram, scarcely straying inland and west over the dunes and along the undulating rabbit-runs.

And when the tide is on the drag and halfway out, carefully assessing when it will turn and make again , you can walk there past Deadman's Hole and across the shining slakes and sandflats, or along the cocklepath through the saltmarsh.

Stretching miles east and west, the marshes are, I suppose, little more than a pocket wilderness, never more than a couple of miles wide, but they're chancy, they're sticky (locals used to call marsh mud *plick-plack*), sometimes misty. The Byzantine network of little creeks penetrating them have high, crusted, muddy banks, and to edge your way up them in a canoe or a rowing-boat is like entering the narrow neck of a canyon. And the marsh paths: that's where Shuck, the hellhound, prowls, and heaven help any child who sees him and says he has done so within a year and a day. Often enough, the marshes look desolate and rather forbidding, and yet in season they're purpled with great reaches of sea-lavender and strewn with almost luminous green samphire.

Across the sand, then, or through the marsh, or along the leggy dyke to the wide sands and Point east of the island... Whichever way you choose, it's still always a matter of wading shin-deep, knee-deep, thigh-deep, across to Scolt Head.

"It is the morning," my little grandson told me early today with a sense of wonder and pleasure, and of limitless possibility. Exactly! That's the feeling I have each time I step on to the island.

Drift: is it two syllables long? Three? You can't hurry it.

Sea-and-sand-and-snow-drift. A drift of birds. Drift-weed. Drift-wood.

Longshore drift is of course the phenomenon whereby shingle, driven by winds and tides, slowly shunts along a beach. By and large, it's the western end of Scolt Head that is growing, but only slowly, while the eastern end is eroding.

Nowhere on Scolt Head is the shingle very thick, and only here and there is it graded. But allowing for longshore drift, there's one place along the north side where the conflict of salt water and shingle makes the most powerful arrhythmical sound. I was going to write tone, but this sound is not pitched.

First there's the explosive noise of something akin to a sledgehammer pounding concrete. Once or twice; three times. But no more than that. And almost at once a sound like air when you draw it back through your teeth. Arnold's "melancholy, long, withdrawing roar".

Try it!

This sound, broadcast at full blast along the foreshore, is the nearest thing I've heard to the sound and irregular pulse of Anglo-Saxon poetry. And it is tremendous. First the hefty punch of three stressed syllables, one or both of the first two alliterating with the third. Then the dying fall of the fourth stress, the one that never alliterates with the first three.

Isn't this prosody – so often gruff, so often terse, yet far from incapable of being lyrical – the very sound of poetry itself: always controlled, always variable, but here undressed and stripped to the bone?

In the end, each of us stands exposed and alone. Social animals as we may be, and I certainly am, each of us needs, and knows we need, such places, and the pounding of waves on a desolate and stony shore. That is the meaning of their meaning.

For much of my teens, I thought it likely that I would be ordained. And on Good Friday after Good Friday, by way of silent protest against my family's loose ways, I sanctimoniously trudged up to the island, spent all day alone there, and did not break my fast until after the ninth hour!

This religiosity is at the heart of 'Confessional', written when I was twenty, in which I described how harsh Scolt Head and the surrounding marshland insists that "I know who I am", and will rid me of superfluity, so –

> I can go, prepared for the possible;
> Dream and bone set out from the confessional.

But of course, of *course* the way, chastening but not entirely unwelcome, in which such places expose us is offset by everything that makes them magical. In the case of Scolt Head, I think first of the headiness, the intoxication induced by the ozone-rich air; and then the light, "creation light" I call it, "honed on a northern whetstone", at times so edgy that it makes nonsense of distances and has you thinking you can see almost to the ends of the world; those and the immense skyscapes, and often three or four simultaneous and quite different theatres of action. Yes, and the breathtaking birdscapes (no fewer than three hundred species at one time or another), some living on the island, some overwintering, some like you and I just visiting.

These components, and flux, and danger, the bitterly cold winds and sea-slam, underpin many of my north Norfolk poems, as do the lives in my Waterslain poems of some of the local people I knew from my frequent boyhood visits: But with my cycle *Moored Man* I waded into deeper water. He's the embodiment of the north Norfolk coast, a virile and beautiful trickster who embodies its warring elements. He shapes the dykes and dredges the creeks, but is also a dangerous customer who drowns unwary children and seduces women.

In one poem, Moored Man recounts how he created Scolt Head. Scratching and scraping at the sea bed, "like a wild sea-cat covering its fæces, until his ankles were bloody and raw", he literally hoofed it into being.

> The gravel flew and dropped,
> it swarmed and swirled like chaff
> in the murky water.
>
> Longshore drift did the rest.
> Pebbles and grit swam
> and settled in new stations.
> They rose above themselves
> out of the water.

Asking himself why he created it, Moored Man says that it was so he could see "felicity". To realise a dream, that's to say.

This, however, is not quite how experts in physical geography see things.

They tell us the sea-level around the north Norfolk coast has fluctuated only a couple of metres during the past four thousand years – something difficult to credit, given the present rate of erosion, the breakthroughs and the way our entire island seems to be on a tilt. They say an enormous amount of glacial sand and gravel swept south six or seven thousand years ago, and settled in our inshore waters, and that Scolt Head is a barrier island composed of this sediment, and was once part of a longer barrier system. Some of the saltmarshes are millennia old while the sandflats that emerge at each ebb-tide, and change shape and position from year to year, probably accumulated only about nine hundred years ago.

All this speaks of the gradual, and that I suppose is the scientific truth of Scolt Head – but it has been regularly interrupted by the sudden. In 1833 and 1893 and 1953 and 2013, strangely in each case a period of sixty years, the east coast of England and the Netherlands were savaged by floods many metres above the highest of high spring tides, because powerful north winds induced a storm-surge, and one tide was unable to ebb before the next came in on top of it.

I remember seeing in 1953 two breaches all of fifty metres long on the first leg of Burnham dyke. And on Scolt Head the sea poured through the 'Low Hills' halfway between the East End of the island and the Chestney Hut. Since then, they've also been known as the Flat Hills, and that's what they are!

There is plenty of uncertainty about the name Scolt. In his magisterial work *Scolt Head Island*, J. A. Steers notes that various names occur on nineteenth-century maps, including Scolt, Scolts, and Scald. Perhaps the most likely derivation of the word is from the Anglo-Saxon *sceald* and Low German *scheldt*, meaning shallow water at a harbour mouth. But the old Norfolk word *scaldy* was once used to describe land affected by drought. "There is something to be said for this derivation," wrote Steers. "A sand-hill is certainly dry, and the headland is also the highest part of the island and, what is more, the highest dune in Norfolk".

Perhaps it's more rewarding to list here a small part of the suggestive litany of names recorded on Steers' map in 1934 charting all the components of the island, some of which I've used in my own poems: Cockle Bight, Wire Hills, Missel Marsh, Butcher's Beach, The Nod, Smuggler's Gap, Plover Marsh, Low Hills, Norton Creek, Plantago Marsh, The Sloughs also known as Great Aster Marsh…

My own interest has been so much in human interaction and the passage of generations – with society, that's to say – that I find it strange to be writing now about a virtually uninhabited island. Not that it was always quite so. During the 1930s and early years of the war, there was a raggle-taggle township of shacks and bungalows and even a white two-storey house at the eastern end of Scolt Head, which was owned by the Earl of Leicester, but they were all burned or demolished when the War Office requisitioned the island as a gunnery range.

But the real inhabitants, of course, are the birds – the constantly fluctuating concourse, the parties, the assemblies of fowls. And we humans are the interlopers.

You can't live here without developing at least some small knowledge of birdlife. And the arrival of greylags and Brent geese (often described as the 'real wild birds, the northern birds'), and above all thousands and thousands of squeaking-and-croaking pink-footed geese (known as 'pinks'), flying in from Greenland and Iceland and Spitzbergen, brings people to their doorsteps, and tugs at the heart.

But we're blessed now with a whole parliament of ornithologists and naturalists well versed not only in science, but in literature and art and music, infinitely better placed than I to suggest how to observe and think about birds, birdlife, birdsong, and to show us some of the ways we have imaginatively responded to them, and in this short eulogy I leave it to them: Jeremy Mynott, Tim Dee, Mark Cocker, and Adam Nicholson, and many another.

From time to time I've been told that, somewhere in the heart of Scolt Head, there's a rose-garden, but not one of Burnet Rose (*Rosa pimpinellifolia*) or Japanese Rose (*Rosa rugosa*), both of which flourish around House Hills, near the midpoint of the island, where there was some experimental planting of shrubs almost one hundred years ago. People say that it's a defined little area, well sheltered, maybe bordered by a low wall or by boundaries of shells, maybe simply fenced from intruders by air – like the garden in the medieval romance, 'Erec and Enide', so that "nothing could enter it, any more than if it were ringed about by iron, unless it flew in over the top".

Maybe it's akin to a garden in folk tale that only reveals itself to the chosen one. And should someone stumble upon it and fail to recognise it, its defence of shells will rise and grow monstrous and jagged; one of a piece with the gardens in 'Sleeping Beauty' and 'Jorinda and Joringel'.

But where is it, this garden? As with the island itself, where sometimes earth and air and water become one lung, it seems simply to be there and not there.

An enigma and a dream.

It will connect me with the spiritual world... and develop my sense of curiosity... protect me against myself... stimulate my sense of compassion and my creativity...

What's this? Just part of a long list of the desirable qualities attributed to the form of chalcedony know as carnelian, or cornelian as I've always called it. In aiming to be comprehensive, such lists tend to contradict themselves, and they too readily grant our deepest wishes: "Pink carnelian, especially, can encourage love between parents and children, and between parent and parent."

Ranging in colour from palest (lime?) marmalade through orange and blood-red to sluggish red-brown, carnelian differs from the millions (and millions) of pebbles on Scolt Head's shingle patches and occasional ridges in being transparent, or semi-transparent.

And it differs also in being rare and semi-precious.

My family and I have been cornelian-hunters for as long as I can remember, and our childhood photograph albums are peppered with snaps of my sister Sally and me searching, and hurtling to our father with our latest find only for him to half-smile and allow "second grade", or "well, third grade", and for us to protest with "Not when it's wet" and "Let me lick it!"

The trick is this: walk at a regular, unhurried pace, preferably at an angle to the low or setting sun, and along wet shingle. Don't suppose that a piece of cornelian lies buried by other pebbles. It never does. When your neck begins to ache, or every single pebble looks much the same brownish colour, call it a day. But when you do see a piece, you won't doubt it – not for one moment. The light, the gleam, the colour of it! As if lit from within. It's genuinely thrilling to stoop, and pick it up, and nestle it in the palm of your hand.

I'm custodian of an oblong glass tray piled with the pieces of cornelian found by four generations of our family. Some are rounded, some slivers, some smooth, some abraded, and most of them are small or smaller than fingernails or regular marbles.

But I well know the piece of pieces, the *pièce de résistance*, is out there, still waiting for me. Of course I do.

And so does Moored Man. At first it's no more "than a glint in the corner of his bloodshot eye", but then, all at once, there it is:

Utter,
transparent and unblinking

Between his rough fingers he holds it up.
He raises it,
free and shining,
quite clear of time.

But he knows what he has to do...

Moored Man has to draw back his arm, hurl the precious stone deep into the water's throat, and begin the labour of searching for it all over again. His task is Sisyphean. It's the searching that counts.

Scolt Head – it's where I go, day by day, as a believer more dutiful than I will go to prayer. It's where I go, sometimes in my daydreams, and sometimes in my night-dreams. And unsystematically but hungrily reading the work of naturalists, ornithologists, historians who converge on the island, I learn more and more:

Thus: at much the same time during the Second World War as the SS Nina was deliberately sunk off the west end of the island, and used for artillery practise, a Graf Zeppelin roared over Scolt Head on a mission to inspect new radar stations along the east coast. A Wellington bomber, meanwhile, landed on the island when unable to find its way back to a nearby airfield, and still lies buried in the sand some four hundred metres to the west of Chestney Hut.

Recently, one of my friends found on Scolt Head the huge femur of a mastodon. And at the west end of the island, I've sometimes picked up a lump of peat washed eastwards from the five-thousand-year old peat beds of the primeval forest west of Titchwell and Thornham – the site of Seahenge erected, say archaeologists, in the spring or summer of 2049 BC.

Et nova et vetera!

And now, the main threat to the east coast may be coastal erosion, and the shortage of public funding for sea-defence. But others see it as the amount of plastic waste in the sea, or as the very rapid increase of offshore wind farms, aggressively introducing verticals into a seascape that, like the island and marshes, is horizontal, and limiting a horizon apparently limitless...

So yes, I'm a magpie of the foreshore, and for me – a jack-of-many trades but specialist in none – the island of Scolt Head is my primary dream-and-word reserve:

Go back at last to the lost beginning
and you will find them waiting not hidden
strewn among pink stars on the saltmarsh
in shallow scrapes beside the speckled eggs
of the little divebombers and shocking
as drops of blood on the shingle rashes.

In this place you've always known and thought
you knew – beyond the Nod, no further than Missel,
all bindweed bells now, blite, blue-green holly:
pick up your old pointer beneath this torrent
of fervent light, ready yourself again
to winnow and to pitch, and prick out.

Until the Dragon Comes

When I was nineteen, and everything was fleeting and little seemed impossible, I borrowed a car, beetled over Snowdonia, grazed a sheep, and paid a pilgrimage to the first poet to set me on fire: R. S. Thomas. Later, I became his editor at the publishing house of Macmillan:

> Life is not hurrying
> on to a receding future, nor hankering after
> an imagined past. It is the turning
> aside like Moses to the miracle
> of the lit bush, to a brightness
> that seemed as transitory as your youth
> once, but is the eternity that awaits you. ('The Bright Field')

Thomas wrote another wonderful short poem, 'Arrival', about how, without being conscious that he had been seeking for it, a traveller comes upon a village in the Welsh hills that shows him who he is, a traveller "who has arrived / after long journeying where he / began, catching this / one truth by surprise / that there is everything to look forward to."

Being fired by "the miracle of the lit bush", and recognising that I had found something I didn't know I'd been seeking: these two elements are precisely what underlay my own immediate engagement with Anglo-Saxon poetry.

Both my parents, followers of Ouspensky, had (so to speak) tilled me. The very first words in my father's *Music in Wales* (1948) – he edited it and wrote the first chapter – are:

The birds of Rhiannon sang to the seven warriors of the Island of the Mighty a certain song, and all the songs that they had ever heard were unpleasant compared thereto, and the singing was so sweet that the warriors remained spellbound for eighty years together listening to the birds.

When as a teenager I began to take a serious interest in being ordained, his and my mother's response was to introduce me to other world religions and philosophies, more especially those of Gurdjieff and Krishnamurti. And it was my mother who despatched me to a high village in the Alps to meet the philosopher, traveller and Olympic sportswoman, Ella Maillart.

I won a place at St. Edmund Hall, Oxford to read English on the strength of being a tennis-playing ordinand – many the doors long since locked and bolted! – only to fail my Anglo-Saxon prelims. But I'd already begun to translate the attractive metaphorical riddles. I was drawn by poems like 'Deor' that contain memories of mythical figures such as Wayland the Smith. And I was thrilled by passages in the elegiac poems in which their poets are searching – searching for meaning, searching for their place in this world, aware that nothing truly worthwhile is ever easily won:

>   Forþon nu min hyge hweorfeð   ofer hreþerlocan,
>   min modsefa   mid mereflode
>   ofer hwæles eþel   hweorfeð wide
>   eorþan sceatas,   cymeð eft to me
>   gifre ond grædig,   gielleð anfloga,
>   hweteð on hwælweg   hreþer unwearnum
>   ofer holma gelagu.
>
>   my heart leaps within me,
>   my mind roams with the waves
>   over the whale's domain, it wanders far and wide

across the face of the earth, returns again to me
eager and unsatisfied; the solitary bird screams,
irresistible, urges the heart to the whale's way
over the stretch of the seas.

I'm not by profession a student of myth. And I'm not a folklorist either. Rather, I'm a poet, translator and author for children who has from the first been influenced by myth and folk tale, by history and by place — a writer who, when he encountered Anglo-Saxon poems and subsequently Norse mythology, felt — more than felt, knew — that he'd come home.

Covered in cigarette ash, holes in his pockets, wrinkled and crumpled — maybe it never really does to meet one's heroes! — it was W. H. Auden who first counselled me to immerse myself in the early literature of north-west Europe, the myths, the skaldic poems, the sagas, and the heroic legends.

I did. And I was stunned. Above all, I was fascinated by the myths for which our main (though by no means only) source is Snorri Sturluson in his *Prose Edda*. What a man he was: historian, biographer, poet, mythologist, politician — lawgiver at the Allthing, a position equivalent to that of the Speaker of the House of Commons. In his racy, ice-bright account of the creation and cosmology of the tricentric universe, with its axis of a mighty ash-tree, Yggdrasill, and in his account of the activities and relationships of the gods and goddesses, the giants and dwarfs and spirits and animals, Snorri naturally brings into play all kinds of familiar motifs.

Loki is the trickster, the yeast in the mix of the myths. The deities and giants and dwarfs are relatively static; shape-shifting Loki is not. As Snorri says, he is handsome and fair of face, but has an evil disposition and is very changeable of mood. He excelled all men in the art of cunning, and he always cheats." To begin with, Loki helps the gods out of the difficulties into which he has led them, but his jealousy and spleen grow, and as we have seen it is he who guides the mistletoe dart that kills the most virtuous of all the gods, Balder.

By no means confined to Celtic and Norse mythology, the anarchic trickster is a figure very much alive and kicking, and in one form or another present in contemporary culture. Not long ago, I collaborated with the distinguished artist Norman Ackroyd in an attempt to portray the moody, beautiful, dangerous, shapechanging saltmarshes of north Norfolk in an embodied form, Moored Man. This short poem, 'Trickster', forms part of that sequence:

> As though he were the son
> of apparent light and the mimic jay:
>
> he quivers and glares,
> he unrolls carpets of sticky mud,
> then spits laughter as he laces
> fine sand with pointed stones.
>
> And as though he were screaming quicksilver:
> he rises to the moon,
> drags the lumpen tides
> until the creek's swollen and impassable...
>
> But tricksters turn to darkness.
> He licks oozing blood,
> rubs salt into wounds;
> he cracks and snaps bones.
> In the evening he drowns little children,
> and then he howls with remorse.
>
> Old and wild and angry,
> child of mayhem, father of grief.

It is not difficult to isolate motifs, in some instances common to both mythologies, that continue to influence writers, artists, composers, craftsmen, thinkers, naturalists.

There is the Tree of Life, the green growth without which there cannot be life here on earth. Yggdrasill is a timeless tree, an evergreen ash. It has one root in each of the three worlds, and Snorri says "its branches spread out over the whole world and reach up over heaven". Known as the Guardian Tree, Yggdrasill nourishes and suffers from all the animals and birds that inhabit it. The three Norns or goddesses of destiny sit beside one root. Odin hangs on the tree for nine nights, his side gashed with a spear, in order to learn the wisdom of the dead. And while the Christ analogy is obvious, the date of this Norse myth is far from certain, and thus whether or not it preceded the late arrival of Christianity in the north.

There is the ring, the gold ring cursed by the dwarf Andvari which passes from him to Loki to Odin to Fafnir to Sigurd, and which is central to the work of Richard Wagner and J. R. R. Tolkien. Sigurd the Volsung, and his German cognate Siegfried, (the form already used in the *Nibelungenlied*, first written down in about 1200 AD) was to the Northern world as Arthur has been to the British Isles and France and Germany, the magnet of many unrelated stories. William Morris said of the *Volsunga Saga*:

> This is the Great Story of the North, which should be to all our race what the tale of Troy was to the Greeks – to all our race first, and afterwards, when the change of the world has made our race nothing more than a name of what has been – a story too – then should it be to those that come after us no less than the Tale of Troy has been to us.

The trickster, the tree, the ring... What else? What other motifs in the myths have continuing power? Well, there are the stars and especially the evening star Aurvandil – that's to say Rigel in Orion – which was a frozen human toe hurled by Thor into high heaven. The Anglo-Saxon name for this star is Éarendel, and J. R. R. Tolkien said that when he first heard the lines from Cynewulf's 'Christ I' –

> Éalá Éarendel,   engla beorhtast
> Ofer middangeard   monnum sended
>
> Hail Éarendel, brightest of angels
> sent to men across Middle Earth

— they invoked in him "a curious thrill, as if something had stirred in me, half wakened from sleep". He imagined Éarendel as a mariner, and one of his earliest poems, written in 1914, begins

> Éarendel sprang up from the Ocean's cup
> In the gloom of the mid-world's rim;
> From the door of Night as a ray of light
> Leapt over the twilight brim.

Yes, and more besides: birdsong, and the ability to understand it; the cauldron, in Celtic of rebirth, in Norse of wisdom and the gift of poetry; the supernatural female warriors known as 'shield-girls' or 'Valkyries'...

And then there is the dragon: the enemy of all enemies, the ultimate challenge confronted by many a hero in children's books. In the Anglo-Saxon *Beowulf*, for which there are of course many partial analogues, there's all the difference in the world between the monsters Grendel and his mother (who are the seed of Cain, effectively humans gone wrong) and the dragon, who as we have seen is the embodiment of time – time that we may defeat by winning a reputation that survives us, but that will also defeat each one of us.

Many of you will recognise Tolkien's unforgettable words:

> If the funeral of Beowulf moved once like the echo of an ancient dirge, far-off and hopeless, it is to us as a memory brought over the hills, an echo of an echo. There is not much poetry in the world

> like this; written in a language that after many centuries has still essential kinship with our own, it was made in this land, and moves in our northern world beneath our northern sky, and for those who are native to that tongue and land, it must ever call with a profound appeal—until the dragon comes.

When the dragon comes, he comes after the axe-age and the sword-age, the wind-age and the wolf-age, in the form of Ragnarok, the destruction of the powers, the apocalyptic final battle in which all created beings destroy one another and the nine worlds are submerged. There could not be a motif, an archetype more pertinent to our own time.

And yet... and yet... two humans will hide themselves inside Yggdrasill: Lif and Lifthrasir.

> Surt's fire will not scorch them; it will not even touch them, and their food will be the morning dew. Through the branches, through the leaves, they will see light come back...
> Lif and Lifthrasir will have children. Their children will bear children. There will be life and new life, life everywhere on earth. That was the end; and this is the beginning.

One can point to very good or even great literature, music, and painting rooted in or drawing on Nordic mythology: Thomas Gray's 'The Fatal Sisters', and 'Sigurd the Volsung' by William Morris, and Arthur Rackham's unforgettable illustrations for the Ring cycle; W. H. Auden's 'Journey to Iceland' and Louis MacNeice's 'Iceland'; stirring novels by Cecilia Holland, Henry Treece, and Rosemary Sutcliff; Seamus Heaney's *North* and 'Bone Dreams', and, more recently, the poet John Greening's 'Valhall' and 'The Norns'; Joanne Harris's novel *The Gospel of Loki* and A. S. Byatt's *Ragnarok*, one in a series of short novels reinterpreting bodies of myth.

To this can perhaps be added paintings by Burne-Jones, and Paul Nash; compositions by Grieg, and Elgar, and the Laureate Judith Weir, and the oratorio 'The Death of Balder' by the fine younger composer Bernard Hughes – all this, let alone the magnificent work produced in Scandinavia itself and whatever we conceive of as the wider Nordic world. There has also been an increase in the number of translations of the mythological and heroic poems that comprise the *Elder Edda*, including a good recent one by Andy Orchard. And yet as I write this, I feel as if I am almost pleading that artists should more often look north, and conceding that any Nordic revival since Wagner and the jingoism he inspired in Germany in the 1920s and 1930s has been no more than sporadic and largely limited to fantasy literature and film, including the highly popular *Thor* series (based on the Marvel Comics character), still in the making. The truth is that within the British Isles at least, there is by no means a substantial body of creative work to compare with that generated by the Arthurian legends (some of them of course descended from *The Mabinogion*) in the nineteenth and early twentieth centuries: Tennyson ('Idylls of the King'), Arnold ('Tristram and Iseult'), William Morris again, Swinburne, Edward Arlington Robinson ("too good a poet to be widely popular," said Robertson Davies, "too good to be forgotten"), Charles Williams; James Archer, Holman Hunt, J. W. Waterhouse, Frederick Sandys, Dante Gabriel Rossetti, and Aubrey Beardsley; and Arnold Bax at Tintagel.

A mountain top, an avalanche, an earthquake, a flood, a mighty wind – yes, these are places and events where the human may meet the divine – and let us not forget the humdrum either: our first names, the days of the week. Wherever we go, the gods are standing at our shoulders. But I want to return to the matter of place, and I have written elsewhere of my own *temenos*, the tidal island of Scolt Head, off the north Norfolk coast. It is a crossing-place, a borderland, and I have been spellbound by it since I was a small boy.

Places that matter a very great deal to us become much larger than they are because they occupy such an area of thought, emotion, memory, dream. As a teenager, I discovered a hidden, a secret meadow in the Alps – a borderland between the human and divine – and it turns out I have never left it.

> Well above the hamlet on its tipsy ledge
> there was a meadow. One path scrambled up to it.
> It was passionate with wildflowers and unvisited,
> innocent of whatever was happening below.
> On hands and knees I crawled along the side
> where you could drop off the edge of the world.
>
> Long ago, waking hot and hectic
> or shocked by some dream, I used to splash
> my face with water biting as a mountain stream,
> lie back and climb that rocky path again.
> Turbanned lily, gentian, orange poppy,
> soldanella… names I no longer remember.
>
> Each breathing midnight now, unsure I'll return,
> I realise I'm doing the same. I'll do the same.

Scolt Head and La Plaine de la Madeleine are actual places. It is David Jones who reminds and shows us that each and every place is charged with time and memory, and that each waits on you and on me, unhurrying, to reveal its divine spark. In an essay entitled 'The Myth of Arthur' in his *Epoch and Artist* (1959), Jones writes:

> To conserve, to develop, to bring together, to make significant for the present what past holds, without dilution or any deleting, but rather by understanding and transubstantiating the material, this is the function of genuine myth, neither pedantic nor popularising,

nor indifferent to scholarship, but saying always 'of these thou hast given me have I lost none'.

So here are the last lines of Jones's 'The Sleeping Lord':

> yet he sleeps on
> > very deep is his slumber:
> how long has he been the sleeping lord?
> are the clammy ferns
> > his rustling vallance
> does the buried rowan
> > ward him from evil, or
> does he ward the tanglewood
> > and the denizens of the wood
> are the stunted oaks his gnarled guard
> > or are their knarred limbs
> strong with his sap?
> Do the small black horses
> > grass on the hunch of his shoulders?
> are the hills his couch
> > or is he the couchant hills?
> Are the slumbering valleys
> > him in slumber
> > are the still undulations
> the still limbs of him sleeping?
> Is the configuration of the land
> > the furrowed body of the lord
> are the scarred ridges
> > his dented greaves
> do the trickling gullies
> > yet drain his hog-wounds?
> Does the land wait the sleeping lord
> > or is the wasted land
> that very lord who sleeps?

Festival of the Phoenix

Trumpeters raise the roof; the MC bellows into his mike while his partner stands tall in her pencil-thin stilettoes, and bares her perfect teeth; and to the sound of rhythmical clapping from the four hundred feasters, Lyudmila Putin – wife of the president of Russia – and her guest Cherie Blair process out of the hall.

No sooner have they done so than the seemly after-dinner entertainment (folk-dancers, folk-singers and a conjuror) rapidly begins to go downhill. The floor of the Central Concert Hall in Moscow's Rossiya hotel – the largest and probably the ugliest hotel in the world – is invaded by rock bands, scantily-clad beauties wearing peach-pink and lime-green rags, men in peacock and mustard leotards leaping and lording, and couples whirling and cavorting, simulating copulation.

Not quite the dainty dish, maybe, to set before the wives of our leaders, but how the feasters loved it. They were school librarians gathered in Moscow from the length and breadth of Russia, and this was just one part of the lavish entertainment laid on for them.

The four-day Festival of School Libraries in Moscow is one of the most improbable events I've ever attended. Its purpose was to encourage a passion for reading in children, and to underscore the importance of school libraries as a resource.

The front-woman, attending and speaking at almost all the events, was Lyudmila Putin, pink and pretty as a pale-skinned Matryoshka doll. And at her invitation, the festival was attended by four other First Ladies: Cherie Blair, Laura Bush (herself once a children's librarian), Bella Kocharian from Armenia, and Zorka Pyrvanova from Bulgaria.

Each of the visiting First Ladies brought with her a couple of children's authors.

Laura Bush was accompanied by R. L. Stine, author of the world-bestselling *Goosebumps* stories as well as Louis Sachar, author of *Holes*. Michael Morpurgo, our admirable and forthright Children's Laureate, and I went in to bat from Britain.

When Cherie Blair introduced Michael and me and our work to the other First Ladies and the horde of observing librarians, she also spoke movingly about her own passion for reading as a girl, and how she got special dispensation to borrow books from the adult section of her local library after she'd read just about everything written for children.

Then I conducted a workshop with a group of ten-year-olds and, wearing helmets and brandishing swords, they staged a cameo production based on my Arthur books. They spoke in English; they remembered their lines: they never batted an eyelid.

I told the audience about my intense excitement on the day I discovered I was the possessor of a crusader shield presented to me by my grandfather for my childhood museum; and I explained my writing process.

"When I think I've finished," I said, "I show my manuscript to my wife, Linda, and she bluepencils another ten per cent."

Everyone laughed, and Cherie Blair turned round to get a better look at this Valkyrie.

"And I expect some of you here are wondering whether Mrs Blair gets a chance to bluepencil her husband's speeches," I added.

There was a moment of silence, as if I'd committed some act of lèse-majesté, and then a gale of laughter. Mrs Blair threw back her head and laughed the loudest.

When I met Mrs Putin after my workshop, the first thing she did was to congratulate me on bringing my wife! The first thing I did was to congratulate her on prevailing on her four peers to leave behind their husbands. More seriously, I added that I hoped this festival would become never-ending, moving from country to country, always reborn. "You could call it the Festival of the Phoenix," I suggested.

During four action-packed days, the school librarians were feasted in the Grand Kremlin Palace (red caviar, black caviar, champagne and all), and addressed by their President. They sat in the stalls at the stunning Bolshoi Theatre, and were treated to a gala performance of 'Don Quixote'; they were mightily entertained by top TV acts – all this in addition to a daily diet of workshops, award ceremonies, talks, and readings.

With the help of interpreters, I chatted to some of the librarians, most of whom were women. Many of them had never been to Moscow before, or anywhere near its magnificent gilded domes. Some, touchingly, had delved deep into their meagre savings to bring a daughter or a son with them. And some had addresses that smacked of the back of beyond: The Orphanage School, near the Sugar Beet Factory, near Kushkushara, near Archangel...

In one speech, Cherie Blair noted how many of the librarians' awards had been scooped by Siberians, and said she hoped to come back and see some of the initiatives there for herself. Was this just a throwaway remark? Or was she pointing to the importance of decentralisation – so desirable in Britain, absolutely crucial in a country the size of Russia?

What I saw with my own eyes is that people who do sterling work in unglamorous jobs, and who are seldom praised let alone lionised, turned for home feeling good about themselves and good about their jobs. The impact of the festival, actually organised by the lively Centre for Russian Language Development, and strongly supported by the British Council, will resonate for a long time to come.

Not that the next posse of librarians will have all that long to wait.

I ran into Cherie Blair for the fourth time in three days, this time by chance, at the clapperboard house where Tolstoy argued with his wife Sonya, and cobbled shoes, and wrote *The Life of Ivan Ilyich*. English china sat on the dinner table; outside, orange-and-yellow maple leaves cascaded.

"Mrs Putin has decided to hold another festival in just a couple of years' time," she told me, "and we do hope you'll be able to come."

You bet!

But actually. what are we waiting for?

For all our admirable literacy programmes, school libraries in Britain are woefully underfunded, while hard-working school librarians are underpaid and underpraised.

I'd like to see the Festival of the Pheonix reborn as soon as possible in this country. In fact, I'm already giving thought to the entertainments!

In a Norfolk Garden

An Idyll for Peter and Margaret Scupham

Little clusters of guests are sitting
beneath the tortured oaks, a few on tartan rugs,
most on the jaundiced grass,
and others are lined up on recliners
like survivors from some TB sanatorium
soaking in this late August sunlight.
Something's going on in front of them:
a pair of ancients, gesticulating.
Their backs are turned but I can hear
their words, even at this distance.

> *Jesu, Jesu, the mad days that I have spent!*
> *And to see how many of my old acquaintance*
> *are dead... We shall all follow, cousin...*

Got it! It's those two country justices.

> *Certain, 'tis certain; very sure, very sure.*

*

While I'm still listening to these two truth-tellers,
hollow-eyed and glum, playing at playmaking,
a wizened monk, maybe a Carthusian
or some Carmelite home from the Holy Land,
grabs my collar and he croaks

> 'Norfolk! Norfolk!
> Satan on the road to Hell
> ruined Norfolk as he fell.'
> His breath

smells of honey. I readjust my sprig
of sea-lavender, and politely refer him
to Sir John who's on his way

with his old flame, Billa,
and expected around teatime.

*

Over there, that's George Barker,
black drill-eyed, well oiled already
and the sun's not yet at the zenith.
He's hectoring the pinstripe murderer
who awarded me a bar to my DFC,
then finished me off at Biggin Hill,
presently strangling a very pretty
young whitebeam with his spider fingers.
Why are they pincering poor George Szirtes?
What's going on? Is this some nomen league,
celebrants of a tribune martyred
in Nicomedia, venerated only
in England, Portugal and Albania?

*

Surrounded by cats and herbs, mossy statues
and stagnant little pools fringed with white lace,
what grows in this sacred space
are words, well-watered, thinned
and pleached and flowering – year upon year
of readings and recitations grave and gay
by lights very bright and distinctly limited,
generations of poets, some with their families,
attending to their roots and calling.

*

You'd heard that several guests had died,
some long since, and that's the case,
but it's scarcely surprising to be surrounded
by like minds and 'affable presences'.
Almost everyone's present at this assembly
they wouldn't miss for anything.

Look! There's Skelton, our first laureate, rapping
with a young man who spent all morning
choosing which cravat to wear
(mauve, yes, mauve, I think so), and then how to tie it.
But who's that with bells on his ankles,
hopping and skipping between the weedy beds
and warbling in his annoying falsetto:

> *A Country Lasse browne as a berry…*
> *something, something… heart as merry,*
> *Cheekes well fed and sides well larded,*
> *Every bone with fat flesh guarded…*

Got it again! It's Will Kemp,
darling of the groundlings
and dancer all the way from London to Norwich,
his eyes always sharp for the next chance,
a 'Marrian in his Morrice daunce'.

*

As for Old Hall, and its 'long marriage
of queen strut, king post', its mysteries
'exposed by sweat, patched together with lime,
stage-paint, a little imagination',
let it rest today on its laurels.
Our paths lead out from it,
all our words came home to it
and its 'gatekeepers and custodians'.
Everyone here knows that.

> *Love it. Choose it. Whatever the words mean*
> *Hauled from the moil, the tumult in the head*
> *And heart.*

*

Our host rises, gleaming and genial,
bent double almost. First he rehearses a few
regrets and no-shows, among them Frances Cornford,

Lilias Rider Haggard and dear Wystan,
then announces a couple of surprise arrivals:
two more Georges, on horseback,
both from silly Suffolk. Very strange.

> *When tides were neap, and, in the sultry day*
> *Through the tall bounding mud-banks made their way,*
> *Which on each side rose swelling, and below*
> *The dark warm flood rose silently and slow...*

Ah, Crabbe! George Crabbe, my words, hard-won,
echo your own. My creeks and staithes of Brothercross,
their small gains shored against struggle and loss...

*

The quick and the dead,
home-grown and foreigner,
seventeen poets now stand and deliver.
Several of them are audible.
Sail and Brownjohn, Mole and Griffiths and Underwood
and last, as befits our senior poet:

> *Speaking as best I may, or as I might.*
> *If the day failed and all there was was night,*
> *I look for something which could still be light.*

Yes, that's Anthony Thwaite.
It's very nearly too late.

*

'Where's William Cowper?' I ask my host.
'My namesake on my mother's side.
'A sage beneath a spreading oak.'
He gives me a melancholy look. 'Is that so?
'I don't rightly know. Neither does he.'

*

This blistering heat. These tumblers of red wine.
Butterfly flicker...
Dear creatures, marinade those hours.

Where, pray, in this whole kingdom
is there any living ancient place,
any garden trained, still wild, a dream
of an assembly in the least like this?

Old Hall Poetry Picnic, South Burlingham

Bibliography and quoted works

Storytelling

We, the Story: Traditional Tales that Relate Us

'Law Like Love' from *Another Time*. W. H. Auden (Random House, New York, 1940)
Hungry Mind Review (*Children's Book Supplement*, Summer 1992)
America in 1492. Edited by Alvin M. Josephy, Jr. (Knopf, New York, 1992)
'in white america' from 'singing' in *Next: New Poems*. Lucille Clifton (BOA Editions, Ltd., Brockport, 1987)
The Hidden Wound. Wendell Berry (North Point Press, San Francisco, 1989)
Confucius: The Unwobbling Pivot / The Great Digest / The Analects. Ezra Pound (New Directions, New York, 1969)
The Norse Myths. Kevin Crossley-Holland (Pantheon, New York, 1980)
Christian Schiller in his own words. Edited by Christopher Griffin-Beale (A. & C. Black, London, 1979)
Black Elk Speaks as told through John G. Neihardt (William Morrow & Company, 1932)
Sage und Märchen: Erzählforschung heute. Lutz Röhrich (Herder, Freiburg, 1976), translated by Maria Tatar in *The Hard Facts of the Grimms' Fairy Tales* (Princeton University Press, 1987)
'Napoleon' from *The Fly*. Miroslav Holub, translated by Ewald Osers (Bloodaxe Books, Newcastle, 1987)
To Hold Us Together: Seven Conversations for Multicultural Understanding. Linda Crawford (The Origins Program, Minneapolis, 1990)
The Wildman. Kevin Crossley-Holland (André Deutsch, London, 1976)
Sea Tongue. Kevin Crossley-Holland (BBC/Longman, London, 1991)
The Book of Counsel: The Popol Vuh of the Quiche Maya of Guatemala. Munro S. Edmonson (Middle America Research Institute, Tulane University, 1971)
'Here Be Dragons' from *The Price of the Ticket*. James Baldwin (St. Martin's Press/Marek, New York, 1985)

On Katharine Briggs' *Folk Tales of Britain*

Remaines of Gentilisme and Judaisme. John Aubrey (The Folk Lore Society/W. Satchell, Peyton & co., London, 1881)
Legendary Fictions of the Irish Celts. Patrick Kennedy (Macmillan and Co., London, 1866)

The British Folklorists: A History.
Richard Dorson (Routledge &
Kegan Paul Books, Oxfordshire,
1968)

Different, – but oh how like!

'Diz' from *Waterslain*, Kevin
Crossley-Holland (Hutchinson,
London, 1986)

Popular Tales of the West Highlands,
Volume 3. John Francis Campbell
(Edmonson & Douglas,
Edinburgh,1862)

Sea Tongue. Kevin Crossley-Holland
(BBC/Longman, London, 1991)

*Traditional Tales: A 'Signal'
Bookguide.* Mary Steele (Thimble
Press, 1989)

Akenfield. Ronald Blythe (Allen
Lane, London, 1969)

**Which Eye Can You See Me With?:
Interpreting Folk Tales**

Kinder- und Hausmärchen. Wilhelm
and Jacob Grimm (Reimer, Berlin,
1812)

*Fairy Legends and Traditions of
the South of Ireland.* T. Crofton
Croker, Esq. (John Murray,
London, 1825)

'The Story of the Three Bears' from
The Doctor. Robert Southey
(Longman, 1837)

English Hours. Henry James
(Heinemann, London, 1905)

British Folk Tales: New Versions.
Kevin Crossley-Holland (Orchard
Books, 1987)

The Wildman. Kevin Crossley-
Holland (André Deutsch,
London, 1976)

Anglo-Saxon Poetry

Word ond Andgiet: **On Translating
Anglo-Saxon Poetry**

Beowulf. Translated by Kevin
Crossley-Holland (Macmillan,
London, 1968)

The Seafarer. Translated by Kevin
Crossley-Holland (The Old Stile
Press, Wales, 1988)

The Anglo-Saxon Elegies

Beowulf. Translated by Kevin
Crossley-Holland (Macmillan,
London, 1968)

*The Battle of Maldon and Other
Old English Poems.* Translated
by Kevin Crossley-Holland
(Macmillan, London, 1965)

The Anglo-Saxon World. Translated
by Kevin Crossley-Holland
(Boydell Press, 1982)

The Exeter Book Riddles

Rhetoric. Aristotole, Translated by
James Edward Cowell Welldon
(Macmillan, London, 1886)

The Anglo-Saxon Poetic Records.
George Philip Krapp, Elliott
Van Kirk Dobbie (Columbia
University Press, 1931)

*The Germany and the Agricola of
Tacitus.* Cornelius Tacitus (David
McKay, Philadelphia, 1897)

**The Cross Crucified: An
Introduction to 'The Dream of the
Rood'**

*The Battle of Maldon and Other
Old English Poems.* Translated
by Kevin Crossley-Holland
(Macmillan, London, 1965)

The Anglo-Saxon World. Translated by Kevin Crossley-Holland (Boydell Press, 1982)

Beowulf. Translated by Kevin Crossley-Holland (Macmillan, London, 1968)

Authors and Books

Rosemary Sutcliff: *The Eagle of the Ninth*

The Eagle of the Ninth. Rosemary Sutcliff (Oxford University Press, 1954)

T. H. White: *The Once and Future King*

The Once and Future King. T. H. White (Collins, London, 1958)
The Sword in the Stone. T. H. White (Collins, London, 1938)
The Witch in the Wood. T. H. White (Collins, London, 1940)
The Ill-Made Knight. T. H. White (Collins, London, 1941)
The Book of Merlyn. T. H. White (Fontana/Collins London, 1978)
The Golden Age. Kenneth Grahame (The Bodley Head, London, 1895)
Dream Days. Kenneth Grahame (John Lane/The Bodley Head, London, 1898)
The Midnight Folk. John Masefield (Heinemann, London, 1927)
Mistress Masham's Repose. T. H. White (Jonathan Cape, London, 1947)
The History of the Kings of Britain. Geoffrey of Monmouth (Penguin, London, 1978)
Sir Gawain and the Green Knight. Translated by Keith Harrison (The Folio Society, London, 1983)
Idylls of the King. Alfred Lord Tennyson (Edward Moxon & co., London, 1859)

The Sleeping Lord: And Other Fragments. David Jones (Faber & Faber, London, 1974)

George Crabbe: 'Peter Grimes'

The Borough: A Poem, in Twenty-Four Letters. George Crabbe (J. Hatchard, London, 1810)
The Life and Poetical Works of the Rev. George Crabbe by his Son. Rev. George Crabbe (John Murray, London, 1854)

Footprints on the Grass: Of Gardens and Children's Books

The Oxford Dictionary of English Etymology. Edited by C. T. Onions (Oxford, 1966)
De cultura Hortorum. Walafrid-Strabo
The Englishman's Flora. Geoffrey Grigson (Phoenix House Ltd, London, 1955)
'The Flowers' from *Selected Poems*. Robert Louis Stevenson (Penguin, London, 1999)
Kinder- und Hausmärchen. Wilhelm and Jacob Grimm (Reimer, Berlin, 1812)
Remaines of Gentilisme and Judaisme. John Aubrey (The Folk Lore Society/W. Satchell, Peyton & co., London, 1881)
Puck of Pook's Hill. Rudyard Kipling (Macmillan, London, 1906)
Lob Lie-by-the-Fire. Juliana Horatia Ewing (Society for Promoting

Christian Knowledge, London, 1883)
Lob. Linda Newbery (David Fickling, London, 2010)
Thursday's Child. Sonya Hartnett (Walker Books, London, 2002)
Fireweed, Jill Paton Walsh, (Macmillan, London, 1969)
Arthur. King Of The Middle March. Kevin Crossley-Holland (Orion Children's Books, London, 2003)
Minnow on the Say. Philippa Pearce (Oxford University Press, 1955)
Tom's Midnight Garden. Philippa Pearce (Oxford University Press, 1958)
Autobiography. G. K. Chesterton (Hutchinson & Co., London, 1936)
Jackdaw Summer. David Almond (Hodder Children's Books, London, 2008)
I Never Saw Another Butterfly: Children's Drawings and Poems from Terezin Concentration Camp, 1942–1944. Compiled by Hana Volavková (Schocken Books/ Penguin Random House, London, 1994)
Harding's luck. Edith Nesbit (Hodder and Stoughton, London, 1909)
The Summer Book. Tove Jansson (Hutchinson, London, 1975)
The *Green Knowe* series books. Lucy M. Boston (Published from 1954 to 1976 [various publishers])
The Adventures of Tom Bombadil. J. R. R. Tolkien (George Allan and Unwin, London, 1961)
Linnets and Valerians. Elizabeth Goudge (Brockhampton, London, 1964)

The Secret Garden. Frances Hodgson Burnett (Heinemann, London, 1911)

Michael Longley: Breathing on the Embers

No Continuing City: Poems 1963 to 1968. Michael Longley (Dufour Editions, 1969)
An Exploded View. Michael Longley (Gollancz, London, 1973)
Man Lying on a Wall. Michael Longley (Gollancz, London, 1976)

The King Within Each of Us

Arthur. King Of The Middle March. Kevin Crossley-Holland (Orion Children's Books, London, 2003)
Sir Gawain and the Green Knight. Translated by Keith Harrison (The Folio Society, London, 1983)
Le Morte d'Arthur. Thomas Malory (William Caxton, 1485)
Catherine, Called Birdy. Karen Cushman (Clarion Books, London, 1994)
The Holy Grail, imagination and belief. Barber, Richard (Allen Lane, London, 2004)

A Sort of Song of Everything: *Gatty's Tale* and Music

Wordhoard. Jill Paton Walsh and Kevin Crossley-Holland (Puffin Books, London, 1972)
Wulf. Kevin Crossley-Holland (Faber & Faber, London, 1988)
Heartsong. Kevin Crossley-Holland, illustrated by Jane Ray (Orchard Books, London, 2015)
Gatty's Tale. Kevin Crossley-Holland (Orion Children's Books, London, 2006)

In Tandem

Collaborations with Artists

Havelok the Dane. Kevin Crossley-Holland (Macmillan, London, 1964).

The Green Children. Margaret Gordon and Kevin Crossley-Holland (Macmillan, London, 1966)

Norfolk Poems. Kevin Crossley-Holland and John Hedgecoe (Academy Editions, London, 1970)

Oenone in January. Kevin Crossley-Holland with illustrations by John Lawrence (The Old Stile Press, Wales, 1988)

The Road to Canterbury: Tales from Chaucer Retold. Ian Serraillier with illustrations by John Lawrence (Kestrel, 1979)

The Old Stories: Folk Tales from East Anglia and The Fen Country. Kevin Crossley-Holland with illustrations by John Lawrence (Colt Books, Cambridge, 1997)

The Telling Line. Douglas Martin (Julia MacRae Books, London, 1989)

The Once and Future King. T. H. White. Introduction by Kevin Crossley-Holland with illustrations by John Lawrence (The Folio Society, London, 2003)

The Arthur Trilogy – 3 Volume Set. Kevin Crossley-Holland with illustrations by John Lawrence (The Folio Society, London, 2009)

The Stones Remain. Kevin Crossley-Holland with illustrations by Andrew Rafferty (Rider & Co, 1989)

Seahenge: A Journey. Kevin Crossley-Holland with illustrations by Andrew Rafferty (Kailpot Press, 2019)

Norse Myths: Tales of Odin, Thor and Loki. Kevin Crossley-Holland with illustrations by Jeffrey Alan Love (Walker Studio, London, 2017)

Norse Tales: Stories from Across the Rainbow Bridge. Kevin Crossley-Holland with illustrations by Jeffrey Alan Love (Walker Studio, London, 2020)

Moored Man: Poems of North Norfolk. Kevin Crossley-Holland with illustrations by Norman Ackroyd (Enitharmon Editions, London, 2006)

King Horn. Kevin Crossley-Holland with illustrations by Charles Keeping (Macmillan, London, 1965)

Charles Keeping: An Illustrator's Life. Douglas Martin (Julia MacRae Books, London, 1993)

Beowulf. Translated by Kevin Crossley-Holland with illustrations by Charles Keeping (Oxford University Press, 1982)

Collaborations with Composers

Nujeen: One Girl's Incredible Journey from War-torn Syria in a Wheelchair. Nujeen Mustafa, Christina Lamb (Collins, London, 2016), later retitled *The Girl from Aleppo* (Collins, 2017)

On Writing a Libretto

The Wildman. Kevin Crossley-Holland (André Deutsch, London, 1976)

Norse

Look North

'The Oak and the Olive' from *The Oxford Book of Travel Verse*. Edited by Kevin Crossley-Holland (Oxford University Press, 1989)

Letters from High Latitudes. Lord Dufferin (John Murray, London, 1858)

Icelandic Journals. William Morris (Centaur Press Ltd., London, 1969)

Letters from Iceland. W. H. Auden and Louis MacNeice (Faber & Faber, London, 1937)

The Idea of North. Peter Davidson (Reaktion Books, London, 2004)

Bracelet of Bones. Kevin Crossley-Holland. (Quercus Children's Books, London, 2011)

Scramasax. Kevin Crossley-Holland (Quercus Children's Books, London, 2013)

Gods and Myths of Northern Europe. H. R. Ellis Davidson (Penguin Books, London, 1965)

Axe-age, Wolf-age

'The Sermon of the Wolf to the English' taken from *The Anglo-Saxon World*. Translated by Kevin Crossley-Holland (Boydell Press, 1982)

On Ian Crockatt's *Crimsoning the Eagle's Claw*

Crimsoning the Eagle's Claw: The Viking Poetry of Rognvaldr Kali Kolsson, earl of Orkney. Ian Crockatt (ARC Publications, 2014)

Places

On *The Oxford Book of Travel Verse*

The Oxford Book of Travel Verse. Edited by Kevin Crossley-Holland (Oxford University Press, 1989)

The History of Jerusalem AD 1180. Jacques de Vitry. Translated by, Aubrey Stewart. (Palestine Pilgrims' Text Soc., 1895)

The Kings of the Irish

Twenty Years A-Growing. Maurice O'Sullivan (Chatto & Windus, London, 1933)

'Going into Exile' taken from *The Sniper, Spring Sowing, Going Into Exile*. Liam O'Flaherty (Cambridge University Press, 1978)

Let There be Light

Money For Nothing. P. G. Wodehouse (Herbert Jenkins, London, 1928)

Devices and Desires. P. D. James (Faber & Faber, London, 1989)

Watercolour Sky. William Riviere (Sceptre, London, 1991)

The Story of a Norfolk Farm. Henry Williamson (Faber & Faber, London, 1941)

At Thurgarton Church: A Poem With Drawings. George Baker (Trigram Press, London, 1969

The Hound of Baskervilles. Arthur Conan Doyle. (George Newnes, London, 1902)

The Seafarer. Translated by Kevin Crossley-Holland (The Old Stile Press, Wales, 1988)

Scolt Head

Moored Man: Poems of North Norfolk. Kevin Crossley-Holland with illustrations by Norman Ackroyd (Enitharmon Editions, London, 2006)

Scolt Head Island. Edited by J. A. Steers (W. Heffer & Sons Ltd, Cambridge, 1934)

Until the Dragon Comes

'The Bright Field' from *Selected poems, 1946-1968*. R. S. Thomas (Hart-Davis MacGibbon, London, 1973)

'Arrival' from *Later Poems*. R. S. Thomas (Macmillan, London, 1983)

Music in Wales. Edited by Peter Crossley-Holland (Hinrichsen Edition Limited, London, 1948)

The Seafarer. Translated by Kevin Crossley-Holland (The Old Stile Press, Wales, 1988)

Moored Man: Poems of North Norfolk. Kevin Crossley-Holland with illustrations by Norman Ackroyd (Enitharmon Editions, London, 2006)

The Story of the Volsungs. Translated by William Morris and Eiríkr Magnússon, (F.S. Ellis, London, 1870)

'Éalá Éarendel Engla Beorhtast' from *The Book of Lost Tales: Part Two*. Christopher and J.R.R. Tolkien (George Allen and Unwin, London, 1984)

The Monsters and the Critics and Other Essays. J. R. R. Tolkien (Harper Collins, London, 1997)

Poems By Mr. Gray. Thomas Gray (J. Dodsley, London, 1768)

The Story of Sigurd the Volsung and the Fall of the Niblings. William Morris (Ellis and White, London, 1877)

Letters from Iceland. W. H. Auden and Louis MacNeice (Faber & Faber, London, 1937)

North. Seamus Heaney (Faber & Faber, London, 1975)

'Bone Dreams' published in *New Poems 1973-1974*. Edited by Stewart Conn (Hutchinson, London, 1974)

'The Norns', published in *Iceland Spar*. John Greening (Shoestring Press, 2008)

The Gospel of Loki. Joanne Harris (Orion, London, 2014)

Ragnarok: The End of the Gods. A. S. Byatt (Canongate, London, 2011)

Epoch and Artist. David Jones (Faber & Faber, London, 1959)

The Sleeping Lord: And Other Fragments. David Jones (Faber & Faber, London, 1974)

SOURCES

Storytelling:

We, the Story: Traditional Tales that Relate Us: The Ronald M. Hubbs and Margaret S. Hubbs Lectures – Number One. University of St. Thomas, St. Paul, 1992; On Katharine Briggs' *Folk Tales of Britain*: *Folk Tales of the British Isles*, Katharine Briggs, The Folio Society, London, 1985. Faber and Faber, London, 1985; Different, – but oh how like!: Oracle Series No.3. The Society for Storytelling. Daylight Press, 1998. *Tales, Tellers and Texts*. Cassell, London and New York, 2000; Which Eye Can You See Me With?: Interpreting Folk Tales: The Helen E. Stubbs Memorial Lectures – Number One. Toronto Public Library, Toronto, 1988; Butterfly Soul: From *Between Worlds: Folktales of Britain and Ireland* (2018). First published as *British Folk Tales* (1987).

Anglo-Saxon Poetry:

An Old House Packed with Memories: *The Wuffings*, a play by Kevin Crossley-Holland and Ivan Cutting. Runetree Press, London, 1999; Word *ond Andgiet*: On Translating Anglo-Saxon Poetry: London Anglo-Saxon Symposium, 2019; The Anglo-Saxon Elegies: The Folio Press, 1988; The Exeter Book Riddles: Enitharmon Press, 2008; The Cross Crucified: An Introduction to 'The Dream of the Rood': *A Passion for Winchester*. Saracen Press, 2008; From 'The Dream of the Rood': *The Anglo-Saxon World*. Boydell Press, 1982 and Oxford University Press, 1984.

Authors and Books:

Rosemary Sutcliff: *The Eagle of the Ninth*: The Folio Society, London, 2005; T.H. White: *The Once and Future King*: The Folio Society, 2003; George Crabbe: 'Peter Grimes': *Peter Grimes the Poor of the Borough*. The Folio Society, 1990; Footprints on the Grass: Of Gardens and Children's Books: The Sixth Philippa Pearce Lecture, Homerton College, Cambridge. September 2013. Previously unpublished; Michael Longley: Breathing on the Embers: *Love Poet, Carpenter. Michael Longley at Seventy*. Enitharmon Press, 2009; Annie's Wonderland: On receiving the Carnegie Medal for *Storm*: Elaboration of speech on receiving the Carnegie Medal, 1985. Previously unpublished; The King Within Each of Us: Journal of Children's Literature, Vol. 31, No.2, Fall 2005; A Sort of Song of Everything: *Gatty's Tale and Music*: IBBYLink 55, Spring 2019, Issue 55; From *Storm*: Storm. Heinemann, London, 1985.

In Tandem:

Collaborations with Artists: Entitled ,Bruder und Schwester wie Wort und Bild?'. Book 2.0, volume 10, Number 2 (2020), reproduced by permission of Intellect Limited 2020; 'Tump' and 'Altar' from *Seahenge*: Seahenge. Kailpot Press, 2019; Collaborations with Composers: 2022. Previously unpublished; The Girl from Aleppo (Everyday Wonders): 'The Girl from Aleppo'. Commissioned by The National Children's Choir of Great Britain. First performance 10 August, 2018; On Writing a Libretto: *The Wildman*. The Boydell Press, 1995; From *The Wildman*: The Wildman. The Boydell Press, 1995.

Norse:

Look North: Previously unpublished; Axe-Age, Wolf-Age: 2022. Previously unpublished; On Ian Crockatt's *Crimsoning the Eagle's Claw: The Viking Poems of Rognvaldr Kali Kolsson*, Earl of Orkney. ARC Publications, 2014; From *The Death of Balder: The Penguin Book of Norse Myths*. First published as *The Norse Myths*, André Deutsch, 1980. Penguin Books, 1982.

Places:

On *The Oxford Book of Travel Verse*: The Oxford Book of Travel Verse. Oxford University Press, 1986; The Kings of the Irish. Drawn from, and combining, *Pieces of Land*, Victor Gollancz, 1974, and Islands Magazine, 1990; Let There be Light: *The Re-Turn of the Tide: North Norfolk's Saltmarsh Coast*. JJG Publishing, 2010; Scolt Head: *Archipelago*. Number 12, Summer 2019; Until the Dragon Comes: Talk to Temenos Academy, 2016. Temenos Academy Review, Number 19, 2016; Festival of the Phoenix: *Moscow Jaunt*. School Librarian, Volume 52, Number 1, Spring 2004; In a Norfolk Garden: An Idyll for Peter and Margaret Scupham: *Gravity for Beginners*. Arc, 2021.

ACKNOWLEDGEMENTS

First, let me sincerely thank those generous friends and colleagues who in different ways have had a direct and substantial bearing on my writing life: Richard Barber, my father Peter Crossley-Holland, Sue Bradbury, Karen Cushman, Lynda Edwardes-Evans, Judith Elliott, Mick Gowar, A. N. Jeffares, Charles Keeping, Nicola LeFanu, Hugh Lupton, Bruce Mitchell, Andrew Rafferty, Stephen Stuart-Smith, Roger Straus, and Jill Paton Walsh.

Then I thank my loving and unfailingly supportive wife Linda for commenting on drafts of all these pieces, written over many years; my very patient PA Karen Clarke for so capably helping to shape and reshape them; and Henry Layte (and his Editor, Thogdin Ripley) not only for publishing this portfolio but suggesting it in the first instance.

And thirdly, I gratefully acknowledge permission to reprint individual poems and pieces from the sundry sources listed in the previous pages.